［巻頭言］

第16回国際犯罪学会大会（神戸）を振り返って

福 島　　至（矯正・保護課程委員長）

　2011年は東日本大震災と福島原発爆発が起きた年として、人類史上に永遠に記録されていくことであろう。仙台で生まれ育った私にとっても、忘れることのできない年になった。そんな困難な状況であったが、国際犯罪学会第16回世界大会が、当初の予定通り、神戸国際会議場を主会場にして開催された。開催に尽力された関係各位のご努力、ご苦労には、この場を借りて敬意を表したい。

　大会4日目の8月8日夜のセッションでは、私も名誉ある報告の機会をいただいた。セッションは、「犯罪学・刑事司法の総合的教育体制（Integrated System of Teaching Criminology and Criminal Justice）」で、報告者はファター名誉教授（カナダ・サイモンフレーザー大学）、クリー教授（ドイツ・フライブルク大学）、パルメンティエ教授（ベルギー・ルーベンカトリック大学）、フィンケナウアー教授（アメリカ・ラトガース大学）、小柳武教授（常磐大学）と私で、齊藤豊治教授（大阪商業大学）が司会の労をとられた。報告内容は、各々の大学の教育プログラムや、各国の犯罪学や刑事司法関係の専門職養成制度などを紹介、評価するものであった。このセッションは、上記プログラムや諸制度について、国際的な比較、検討をする貴重な場となったのである。当日印象に残ったのは、統合的な犯罪学の教育体制を作ってきたアメリカやカナダからの報告であった。

　報告の機会を与えられ、私も改めて、日本の大学における刑事司法や犯罪学の教育システムを、諸外国との比較において検討することができた。以下に私の報告の骨子を紹介することで、巻頭言としたい。

　日本の大学においては、犯罪学部や刑事司法学部など、これら専門に特化

した学部はない。法学部や社会学部などに、犯罪学や刑事政策、犯罪社会学といった授業科目があるだけである。大学院も、これとさほど異なる状況にはない。このことは、大学で犯罪学や刑事政策、司法福祉などを対象とする研究者や学生が、種々の学部に分散して所属していることを意味する。キャンパスが分かれていれば、関連専門図書などの研究・教育資料も同様に分属してしまうことになる。これらの事実は、このような科目が、従来から日本ではあまり重視されてこなかったことの現れとも言えよう。

　しかし、目を転じてみると、社会においては一定の変化が生じてきているように思う。それは、最近の司法改革に伴い、市民の中に犯罪学などへの関心が高まってきていることである。裁判員制度においては、市民が刑事裁判の裁判員に選任され、事実認定ばかりか量刑の決定に関与することになった。この影響を受けて、刑事裁判そのもののみならず、犯罪原因や犯罪者処遇、犯罪心理などに対する関心が高まってきているように思う。しかしながら、テレビのワイドショーや週刊誌上では、相変わらずセンセーショナルな報道があふれている。せっかく高まった関心も、感情的に歪められた反応をもたらしてしまう懸念がある。このような状況に鑑みると、今こそ大学には、犯罪や福祉、刑事司法に対する理性的な思考方法や、的確な知識を提供する社会的責務があると言っていいだろう。

　また、刑務官や法務教官、保護観察官、児童自立支援施設職員、地域生活定着支援センター職員など犯罪者等の処遇・福祉に関係する専門職や実務家の組織的、系統的養成は、次第にその必要性を増していると思われる。矯正・保護の現場においては、福祉との連携が進みはじめている。社会福祉や精神保健福祉に携わる人々が、刑事施設の中でも活躍している。実際に、これらの職を希望する大学生のニーズも堅調である。現在では、こうした仕事に就く希望を持つ学生の多くは、心理学や社会学、法学、精神医学、教育学、社会福祉学など様々な分野の学部でそれぞれの学習を行い、卒業までに公務員試験や資格試験などに合格して、道を進んでいくのが一般的である。かかる教育は、大学内で別々に行われている状況がある。このような人材育成に係る教育についても、大学内でもっと有機的に関連づけて、就職支援に努めるべきであろう。

このような状況を考えるならば、本学に矯正・保護課程が設けられて運営されてきたことは極めて意義深いと感じる。このような職業に就く人たちの養成を目的として、組織的、体系的なカリキュラムを提供し、実際に長年にわたり多くの人材を輩出してきたからである。

　しかしながら、現在の矯正・保護課程は、特別研修講座の一つとして存在しているに過ぎず、総合的な教育を行う体制とはなっていない。たとえば、提供している科目は全体としてまとまりのあるものにはなっているが、どの科目を受講するかは全く学生・院生側の選択に委ねられている。たとえ、学生が矯正・保護課程の科目をトータルに受講したいと思っても、自分が所属している学部等の必修授業と開講時間が重なっていれば、受講を断念せざるを得ない。矯正・保護課程委員会が設けられているが、各学部等教授会から選出された委員が課程の運営をしているにとどまり、ファカルティとして教育・研究者集団を形成しているわけではない。ニーズのポテンシャルが高まっているにもかかわらず、大学の組織が必ずしもそれに十分に対応していない状況があるように思う。

　それでは、どのようにしていけば良いのか。差し当たり、次のような措置が必要ではないかと考える。

　第一は、教育活動と研究活動の密接な連携である。教育なくして研究はなく、研究なくして教育はない。教育実践と研究成果の相互のフィードバックが必要である。矯正・保護課程における取組みは、教育と研究の相互作用の所産であった。矯正・保護総合センターとして統合されたのは、必然であったと言ってよい。今後は、このセンターを母体にした犯罪学部や司法福祉学部を指向することも必要であろう。

　第二は、実務との密接な連携である。上記の教育と研究との密接な連携の必要性は、何も犯罪学にとって固有な要素ではない。しかし、実務との連携は、実際に人間を対象にする犯罪学の教育にとって特に必要な要素であると言える。矯正・保護の分野においては、社会復帰のために様々な人々が関与している。刑務官や法務教官、保護観察官、警察官などの公務員のほか、教誨師や保護司、篤志面接委員などのボランティア、更生保護会や刑事施設視察委員会、自助グループ、被害者支援団体など、多くの人々や団体が活動し

ている。犯罪学に関係する新たな人材育成に努める機関としては、これらの人々や団体の経験を教育に生かしていかなければならないと思う。

矯正講座 第32号 目　次

〔巻頭言〕
　第16回国際犯罪学会大会（神戸）を振り返って
　　　　………………………………………………………福　島　　　至…（ⅰ）

〔特集：龍谷プログラム2011〕
　国際犯罪学会第16回大会・神戸における龍谷大学の活躍
　　　　………………………………………………………石　塚　伸　一…（ 1 ）

〔基調講演〕
　経済危機と犯罪統制政策──財産犯罪と経済犯罪の象徴的操作──
　　　　………………………………………………………石　塚　伸　一…（ 3 ）

〔シンポジウム〕
東アジアと合衆国における死刑
　１．企画の趣旨 ……………………………………石　塚　伸　一…（17）
　２．報　　告
　　　［１］日本の死刑　　　　　　　　　　　　布施勇如　（20）
　　　［２］韓国の死刑制度と廃止への歩み　　　　朴秉植　（27）
　　　［３］台湾における死刑執行の停止と再開：これまでとこれから
　　　　　　　　　　　　　　　　　　　　　　　　謝如媛　（45）
　　　［４］中国はどのようにその死刑制度を改善しているのか
　　　　　　　　　　　　　　　　　　　　　　　　王雲海　（58）

〔テーマセッション〕
日本版ドラッグ・コート構想
　１．企画の趣旨──処罰からハーム・リダクションへ──
　　　　………………………………………………………石　塚　伸　一…（67）
　２．報　　告

［１］日本の薬物問題の現在——刑事司法における
　　　直接強制および間接強制による薬物プログラム——
　　　　　　　　　　　　　　　　　　　　　　丸山泰弘（*69*）
［２］米国ドラッグ・コートの現在　　　　　森村たまき（*72*）
［３］ダルク25年のあゆみ　　　　　　　　　近藤恒夫（*75*）
［４］NPO法人アパリ　　　　　　　　　　　尾田真言（*81*）
［５］JICAにおけるダルクの活動　　　　　　三浦陽二（*84*）
［６］フィリピンの現況と課題：法規制と依存症の
　　　治療への取り組み　　レオナルド・エスタシオ Jr.（*86*）
［７］韓国の薬物依存症の現状と対策　チョウ・ソンナム（*91*）
［８］支援の際の基本的価値とスタッフ教育の重要性について
　　　　　　　　　　　　　　　　　　　　　　市川岳仁（*95*）
［９］薬物依存症と向き合うダルク
　　　——正義ではなく許しと寛容——　　　加藤武士（*102*）
［10］刑事法研究者の立場から
　　　——ドイツの非刑罰化・非犯罪化政策——
　　　　　　　　　　　　　　　　　　　　　　金尚均（*106*）
［11］精神科ソーシャル・ワーカーの立場から　西念奈津江（*109*）
［12］依存症とジェンダー　　　　　　　　　野村佳絵子（*111*）

[Special Issue: RYUKOKU Programs 2011]

"Ryukoku Programs" at 16th World Congress (ISC) in Kobe
　………………………………………………………Shinichi Ishizuka…(*113*)

[Symposium] Death Penalty in East Asia and the United States
　………………………………………………………Shinichi Ishizuka…(*114*)

〔１〕The Death Penalty in Japan …………………Yusuke Fuse…(*121*)
〔２〕Capital Punishment in Korea and Abolition Movement
　　　Against It ………………………………………Park, Byungsick…(*124*)
〔３〕Taiwan's Anti-Death Penalty Movement in
　　　The Local-Global Dynamics ………………Chia-Wen Lee…(*136*)
〔４〕How is China changing its Death Penalty Policy?

....Wang Yunhai...(*165*)

[Theme Session] The Concept of Japanese Drug Court :
from punishment to harm-reduction ....Shinichi Ishizuka
　　　　　　　　　　　　　　　　　　　Yasuhiro Maruyama...(*167*)
　〔1〕 Contemporary Japanese Drug Policy : Compulsory and Coerced
　　　　Treatment for Drug Addicts in Criminal Justice System
　　　　　　　　　　　　.................................Yasuhiro Maruyama...(*171*)
　〔2〕 Drug Courts in the USA   ....Tamaki Morimura...(*178*)
　〔3〕 DARC (Drug Addiction Rehabilitation Center) for 25Years
　　　　　　　　　　　　...Tsuneo Kondo...(*183*)
　〔4〕 What is APARI (Asia-Pacific Addiction Research Center)?
　　　　　　　　　　　　...Makoto Oda...(*188*)
　〔5〕 DARC as a Cooperator of JICA in the Philippines　Yoji Miura...(*191*)
　〔6〕 Current Situations and Agenda in Philippines
　　　　　　　　　　　　..............................Leonardo Estacio, Jr....(*193*)
　〔7〕 Current Situations and Agenda in Korea ....Sung Nam Cho...(*205*)
　〔8〕 Mie DARC's Case : Discussing the Fundamental Value
　　　　Behind Supporting and the Importance of Staff Education
　　　　　　　　　　　　..Takehito Ichikawa...(*211*)
　〔9〕 DARC Faces Drug Addiction : Forgiveness and
　　　　Tolerance Instead of Justice ....Takeshi Kato...(*216*)
　〔10〕 Decriminalization and Depenalization of Drug Abuse
　　　　and Possession in Germany ....Sangyun Kim ...(*220*)
　〔11〕 Drug Addiction for a Psychiatric Social Worker
　　　　　　　　　　　　...Natsue Sainen...(*222*)
　〔12〕 Dependency and Gender ....Kaeko Nomura...(*224*)

〔矯正施設参観記〕
　2011年度「矯正・保護課程」共同研究・施設参観報告
　　　　　　　　　　　　..加　藤　博　史...(*227*)
　1　福井刑務所参観記 ....青　木　恒　弘...(*232*)
　2　更生保護法人「福井福田会」参観記.........宮　内　利　正...(*237*)

3	更生保護法人「福井福田会」参観記	井上見淳	(242)
4	湖南学院訪問記	板垣嗣廣	(245)
5	金沢刑務所参観記	畠山晃朗	(252)
6	富山刑務所	池田静	(261)

〔活動報告〕

〔編集後記〕

　　　　　表紙題字　元・浄土真宗本願寺派総長　豊原大潤
　　　　　表紙のスケッチ　ISHIZUKA, Shinichi

〔特集：龍谷プログラム2011〕

国際犯罪学会第16回大会・神戸における龍谷大学の活躍

http://hansha.daishodai.ac.jp/wcon2011/index.html

　龍谷大学は、1939年の創設以来、浄土真宗の精神に基づき、社会的な少数者や被排除者の支援の貢献に努めてきた。犯罪者や非行少年もその例外ではない。わたしたちは、1977年に、教育プログラムとしての矯正・保護課程を、2001年には研究機関としての矯正・保護研究センターを設置した。2010年4月、これらの機関とそれ以外の社会的機能を統合して、矯正・保護総合センターを開設した。

　わたしたちは、今回の組織刷新を記念して、「龍谷プログラム」を提案し、2011年8月5日から9日に神戸で開催される第16回国際犯罪学会において、多くの研究者や実務家のみなさんとともに、刑事政策や犯罪をおかしてしまった人の社会復帰に関するさまざまなテーマについて議論をする機会を提供することにした。

　以下が、本プログラムが提供した講演、セッションおよびラウンドテーブル・ディスカッションである。

1．〔基調講演〕「世界的経済危機と犯罪学」　　　　　　　　　　（石塚伸一）
2．死刑問題
　「東アジアと合衆国における死刑」
　「ワールドワイドの視点から見た死刑」
　　　　　　　　　　　（石塚伸一、D・T・ジョンソン、布施勇如、浜井浩一）
3．ドラッグ問題
　「日本版ドラッグ・コート構想
　　　――処罰からハーム・リダクション（有害性の縮減）へ――」

　　　　　　　　　　　　　　　　　　　　　　　　　（石塚伸一＝丸山康弘）
　　「薬物政策についてもっと話そう」　　　（石塚伸一、丸山泰弘、金尚均）
4．「犯罪学・刑事司法教育の統合的教育体制」　　　　　　　　（福島至）
5．「ヨーロッパ社会調査における『司法への信頼』に関する新たな調査モ
　　デル——刑罰ポピュリズムの測定」　　　　　　　　　　（浜井浩一）
6．「刑罰を超えて——刑事司法と社会福祉の協働」　　　　（浜井浩一）
7．「学校における公開と安全の考察——こどもの安全に焦点を当てて」
　　　　　　　　　　　　　　　　　　　　　　　　　　　　（浜井浩一）

　本特集では、1、2および3を紹介することにする。

〔基調講演〕

経済危機と犯罪統制政策
── 財産犯罪と経済犯罪の象徴的操作 ──

石　塚　伸　一（龍谷大学：京都）

はじめに
1．「富士山曲線」と象徴主義
2．「危機」概念について
3．経済的危機と犯罪者・受刑者
4．古典的財産犯と経済・財政犯罪
　4．1．古典的財産犯
　4．2．後期資本主義における経済・財政犯罪
5．「バブル経済」崩壊後の犯罪と犯罪統制政策
6．結　論
　6．1．質問に対する答え
　6．2．相対主義（Relativism）と関係主義（Relationism）
　6．3．「3．11」の前と後
　6．4．21世紀の存在拘束性
　　　　──ポスト「バブル経済」とポスト「3．11」の社会を生きる──
　6．5．刑事政策と犯罪学者

はじめに

　ようこそ日本にいらっしゃいました。わたしたちは、2011年3月11日以来、一連の破局的災害を体験しています。すなわち、地震、津波そして原子力発電所の破壊です。
　わたしに与えられたのは、下記のテーマです。すなわち、「世界的経済危機と犯罪統制：地域間および国家間の比較」です。このテーマは、犯罪学が「世界的経済危機ならびに国家および社会の構造的諸変化にどう対応してき

たか」を問うものです。おそらく、ここでの世界的経済危機とは、2008年9月15日の「リーマン・ショック」を指すのでしょう。本報告は、日本が、リーマン・ショック後の世界的変化に対応するために、どのような犯罪予防戦略を採ってきたかを考えるものです。

具体的に答えられるべき問いは、つぎの3つです。すなわち、【質問1】日本の犯罪および犯罪予防戦略の状況は変化したか？【質問2】世界的経済危機は、日本の国家および社会に重要な構造的変化をもたらしているか？【質問3】これらの変化は、日本の犯罪状況に影響を与えているか？

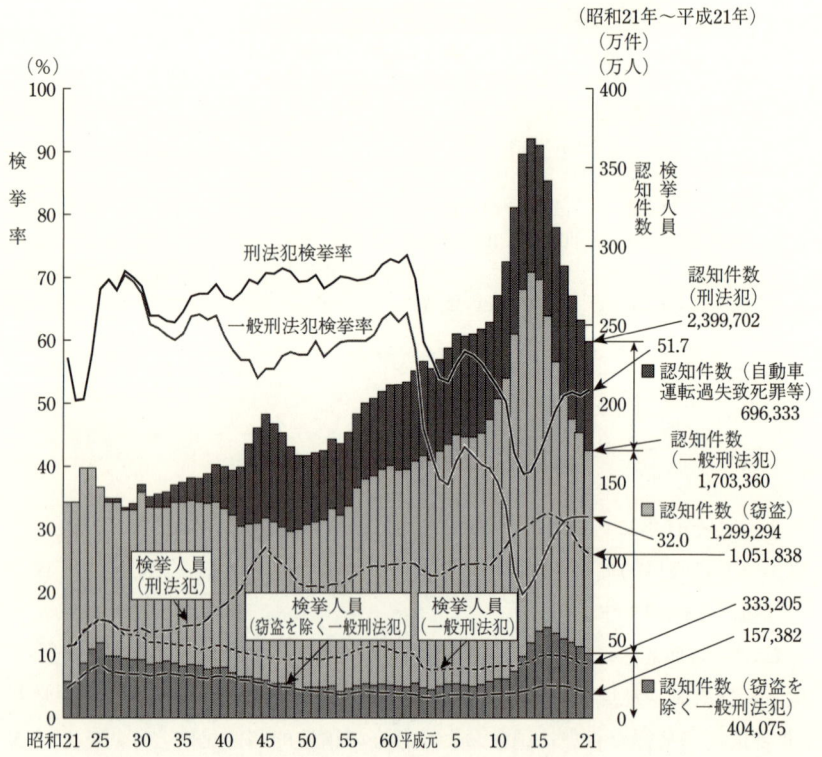

【グラフ1】法務総合研究所編『2010年版犯罪白書』

【グラフ２】 刑法犯の認知件数および検挙人員における富士山曲線

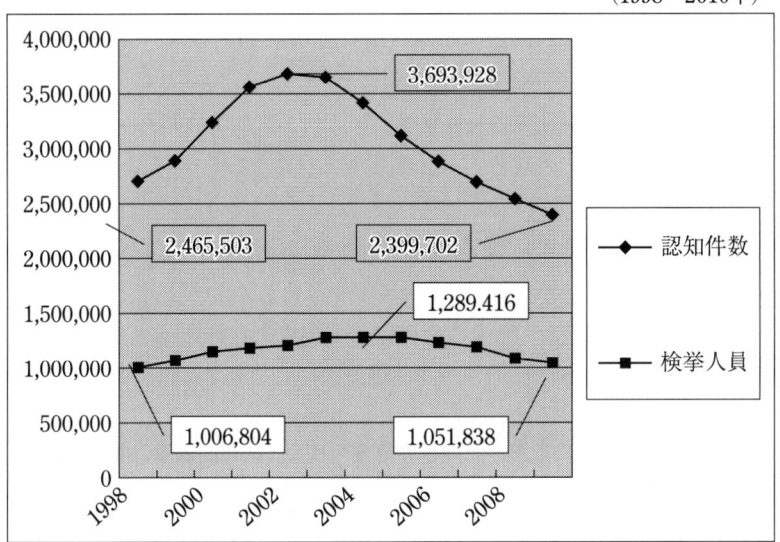

(1998～2010年)

1．「富士山曲線」と象徴主義

　刑法犯認知件数は、1996年に約247万件を記録して以来、毎年、記録を更新し、2002年には約370万件を記録した（49.8％増）。しかし、2003年から減少に転じ、2009年には約240万件にまで減少した（35％減）。検挙人員については、1998年に約101万人を記録し、その後も毎年増加して、2004年に約129万人まで増えたが（28.1％増）、2005年からは減少に転じ、2009年には約105万人にまで減少した（18.4％減）。
　わたしは、ここで、1998年から2009年にかけての、犯罪統計上の曲線を「富士山曲線」と呼ぶことにする（法務総合研究所編『2010年版犯罪白書』参照）。果たして、この富士山は、この間の犯罪と犯罪者の実態を反映しているであろうか。

刑法典に「強制執行妨害罪」(刑法第96条の2) という規定がある。この犯罪類型は、ときの政策決定権者や政府、検察庁、警察庁などの法施行機関によって、刑事政策の象徴として操作されてきた。当初この犯罪類型は、戦時中の国家的法益侵害犯罪としてつくられた (1941〜45年)。ところが、高度経済成長期には財産犯罪として用いられ (1952〜72年)、さらには、バブル経済崩壊後には経済犯罪・財政犯罪として利用された (1996〜2005年)。

2.「危機」概念について

世界の歴史を見ると、「経済の危機は、正統性の危機を招来する」という一般的傾向がある。わたしたちが「危機」について語るのは、社会の構成員

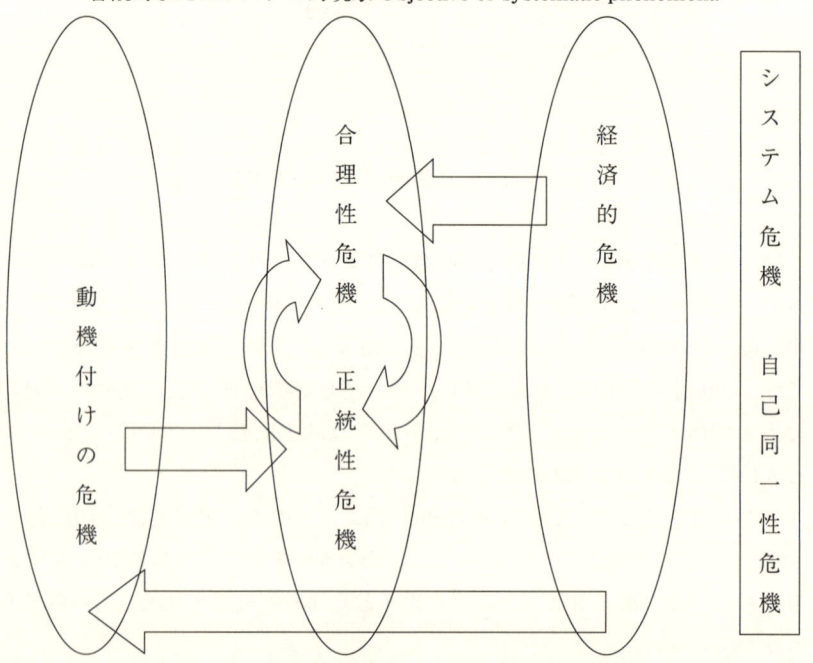

【図1】経済的危機=正統性の危機=社会・文化的危機の関係

たちが構造的な変動をその存続にとって危機であると経験し、みずからの社会的自己同一性を脅かされていると感じたときである（J・ハーバマース 1973/1975年、3頁）。したがって、危機とは、たんなる客観的またはシステム的な現象ではなく、主観的または規範的な現象なのである。

経済危機が政治システムに変化を要求するのは、規範構造が変化していないにもかかわらず、行政的および政治的な権力が正統性の要求を充たすことができない場合、すなわち、合理性および正統性の危機が生じている場合である。同時に、動機付けの危機は、他方での社会＝文化システムそれ自体の変化の帰結である（上掲書、48頁）。

3. 経済的危機と犯罪者・受刑者

一般的にいえば、経済不況は、直接失業率の上昇をもたらし、その結果として、貧しい成人や少年による財産犯を増加させるという現象をもたらす。近代初期（重商主義の時代）と自由な資本主義社会にはこのような現象が起こった。アムステルダム初期「懲治場」の創設期には、労働市場の状態は、受刑者の数と密接な関連を有していた（G・ルッシェ 1933年；Th・セリン 1944年）。経済システムは、労働と資本を入力し (input)、使用価値を出力する (output)。入力の不足によってもたらされる危機は、資本制生産様式に典型的な危機ではない。自由な資本主義を破壊する本当の危機は、出力の危機である（ハーバマース、上掲書、45頁）。

産業革命後、救貧政策が導入され、経済不況と失業が受刑者の増加をもたらすという傾向が弱くなり、救貧政策の対象者の数が増えるようになった。とりわけ、周期的な経済的危機を経験し、その対応策として、多様な社会政策が導入された19世紀末から20世紀初頭の福祉国家の諸制度の確立後には、政府は、プロレタリアート階級に属するハイリスクの潜在的犯罪者（フォン・リスト 1897年）をプロベイション（保護観察）やパロール（仮釈放）によってコントロールするようになった（G・ルッシェ＝O・キルヒハイマー、1939年）。犯罪学者たちは、一方でこれらの諸政策を「社会統制の網の拡大」と呼ぶこともできれば、他方でこれを福祉国家の発展と呼ぶこともできる。その結果、

労働市場は、財産犯や受刑者の数と直接的な相関関係をもたなくなった。

4．古典的財産犯と経済・財政犯罪

4.1．古典的財産犯

　自由な資本主義社会において最も基本的かつ本質的な社会統合の基盤は、市民法体系の存在である。すなわち、それは、①独立で平等な主体としての法人格（生命と身体）、②絶対的支配の客体としての財産権（財産）、そして③主体の自由意志の自立としての契約の自由権（自由）を保証している。

　第二次規範である古典的刑法典は、3種類の利益を保護することによって、上記の市民法体系を支えている。すなわち、【カテゴリー1（個人的法益）】は、市民の自由な社会における諸原則としての個人の利益である。【カテゴリー2（社会的法益）】は、市民の自由な市場社会の基盤としての、公共

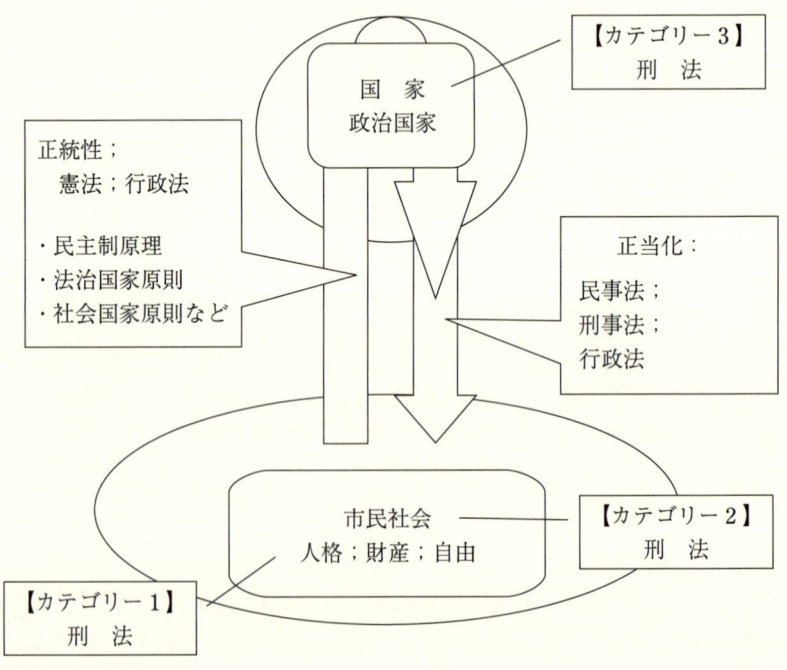

の安全と安心、商品交換の諸手段およびそれを支える倫理と道徳という利益である。【カテゴリー3（国家的法益）】は、政治国家における諸原則としての国家の統合と統治という利益である。

　刑法典は、上記の【カテゴリー1】について、3つの客体に対する犯罪を処罰している。すなわち、①生命および身体に対する罪（例　殺人罪、傷害罪、過失傷害罪、堕胎罪、遺棄罪など）、②財産に対する罪（例　窃盗罪、強盗罪、恐喝罪、器物損壊罪、隠匿罪など）、および③自由に対する罪（例　詐欺罪、強要罪、監禁罪、脅迫罪、誘拐罪など）である。

4.2. 後期資本主義における経済・財政犯罪

　後期資本主義の社会において政府は、伝統的犯罪統制に比べ、はるか広汎に市民社会に介入する。その介入の道具のひとつが、経済犯罪あるいは財政犯罪というカテゴリーによる犯罪統制である。日本におけるこの種の犯罪には、下記のものがある。すなわち、①租税犯罪、②狭義の経済犯罪（商法・会社法・独占禁止法・証券取引法等の違反）、③財政犯罪（投資法・金融規制法等の違

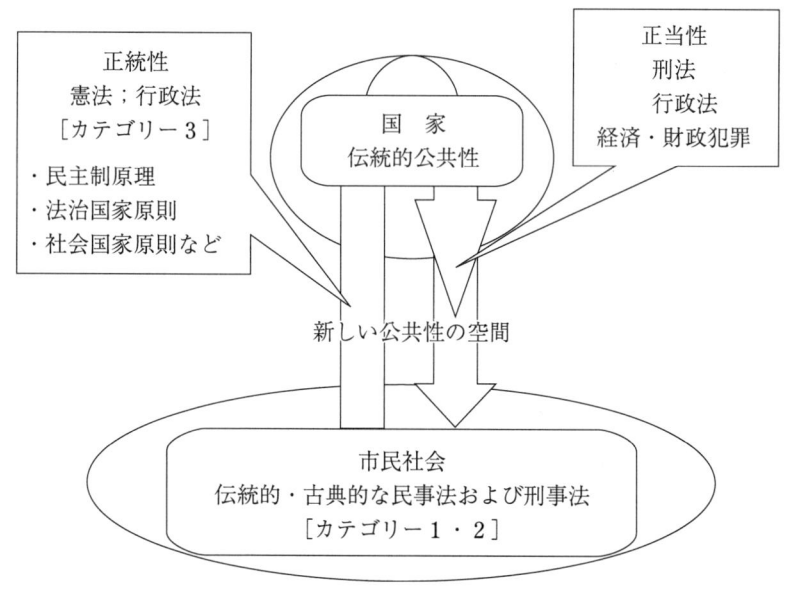

【グラフ3】 強制執行妨害罪の適用状況（1989〜2007年）

	1989	1990	1991	1992	1993	1994	1995	1996	1997	1998	1999	2000	2001	2002	2003	2004	2005	2006	2007
不起訴	24	12	14	15	10	19	10	15	30	29	20	28	30	33	17	46	31	16	14
起訴	2	1	3	1	1	1	1	12	18	19	14	16	7	11	16	15	5	2	2
起訴率	7.7	7.7	21.4	6.3	9.1	5	9.1	44.4	37.5	39.5	41.2	36.4	18.9	25	48.5	24.6	13.9	11.1	12.5

反）、④知的財産犯罪（有価証券法・著作権法・特許法・意匠法等の違反）、⑤倒産関連犯罪（刑法の強制執行妨害〔96条の2〕・競売妨害罪〔96条の3〕、倒産法違反など）、⑥その他新たな形態の経済犯罪（貸金業改正法な等）である。

　刑法96条の2の強制執行妨害罪は、1940年代に古典的刑法の国家的法益犯罪として導入されたが、1960・70年代に個人的法益犯罪として利用され、さらには1990年代後半経済犯罪と解釈されるなどその適用方針は揺れ動いたが、2000年はじめに再び国家的法益犯罪にしようと政府は立法を試みたが、それは失敗に終わった。（2011年6月24日法律第74号による刑法一部改正の結果、同罪は国家的法益犯罪に重点を移行させた。）

5．「バブル経済」崩壊後の犯罪と犯罪統制政策

　他の要因が等しければ、(a) 経済システムは、必要量の使用価値を生産しない。(b) 執行システムは、必要量の合理的決定を生産しない。(c) 正統性システムは、必要量の一般化された動機付けを提供しない。そして、(d) 社会＝文化的システムは、必要量行為を動機付ける意味付与を創造しない。以上の命題は、資本主義システムの根本的矛盾の諸帰結である（ハーバマース、上掲書、49頁）。

　日本の社会と政府は、20世紀以降、1929年、1945年、1972年、1993年およ

【グラフ４】1980年を100とする危機指標（1980〜2008年）

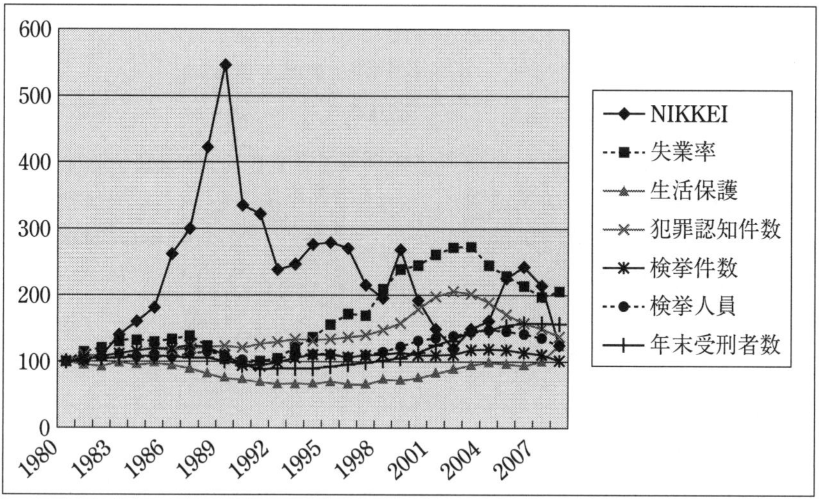

び2008年に経済的危機を経験した。本報告の文脈において、本来の意味での経済危機（恐慌）は、1993年の危機だけである。なぜなら、バブル経済の崩壊は、国内の過剰な出力によって、経済システムが瓦解したからである。

　システム統合の撹乱は、社会の統合を危殆化し、システムの存続それ自体を危うくする。規範構造の合意的基礎に障害が生じ、社会はアノミーに陥る（ハーバマース、上掲書、3頁）。バブル経済の崩壊によって日本政府は、経済システムに危機が生じただけでなく、政治的危機に陥っていることに気づいた。経済的および政治的な危機は、社会＝文化的システムにも転移した。治安維持組織としての検察庁・警察庁が、社会＝文化的システムと経済的システムに直接介入した。前者の象徴が、オウム真理教（1995年）と金融の「魔女狩り」（1998年）であった。これと併行して政府は、自由な資本主義社会の基盤たる、商品交換体制と労働市場を維持し、市民社会の安全と安心を確保して、社会のアイデンティティー（自己同一性）を維持しようとした。政府は、みずからが正義の実現のために懸命に働き、闘っているという印象を与えようと試みた。その結果、刑法犯検挙人員の増加率は比較的低レベルであったにもかかわらず、その犯罪認知件数、とりわけ財産犯の認知件数が劇的

【グラフ5】財産犯罪（窃盗罪／詐欺罪／恐喝罪／横領罪）

（1998～2009年）

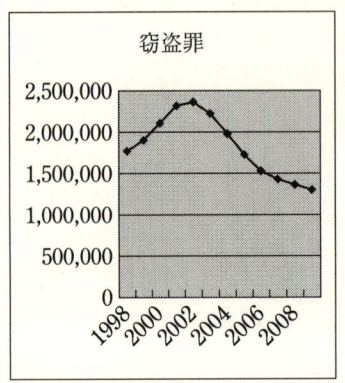
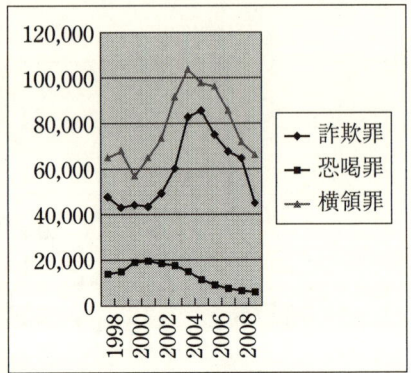

に増加するという現象がもたらされた。政府は、また、金融統制の「敵」に対する仮借のない、そして恣意的な介入を正当化するために、経済犯罪・財政犯罪という新しい犯罪カテゴリーを活用したのである。

以上のように、「富士山曲線」と日本刑法第96条の2の象徴的操作は、「バブル経済」崩壊（1993年）後の経済危機への対応として説明できる。このような犯罪統制戦略の変動を示す例として、以下の例を指摘することができる。すなわち、1999年の少年法改正、2000年被害者保護法、2000年から2007年にかけての死刑および無期懲役刑の劇的な増加、2004年の重罰化に向けての刑法一部改正などである。

6．結 論

6.1．質問に対する答え

わたしは、最初に設定した3つの質問に答えなければならない。

【質問1】日本の犯罪および犯罪予防戦略の状況は変化したか？

〔答〕2008年リーマン・ショック後についていえば「ノー」である。しかし、1993年バブル経済崩壊以後についていえば「イエス」である。

【質問2】世界的経済危機は、日本の国家および社会に重要な構造的変化

をもたらしているか？

〔答〕 2008年リーマン・ショック後についていえば「ノー」である。しかし、1993年バブル経済崩壊以後についていえば「イエス」である。

【質問3】これらの変化は、日本の犯罪状況に影響を与えているか？

〔答〕 2008年リーマン・ショック後についていえば「ノー」である。しかし、1993年バブル経済崩壊以後についていえば「イエス」である。

6.2. 相対主義（Relativism）と関係主義（Relationism）

人はすべて、それぞれ独自の視点をもっている。それは、それぞれの時代と社会における固有のパースペクティヴからの認識を拘束する。K・マンハイムは、このような見方が相対主義（relativism）に陥ることを危惧し、これに対する概念として「関連主義（relationism）」を提案した（Mannheim, K., Ideology and Utopia. 1936, London）。

ある社会の同時代の構成員は、それぞれ共通かつ特有の視点をもつ。これは、その時代、その場所（社会）に応じた共通のパースペクティヴに応じて同一のパースペクティヴからの認識を必然的に拘束するからである。

6.3.「3.11」の前と後

次の2つの絵を見ていただきたい。1番目の絵は、2011年3月11日の前に新幹線の車窓から見た、富士山を描いたものである。多くの人びとのイメージの中で、遠目からは穏やかな山と思われている富士山は、実は、ゴツゴツとして、北東に向かって大きな口を開けた猛々しい山でもある。

記録によれば、富士山は何度か噴火している。800～802年に延暦噴火、864年に貞観大噴火、直近では、1707年に宝永大噴火の記録がある。宝永の噴火では、江戸（いまの東京）に約4センチメートルの火山灰が降り積もり、山では溶岩が流れ出し、上述の大きな口を開けたカルデラができあがった。

3月11日の直後、わたしは、新幹線の車窓から再び富士山を眺めていた。知らずしらずに1番目の上に筆が走り、2番目のような富士山を描いてしまった。山頂付近からは黒煙が噴出し、溶岩状のものが麓に向かって流れて出ていた。

【絵】新幹線から見た富士山

3.11以前

3.11以後

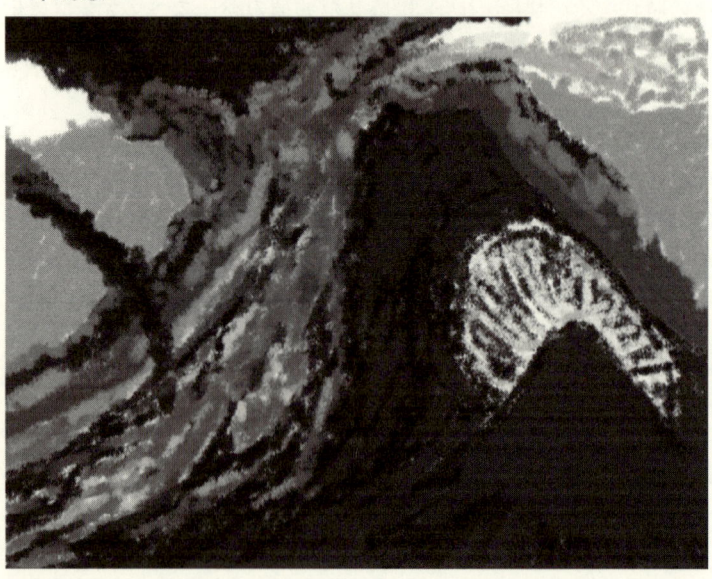

東北大震災以来、わたしたちは、毎日、テレビや新聞を通じて、瓦礫の積み上げられた被災地の画像を眺め、自然と対峙したときの「人間の小ささ」と「文明の空しさ」を感じている。そして、いつ、突然、わたしたちの文明が瓦解するのではないかという「こころの傷」に苛まれている。

6.4. 21世紀の存在拘束性
　　──ポスト「バブル経済」とポスト「3.11」の社会を生きる──

　ポスト・バブル経済時代（1993〜2000年）にいくつかの観念が日本社会を支配するようになった。すなわち、「報償を受けるべきものは報償を受け、罰を受けるべきものは罰を受ける」という信賞必罰の観念である。さらには、人は自らの成功、あるいは失敗の責任を受けるべきであるという自業自得の観念である。

　ところが、わたしたちは、世紀の変わり目にこのような観念を疑いはじめた。なぜなら、社会的格差が固定化し、一度失敗した人は、社会の周縁部に押しやられ、あるいは社会から永久に排除されるように思われたからである。現実の犯罪者・非行少年・受刑者を直視してみれば、その多くは、凶悪なモンスターではなく、社会的に弱い立場にある人たちである。彼らを排除してしまっていのであろうか。

　わたしたちは、3月11日、人智では統制できない、そして、理不尽な災害を経験した。わたしたちは、信賞必罰や自業自得の観念が正しくないということを確信した。なぜなら、被災者・被害者は、個人の自由意志や自己責任では説明のできない悲劇を被っているからである。世の中のすべての事象をその人のせいにすること（誰かに帰属させること）はできないのである。

6.5. 刑事政策と犯罪学者

　政策決定者は、ポスト・バブル経済の時期に財産犯と経済／財政犯罪の観念を操作した。犯罪学者は、関係主義のパースペクティヴから、彼らの象徴操作に気づいた。わたしたち犯罪学者は、敵に対しては厳罰をもってのぞむパースペクティヴを乱用する政策とその決定者を分析し、そして批判しなければならない。なぜなら、このような政策は、ポスト3.11に特有な視点に

適合しないからである。

わたしたちは、これまで以上に寛容なパースペクティヴを導入すべきである。なぜなら、わたしたちの経験は、わたしたちをこのようなパースペクティヴに拘束するからである。

わたしは、まだ、富士山曲線の「登り道」だけしか説明していない。「降り道」については、引き続き議論したいと思う。

[参考文献]

Habermas, J. (1973), *Legitimationzorobleme in Spaetkapitalismus*, Suhrkamp Verlag: Frankfurt am Main, 1975) [trans. by T. McCarty, *Legitimation Crisis*, Beacon Press: Boston, 1975].

Hamai, K. &, T. Ellis (2008), "*Genbatsuka*: Growing Penal Populism and the Changing Role of Public Prosecutors in Japan?" in: "Special issue: Globalized Penal Populism and its Countermeasures," *Japanese Journal of Sociological Criminology*, vol. 33,

v. Liszt, F. (1882), Der Zweckgedanke im Strafrecht (Marburger Universitäts-programm), in: ders. *Strafrechtliche Vorträge und Aufsätze*, Bd. I., Berlin: Walter de Gruyter & Co., 1905, S. 126-179.

Mannheim, K. (1929), *Ideologie und Utopie*, Bonn: Friedrich Cohen.

Rusche, G. (1933), "Arbeitmarkt und Strafvollzug," *Zeitschrift für Sozialforschung*, Bd. 2, S. 63-78 [trans. by G. Dinwiddie, "Labor Market and Penal Sanction," *Crime and Social Justice*, vol. 10, 1978, pp. 2-8].

Rusche, G. & O. Kirchheimer (1939), *Punishment and Social Structure*, New Brunswick, New Jersey, 2003 [originally published in 1939 by Columbia University Press].

Sellin, Th. (1944), *Pioneering in Penology: The Amsterdam Houses of Correction in the Sixteenth Centuries*, Philadelphia: University of Pennsylvania Press.

Ministry of Justice (2010). *White paper on crime in Japan 2010*.
   http://hakusyo1.moj.go.jp/jp/nendo_nfm.html

〔シンポジウム〕

東アジアと合衆国における死刑

(日本犯罪社会学会企画)

8月8日(月)13:15～16:30 (於)神戸国際会議場301号室

司会:石塚伸一＝D・T・ジョンソン

1　企画の趣旨
2　報　　告

1　企画の趣旨

石塚　伸一(龍谷大学)

　まず、コーディネーターである石塚伸一(龍谷大学:京都)から、本企画の趣旨について説明し、その後、日本については布施勇如(龍谷大学大学院:京都)、韓国については朴秉植(東国大学法学部:韓国)、台湾については謝如媛(國立政治大學:台湾)と李佳玟(成功大學法律學系:台湾)、中国については王雲海(一橋大学:東京)が、それぞれの国の近年の状況を報告した。これらの報告を共同司会者のD・T・ジョンソン(ハワイ大学・マノア)が整理した後、F・E・ツィンムリング(カリフォルニア大学:バークレー)と浜井浩一(龍谷大学法科大学院:京都)がコメントした。

　アジア諸国の死刑について要約する。韓国は、10年以上執行が停止され事実上の廃止国になっている。センセーショナルな事件や憲法裁判所の死刑合

憲判決はあったが、執行の再開に振れることはないと思われる。台湾は、一時廃止の方向にむかったが、揺り戻しがあり、執行が再開された。その背景には、政治的な変動とポピュリスティックな報道がある。これにどう対応していくかが廃止運動の大きな課題となっている。中国は、世界で最も多くの死刑を執行している国である。しかし、近年、政府は死刑についての監視を強化し、地方の裁判所の安易な死刑判決が、即座に執行されるようなことを規制しており、死刑判決の数は確実に減ってきている。また、立法のレベルでも死刑を法定する犯罪を減らす努力をしている。即時廃止は無理ではあるが、地道な縮減の努力が進められている。アメリカ合衆国についても、ここ数年間で死刑の判決は半減した。執行も抑制的になっており、死刑確定者の数が増えている。また、薬物注射による執行方法についても、その残虐性が問題となっている。

　このような流れの中で、日本の動きは特異である。2000年代に入って死刑や無期懲役刑の判決が激増し、自民党政権末期には特定の法務大臣が多くの死刑を執行し、「殺人狂時代」と呼ぶにふさわしいような状況にあった。その後、裁判員裁判法の施行や政権交代で、死刑の判決や執行の数は激減した。しかし、昨年、民主党の法務大臣が死刑執行を命令し、多くの市民を失望させた。

　日本では、被害者やその遺族への配慮、世論調査の圧倒的支持が、死刑存置の根拠とされることが多い。しかし、死刑を法定する犯罪の多くは、国に反逆する犯罪や公共危険犯である。憲法上、軍隊を否定している日本では、戦争によって国家が暴力装置であることを示すことができないので、統治者は死刑をなんとしても維持しようとする。日本のような犯罪の少ない国で死刑が存置されているのは、実は治安政策のためである。

　現在、わたしたちは、拘置所の壁の中で行なわれている死刑の現実をなにも知らずに抽象的に死刑を語っている。犯罪学には、科学的な方法で死刑の実像を浮かび上がらせるという重要な役割が与えられている。そのためには、比較の視点はきわめて重要であり、研究者の国際協力が不可欠である。

　本セッションは、龍谷大学がスポンサーとなり同時通訳が付いた。また、これと接合してラウンドテーブル・ディスカッション「世界的視点から見た

死刑」を主催し、悲惨な事件のあった直後のノルウエーの情況をL・シェルダン（ノルウエー大学：オスロ）が、アメリカと日本との比較をJ・クラパーキ（立命館大学：京都）が報告し、活発な議論が行なわれた。

　東アジアおよびアメリカ合衆国における死刑の現状を踏まえ、その廃止・縮減に向けた展望を共有する、という本企画の趣旨は、十分に達成された。

　報告者および参加者のみなさんには、こころより感謝したい。

2 報　告

［１］日本の死刑

布施　勇如（龍谷大学大学院）

はじめに

　日本における死刑の状況は、改善されていないどころか、むしろ後退しているとさえ言うことができ、韓国、台湾、中国、アメリカなどと対比すればそのことはいっそう明確となるであろう。日本は先進工業諸国の中で孤立し、それでもなお、死刑という制度が問い直されることがないという特殊な様相を呈している。

　国際的潮流をよそに、死刑の廃止や見直しの動きは皆無と言っていい。1983年〜1989年に死刑の確定判決が再審によって無罪となった事件が4件もあり、その後3年余り、死刑の執行は中断されたものの、それ以降も死刑制度改革の動きがない。すなわち、死刑が必要な制度なのか、代替刑ではいけないのか、絞首刑という執行方法は本当に憲法の禁じる「残虐」ではないのかについて、本格的な調査や議論は行われていない。

１　死刑を取り巻く大きな「変化」

　死刑制度が旧態依然であるのに対し、ここ数年、死刑に関連する裁判制度、政治体制には大きな変化が起きた。一方で、死刑と直接的には関係しないものの、刑事司法システムへの信頼を根底から揺るがす冤罪の事例が相次いだ。

(1) 裁判員裁判における死刑相当事件の審理、判決

　2009年5月、裁判員制度が始まった。国民の中から抽選で選ばれる裁判員6人と、職業裁判官3人によって評議、評決が行われる制度で、国民が直接、死刑の言い渡しに関わることとなった。裁判員裁判開始後、2010年11月

〜2011年7月に死刑求刑が11件あり、このうち8件で死刑判決が言い渡された[1]。

(2) 民主党政権下における死刑の執行と不執行

2009年8月の衆議院選挙で、1955年以来ほぼ一貫して政権を握っていた自民党に取って代わり、民主党政権が発足した。法務大臣はその後、頻繁に交代し、このうち、死刑廃止論者といわれる2人の法務大臣は対照的な行動を取った。

千葉景子氏は、死刑確定者2人に対する死刑執行を命令し、2010年7月28日に執行され、死刑制度の改革を望む国民の期待を裏切った。現大臣（2011年8月8日時点）の江田五月氏は、2011年1月14日の就任記者会見で「死刑はいろんな欠陥を抱えた刑罰[2]」と述べ、千葉氏の命令から今日まで1年余り、死刑は執行されていない。

(3) 冤罪事件の続発

①足利事件：1990年に当時4歳の女児が誘拐、殺害され、男性が無期懲役刑となった。DNA再鑑定、再審で2010年3月に無罪が確定した。

②大阪地検特捜部による証拠ねつ造事件：郵便制度悪用事件に関し、厚生労働省の局長が虚偽の公文書を作成、行使したとして起訴された。2010年9月に無罪判決が言い渡され、確定した。

③布川事件：1967年の強盗殺人事件で、2人の男性が無期懲役刑となった。再審で2011年6月に無罪が確定した。再審判決は目撃証言の信用性を否定し、捜査段階で犯行を認めた2人の供述についても、捜査官の誘導で作成された可能性があると指摘した。

以上のように裁判制度と政治の変革があり、この国の捜査機関、裁判所が

1　本報告中で言及した裁判は、特に断りのない限り、朝日新聞記事データベース「聞蔵II」で検索、引用した。

2　法務省ホームページ「江田新法務大臣官邸記者会見の概要　平成23年1月14日（金）」http://www.moj.go.jp/hisho/kouhou/hisho08_00112.html で検索。

無謬とは程遠いことが実証されてもなお、死刑が廃止または停止に向かう兆しはない。

2 死刑判決の変遷

最近20年間に第1審で死刑判決を受けた人数を司法統計年報でみると、1991年～1999年は、1995年（11人）を除き、年間1～8人と1桁で推移していた。ところが、2000年～2007年には年間10～18人と2桁が続き、2008年～2010年は年間4～9人と再び1桁に戻った。

死刑判決の多くは殺人罪で、検挙・起訴から第1審の判決までは当然ながらある程度の年月を要する。警察庁の統計によると、殺人で検挙された人数は、1998～2005年が年間1313～1456人、2006～2009年は年間1036～1241人となっており、こうした増減が、2000年以降の死刑判決の傾向と関連していると推測できる。また、2000年代終盤は、裁判員制度導入を控えていた時期であり、裁判が始まる前に争点を整理する公判前整理手続きに時間がかかり、結果として死刑求刑事件自体が減ったとも考えられる。

これに対し、2000年から8年間にわたって2桁の死刑判決が続いた現象を、裁判員制度導入と結び付ける説もある。「大量死刑時代」(An Era of mass-produced death sentences) と名付ける石塚伸一は、「検察庁と裁判所が、裁判員裁判になっても死刑や無期刑を言い渡しやすい客観状況を作ろうとした」と論じ、検察が重罰を要求して裁判所が応える構図が産み出されたとする。石塚はさらに、犯罪被害者・遺族の権利拡充という動きを検察が利用し、裁判所も敏感に反応したとの見解を提示する[3]。

裁判員裁判開始以降、死刑が求刑され、第1審の判決が出た11件（2010年11月～2011年7月）では、概ね、最高裁判所が1983年に示した「永山基準」に沿った判断がなされ、裁判員裁判によって死刑判決が出やすくなった、逆に出にくくなったという傾向は現段階では確認できない。

最高裁判所の確定判決を対象に、永山基準の運用を検証する永田憲史は、

---

[3] 石塚伸一ほか「《座談会》裁判員裁判の下で死刑の縮減・廃止を展望できるか」法律時報82巻7号（2010）13-32頁。石塚伸一「大量死刑時代の終焉？──厳罰主義の後始末」法律時報82巻7号（2010）8-12頁。

死刑になりやすい傾向として、殺害された者が複数、身代金、保険金、性的目的などの殺人、殺害を伴う前科があって再び殺人を犯した場合、複数の被害者を異なる機会に殺害した事例、共犯における主導性、殺害の計画性などを挙げる[4]。裁判員裁判で死刑判決が言い渡された8件では、殺害された者が3人だったケースが3件、2人が3件で、残る被害者1人のケースのうち、1件は2人殺害の前科があった。もう1件は強盗殺人で、出所してから約3か月後の犯行であり、2か月の間に本件のほか、強盗致傷、強盗強姦などを重ね、これらが前科の内容に類似していることから「反社会的な人格傾向が極めて強い」として、死刑選択の一つの理由とされた。

死刑求刑で無期懲役となった判決は11件中2件で、殺害された者はともに2人であった。このうち1件では共犯の従属的立場と判断された。もう1件では、被害者のうち1人に対しては「計画性なし」としたうえで、被告人について「反省の態度を示している」「自分の考え方や行動のどこに問題があったか、苦しみながら考え抜いて、内省を深めていくことを期待すべきではないかとの結論に至った」と述べており、裁判員が主観的要素を重視したとも考えられる。

無罪判決は11件中1件のみで、2010年12月10日、鹿児島地裁のケースであった。「被告人が犯人でなければ合理的に説明することができない事実関係が（状況証拠に）含まれていない」として、2010年4月27日最高裁判決の判断基準に従っており、プロ裁判官の主導によるものと推察される。判決後の記者会見で、裁判員の1人は無罪判決に関し、「遺族の方には申し訳ない」と話したといい、裁判員がこうした特有の感情に左右される危うさも垣間見えた。

3　政治主導

矯正統計年報によれば、最近20年間の死刑執行は、1990年～1992年がゼロで、1993年～2010年は2008年を除いて年間1～9人だった。2008年は15人と唯一2桁を記録した。15人のうち、当時の鳩山邦夫法務大臣は2月に3人、

4　永田憲史『死刑選択基準の研究』（関西大学出版部、2010）21-25頁、136-138頁。

4月に4人、6月に3人と、計10人の執行を命令し、恣意的だとの指摘もなされた。

2009年に政権に就いた民主党は、「政治主導」を旗印に掲げた。

イギリスが1969年に死刑を廃止したのも、アメリカ・イリノイ州が2000年に死刑執行を停止し、2003年に死刑囚全員を恩赦の対象としたのも、冤罪または冤罪の疑いがその契機ではあったが、政権政党や州知事の政治主導によるところが大きい。イリノイ州では死刑に関する調査委員会（the Commission on Capital Punishment）を設け、制度の問題点を洗い出したうえで知事が決断した[5]。

民主党は政権を取ることとなった2009年8月の衆議院選挙のマニフェストで、「終身刑を検討」「死刑制度については、死刑存置国が先進国中では日本と米国のみ。国際的な動向にも注視しながら死刑の存廃問題だけでなく当面の執行停止や死刑の告知、執行方法などをも含めて国会内外で幅広く議論を継続していきます」と明記した。確かに2010年8月、法務省内に「死刑の在り方についての勉強会」が発足したが、その前提として、死刑廃止論者であったとされる千葉景子法務大臣は2人の死刑執行を命令した。結局、「当面の執行停止」に向けた政治の主導力を発揮できずに、依然として官僚主導と思われる状況が続いている。

4　裁判員裁判と死刑の「残虐性」

日本の死刑執行方法は、旧刑法が施行された1882年から絞首刑に一本化され、現在まで続いており、時代に応じて「人道的な」方法に変えてきたアメリカとは対照的である。絞首刑が憲法の禁じる残虐な刑罰に当たるか否かについて、真摯に問われた機会はほとんどない。

1922年、当時の司法省は「行刑制度調査委員会」を設置し、「死刑ノ執行方法」について、判事、司法省の局長、典獄（刑務所長）ら8人が検討、答

---

[5] Buxton, R. J. (1973) "The Politics of Criminal Law Reform : England." American Journal of Comparative Law 21 : 230-244. Governor George H. Ryan's Clemency Address (http://www.law.northwestern.edu/wrongfulconvictions/issues/deathpenalty/clemency/ryanSpeech.html).

申した。絞首刑の残虐性に関し、この国の政府が曲がりなりにも調査を行った唯一の場であった。絞首刑をアメリカ・ニューヨーク州の電気椅子、ガス、化学薬品などによる執行と比較して、「簡易で苦痛が少なく安全」だとし、絞首刑が「適当」と結論づけた。執行方法の「改善」に「工夫」が必要と付言したものの、「身體ノ一部ニ暫時痙攣ヲ目撃スルコト」が「悲哀ヲ催ス」として、「床下ニ黒幕ヲ引キ幕ノ内部ニ身體落下スル様多少其ノ装置ヲ改ムレハ可ナリ」とするにとどまった。不都合な部分は隠せばいいという密行主義の原型が見て取れる[6]。

　1948年3月の最高裁大法廷判決は「死刑制度は合憲」「ただ、執行の方法等がその時代と環境とにおいて人道上の見地から一般に残虐と認められる場合には残虐な刑罰と言わなければならぬ[7]」とし、1955年4月の最高裁大法廷判決も「我が国の絞首方法が、他の方法に比して特に人道上残虐であるとする理由は認められない[8]」と判断した。50年以上経った現在も、これらの判決が合憲の根拠となっている。

　ただ、裁判員裁判で注目すべき事案の審理が間もなく始まる。死刑が求刑される可能性が高い事件であり、絞首刑の残虐性を巡り、弁護側と検察側が公判前整理手続きで対立している。

　弁護側は、絞首刑で頭部が離断する可能性があり、残虐な刑になりうることを、外国の事例や1883年の日本における事例、専門家の証言などを通じ、裁判員の前で立証する方針で、「裁判官、裁判員が、被告人に絞首刑を科すことの相当性を判断するためには、絞首刑の執行の具体的態様を知ることが不可欠」と主張している。これに対し、検察側は「裁判員法は、法令の解釈に係る判断については、構成裁判官の合議によると定めている。憲法適合性判断も、法律専門家である裁判官の判断にゆだねられる」「（証拠調べで）裁判員に対して、死刑に対する心理的あるいは感情的な抵抗感をあおり立て、死刑の量刑をすることに心理的重圧を加える」として、立証を許すべきではな

6　法務図書館所蔵資料「死刑ノ執行ニ就テ」（E-211）、「死刑執行ノ方法ニ就テ　野口委員」（E-214）。
7　最判昭和23年3月12日刑集2巻3号191頁。
8　最判昭和30年4月6日刑集9巻4号663頁。

いと反論している[9]。

　死刑執行の方法にとどまらず、死刑の求刑・科刑の基準などを含め、死刑制度の根本的な見直しは本来、裁判員制度導入前に年月をかけて行うべきことであったはずで、今後は法務省内の勉強会などではなく、第三者による調査委員会を設けて取り組む必要がある。

9　「大阪パチンコ店放火事件」の裁判員裁判で、弁護側はオーストリアの法医学者と日本の元検察官を証人とし、絞首刑に関する違憲性の立証を行ったが、大阪地方裁判所は2011年10月31日、絞首刑は合憲とし、被告人に死刑を言い渡した。

［2］韓国の死刑制度と廃止への歩み

朴　秉植[1]（東国大学）
<small>パク　ビョンシク</small>

1　はじめに

　韓国は「法律上」死刑存置国である。しかし、執行は、1997年12月以来14年間行っておらず、「事実上」の死刑廃止国になっている[2]。

　韓国の死刑制度は日本と酷似している。刑事法のシステムが日本を継受したからである。しかし、死刑制度の中身は相当違う。死刑相当犯罪が日本に比べ遥かに多く、執行もかつては多かった。同じく存置国であっても、韓国はもっと酷かったのである。このような国で執行が14年間も止まっているのは、一体どういうことなのか。

　2010年2月25日、韓国の憲法裁判所は多数意見で、死刑は違憲ではないという決定を下した。しかし、長く続いてきた死刑執行停止が、憲法裁判所の決定によって急に再開されるとは思えない。しかし、どのようなことがいつ起こってもおかしくない国柄の韓国である。安心は禁物である。

　死刑は絶対廃止されるべきだ、と私は確信しており、死刑を廃止するための活動を展開している。私に死刑廃止の必要性と運動の方法を教えてくれたのは日本である。日本で学んだことを韓国で実践してきたのである。ところが、いま韓国は事実上の廃止国になったのに、日本は、ほぼ毎年執行を続ける存置国のままである。非常に残念に思う。

　本稿は、韓国の死刑制度の仕組みについて紹介すると共に、これまで展開されてきた廃止運動と存廃をめぐる最近の動きについて述べたい。

1　東国大学法学部教授・法学博士（明治大学）。近著に朴秉植『死刑を止めた国・韓国』（インパクト出版会、2012年）。
2　韓国が「事実上の死刑廃止国」になったことさえわからない国民が多い。存廃をめぐるネット論争などインターネットの影響もあるなど以前よりは広まっているけれども、まだまだの状況である。

2 韓国の死刑制度

(1) 死刑制度の憲法上の根拠

韓国憲法で死刑を直接定めた明文の条文はない。しかし、「死刑」という単語が出てくる条文はある。「非常戒厳の下における軍事裁判は軍人・軍務員の犯罪や軍事に関する間諜罪の場合と哨兵・哨所・有毒飲食物の供給・捕虜に関する罪の中で法律の定めた場合に限り、単審で裁判することができる。ただし、死刑を宣告する場合にはその限りではない」と規定した、憲法第110条第4項がそれである。憲法裁判所の多数意見は死刑制度の根拠をこの但書きに求め、「文言の解釈上、死刑制度を間接的に認めている」[3]、と主張した。

しかし、憲法の制定史を遡ってみると、多数意見の主張は事実ではない。憲法第110条4項の本文は、戦争や非常戒厳などの国家非常事態において特殊犯罪を軍事裁判で速やかに処罰するために導入されたものであるけれども、同条の但書きは、いくら国家非常事態であっても死刑宣告だけは司法手続きによる不服申立が可能であるよう配慮しろという意味で導入された[4]。つまり、第110条第4項但書きは、死刑を正当化するためではなく、死刑を抑え生命権を保障するために設けられたのである。

死刑制度を認める明文規定は韓国憲法にはない。したがって、死刑が合憲か違憲かは生命権や刑罰制度の目的、人間の尊厳と価値に関する憲法の解釈にかかっているといえよう。

(2) 死刑相当犯罪

韓国と日本の死刑制度は相当違う。韓国の死刑相当犯罪の数は日本よりずっと多い。韓国においてどういう犯罪が死刑相当犯罪なのかをすべて紹介することは無理である。法定刑として死刑を規定している法律は20を超え、条文の数だけで110余りを数えるからである。

刑法には、以下の犯罪について死刑が規定されている。①内乱罪（内乱・

---

[3] 憲法裁判所 1996年11月28日、判例集8巻2号537頁〔544-545頁〕；憲法裁判所 2010年2月25日、公報第161号421頁以下参照。

[4] 憲法裁判所 2010年2月25日、公報第161号440頁参照。

内乱目的の殺人)、②外患罪(外患誘致・与敵・敵国への施設提供・間諜)、③爆発物使用、④現住建造物放火致死、⑤殺人罪(単純殺人・尊属殺人・偽計等による嘱託殺人、⑥強姦殺人、⑦人質殺人、⑧強盗殺人、⑨海上強盗殺人・致死・強姦である(この中で、与敵罪の刑罰は死刑のみになっている)。しかし、死刑相当犯罪は特別刑法などにも多く定められている。法律と罪名だけを述べておく。

「特定犯罪加重処罰などに関する法」
- 常習強盗・常習特殊強盗・常習人質強盗・常習海上強盗
- 強盗傷害・強盗強姦の再犯
- 窃盗組織の首魁
- 報復目的の殺人
- 通貨偽造の加重処罰

「暴力行為など処罰に関する法律」
- 暴力団体構成の首魁

「性暴力犯罪の処罰などに関する特例法」
- 特殊強盗強姦
- 強姦殺人・致死

「国家保安法」
- 反国家団体構成の首魁
- 軍事上機密・国家機密の探知・収集・漏泄・伝達・仲介
- 反国家団体構成員の騒擾・爆発物使用・逃走援助・放火・溢水など
- 反国家団体支配地域からの潜入・脱出
- 軍刑法および内乱・外患罪の特殊加重

「麻薬類管理に関する法律」
- 営利目的の麻薬の輸出入・製造・販売・斡旋など

「麻薬類不法取引防止に関する特例法」
- 業としての不法輸出入・製造など

「保健犯罪取締りに関する特別措置法」

- 不正食品製造致死
- 不正医薬品製造致死

「臓器など移植に関する法律」
- 臓器の摘出による致死
- 脳死の誤判定による致死

「文化財保護法」
- 文化財管理者威力行使致死

「国際刑事裁判所管轄犯罪の処罰などに関する法律」
- 人種の集団殺害
- 民間人住民の殺害
- 人への戦争犯罪
- 追放・監禁・移住などによる致死
- 軍旗・制服の不正方法による致死
- 戦争での国際的保護者の致死
- 禁止武器による生命・身体・財産への侵害

「韓国造幣公社法」
- 不引渡しの貨幣・有価証券の強制取得

「航空法」
- 航行航空機の墜落・転覆・破壊
- 航行航空機の墜落による致死傷

「航空安全および保安に関する法」
- 航空機の破壊
- 航空機拉致による致死傷

「船舶および海上構造物に対する危害行為などの処罰に関する法律」
- 船舶および海上構造物における死刑
- 船舶拉致殺人・致死
- 暴行傷害殺人致死

「原子力法」
- 戦争・天災における原子炉の破壊

「原子力施設などの防護および放射能防災対策法」

- 核物質の所有・保管・使用・運搬による致死

「放射性廃棄物管理法」
- 放射能廃棄物管理施設破壊致死

「化学・生物武器の禁止および特定化学物質・生物作用剤などの製造・輸出入規制などに関する法」
- 化学・生物武器による生命・身体・財産侵害および公安紊乱

「地雷など特定在来式武器使用および移転の規制に関する法律」
- 禁止武器の使用および地雷使用による殺害・傷害

「戦闘警察隊設置法」
- 敵前における勤務忌避目的の自害

「軍刑法」
- （紙面関係上、罪名の記述は省く）

　一般国民はもちろん、専門家にも馴染みのない法律に、死刑相当犯罪がこれほど規定されているのである。名も知らない法律でもっていつ命が奪われるかも知れない。これを果たして「一般予防効果」といってよいだろうか。とりわけ軍刑法の場合、全体の94ヶ条の中の42ヶ条に62の死刑相当犯罪が規定されている。まさに「死刑法」である。韓国は、法律上、死刑の「インフレーション」の状況である。

　1990年代に一時期、死刑相当犯罪を減らす法改正の動きがあった。従来は死刑相当犯罪であった、5千万ウォン以上の収賄や2億ウォン以上の無免許輸出入、1千万ウォン以上の山林窃盗および5万m²以上の山林毀損、ひき逃げによる被害者の死亡などの法定刑を無期刑に引き下げたのである。しかし、死刑を無期刑に引き下げたというまえに、そもそもこのような行為を死刑相当犯罪にした自体がおかしい。

　法務部（日本の法務省にあたる）は死刑廃止の要求に対し、「裁判所は死刑を連続殺人犯や強盗強姦犯など、みずから人間たることを放棄した凶悪犯だけに宣告している」と答えて死刑を正当化している。しかし、前述のように、未だに生命と無関係な犯罪に対しても死刑は規定されている。

　憲法裁判所の合憲決定で、関亨基裁判官は、「凶悪犯や社会的危険を招く

蓋然性が大きい犯罪であっても、生命に対する侵害がなく身体的法益のみを侵害した場合や、放火・破壊・暴行など積極的侵害行為により国家または公共の安全を害する犯罪でも生命・身体に対し侵害がない場合は、たとえその犯罪による公共の危険性が大きくても死刑を規定するのは原則的に過剰刑罰にあたる余地がある」[5]とし、死刑相当犯罪の縮小を主張している。しかし、この基準に従っても、死刑相当犯罪は依然として相当な数にのぼる。

3 韓国の死刑執行

韓国政府が樹立された1948年から最後の執行が行われた1997年までの50年間、死刑で執行された者は902人である。年平均18人にのぼる。その40%が国家保安法あるいは反共法の違反であり、イデオロギーに揺れ動いた歴史の悲惨さを物語っている。最近は国家保安法による死刑宣告はたいへん減ったけれども、南北に分断された朝鮮半島の政治状況を考えれば、イデオロギーによる死刑がこれ以降絶対ないとは言い切れない。

死刑が最も多かったのは、朝鮮戦争の終わった翌年の1954年で、68人が処刑された。ところが、その半分を超える38人は、国家保安法と非常措置令の違反である。また、朴正煕政権では独裁政治に対する反体制運動が盛んだったこともあって、1974年には何と58人が執行されるが、そのうち19人の罪はスパイ容疑である。とりわけ学生運動の主導者をスパイにでっち上げ殺してしまった「人民革命党事件」は、代表的な冤罪として知られる。大法院（日本の最高裁にあたる）の死刑宣告から20時間も経たないうちに執行してしまい、国際的に「司法殺人」という非難を受けた[6]。韓国において死刑の歴史は、政治的コードを抜きにしては語れない。

ソウル西大門区にある旧ソウル拘置所の跡地は、現在「独立公園」となっ

---

5 憲法裁判所2010．2．25。2008憲ガ23、公報第161号436頁以下
6 朴正煕元大統領自身も左翼活動の容疑で死刑判決を受けた人物である。最近、中央日報には、死刑判決を受けて、責任者に命を乞う彼の姿に対する証言が描かれている。「彼の答えは簡単であった。何の飾りもなかった。『一度だけ、生かしてください…』。しかし、彼の声は震えていた。その言葉と一緒に彼は涙を流していた。目元が赤くなったのも見えた」（中央日報2010．8．3記事参照）。

ている。その片隅に死刑を執行した死刑場が史跡として保存されている。日帝時代に多くの独立運動家が処刑され、小泉元総理も参拝したことがある。しかし、この死刑場では数多くの反独裁民主化運動家も処刑されていたのである[7]。「独立公園」は「独立民主公園」に改めるべきである。

しかし、死刑は軍事独裁政権でのみ行われたわけではない。いわゆる「文民政権」を名乗った金泳三政権でも多くの執行が行われた。金泳三自身が民主化運動をしており、軍事政権とは違うから、死刑を廃止するかあるいは執行はしないだろうと予測していた。しかし、彼は、組織暴力団による凶悪事件が起こった1994年、15人を執行したのをはじめ、1995年には19人、そして政権末期の1997年には23人もの命を一挙に奪ってしまう。結果的に金泳三政権では57人が執行されるが、この数字は39人を執行した軍事独裁の盧泰愚政権を上回る。1997年12月30日の金泳三政権の死刑執行は、最後の執行日となっている。

金泳三政権に次いで、金大中政権が開幕した。彼は独裁政権から死刑宣告を受けた死刑囚でもあったし、内外にむけて人権大統領を自称した。それで、多くの人々は、彼の在任中に死刑が廃止されるのではないかと強く期待した。しかしながら、彼にとっても死刑は、自分の波乱万丈な政治的体験を語るための「物語り」に過ぎなかった。死刑廃止については明白な態度をとらず、廃止の具体的な動きも示さなかった。退任後、事実上の死刑廃止国になったのを祝う記念式場に出席し、「今日の死刑廃止国家宣布式は、われわれの人権運動史上、もっとも意義深い日であり、最大の人権勝利を祝うべき日である」[8] と述べたけれども、これもイベントに過ぎない。

ただ、金大中政権において政府機関である国家人権委員会が初めて、死刑廃止を勧告したことは大きな成果である。国家人権委員会は2005年4月6日、全員委員会を開き、死刑制度について検討して、次のような意見を表明

---

7 しかし、ソウル拘置所の展示館には、民主化運動家が処刑されたことを伝えるものはどこにも見当たらない。この公園が軍事政権の盧泰愚元大統領時代に造られたことを勘案すると、民主化運動について語りたくないのは当たり前かも知れない。しかし、その後の金泳三、金大中、盧武鉉政権にも見直されないまま現在に至っている。

8 「連合ニュース」 2007. 10. 10 参照

した。〔ア〕死刑制度は生命権の本質的内容を侵害するものであり、廃止すべきである。〔イ〕死刑廃止後の措置として減刑・仮釈放のない終身刑制度、一定期間減刑・仮釈放のない無期刑制度および戦時における例外的な維持などの法案を考えられるが、採択の内容については国会が立法過程で考慮すべきである[9]。国民人権委員会の死刑廃止勧告は大きな反響を呼び起こし、廃止論の大きな力になった。国家人権委員会は、憲法裁判所の合憲決定の後も廃止意見を維持している。

金大中を継承した盧武鉉前大統領は、死刑について具体的な意見を表明したことがなかったけれども、民主化運動をした経験から執行をすることはしないだろうと期待していた。そして、最後まで執行をしなかった。大統領の任期は5年であり、金大中と盧武鉉政権だけで無事10年が経ち、2007年12月9日、事実上の死刑廃止国になったのである。

しかし、このような雰囲気は李明博政権が出帆してから一変される。大統領選の際に、死刑存廃の意見を聞くアンケート調査に対し、他の候補者は在任中は執行しないと答えたけれども、李明博だけは何の返事もしなかった。そして、2009年の2月、連続殺人事件をきっかけに、死刑執行を具体的に検討するよう指示し、それを受けて党政協議会が開かれた。執行はできなかったけれども、李明博政権の下ではいつ死刑が執行されてもおかしくない状況だということを印象づけた。

韓国の刑事訴訟法によれば、法務部長官は判決の確定日から6ヶ月以内に死刑執行の命令をしなければならず、命令から5日以内に執行することになっている（同法第465条、466条）。法律だけをみる限り、死刑執行は法務部長官の仕事であって、大統領が介入する余地はないように見える。しかし、韓国においては法務部長官が独自に死刑執行命令を出すことはほとんどできない。法務部長官が執行命令にサインをするのは、政治的・社会的に判断し執行を大統領に建議して了解を得てからである。韓国の死刑制度は、政治と深く結びついているのである。

事実上の廃止国になったとはいえ、死刑宣告は現在も続いている。〈表1〉

---

[9] 国家人権委員会「死刑制度についての国家人権委員会の意見」(2005.5.3)

〈表1〉 第1審死刑確定者数と死刑執行者数

年度	第1審死刑確定者	死刑執行者	年度	第1審死刑確定者	死刑執行者
1980	32	9	1995	19	19
1981	33	0	1996	23	0
1982	35	23	1997	10	23
1983	19	9	1998	14	0
1984	18	0	1999	20	0
1985	25	11	2000	20	0
1986	8	13	2001	12	0
1987	18	5	2002	7	0
1988	15	0	2003	5	0
1989	17	7	2004	8	0
1990	36	14	2005	6	0
1991	35	9	2006	6	0
1992	26	9	2007	0	0
1993	21	0	2008	3	0
1994	35	15	2009	6	0

は、1980年以降の第1審死刑確定者と死刑執行者数をあらわしたものである。かつては毎年20〜30人を超えていたが、2002年からは一桁で安定しているのがわかる。現在の死刑囚は60人である。

4 死刑廃止運動とその限界

韓国の死刑廃止運動団体としては、「死刑廃止運動協議会」と「死刑廃止汎宗教連合」を挙げられる。前者は、国連の死刑廃止条約と1989年アムネスティの「死刑廃止の年」宣言に触発され、1989年に発足された。ソウル拘置所の囚人を対象に教化活動を行っていた民間ボランティア（日本の教誨師にあたる）で構成された「ソウル拘置所教化協議会」が母体となっている。死刑廃止に向けた努力と活動は高く評価できよう。

一方、後者の「死刑廃止汎宗教連合会」は2004年カトリック正義平和委員会・キリスト教教会協議会・仏教人権委員会など、宗教組織で発足されたものである。現在の死刑廃止活動は事実上この団体が主導している。

　宗教界が死刑廃止運動を主導するというと、政教分離原則のことを気にするかも知れない。しかし、宗教に対する観念と視角は、日本と韓国とで相当異なる。韓国における宗教界のパワーは想像以上である。殆どの国民がみずから信者をなのり、政治界も投票を意識して宗教界の声に耳を傾ける。憲法における政教分離原則はそれほど問題にならない。宗教者たちが死刑廃止運動を引っ張ったのも、宗教界のパワーにバックアップされているからである。

　宗教界の活動に比べ、市民団体の活動はあまり目立たない。日本でよく見られる「〇〇〇さんを救う会」のような団体は一つもない。政治的な冤罪でもって囚われている人のための救援活動はあっても、特定死刑囚のための救援組織はない。この頃アムネスティ韓国が死刑廃止運動に力を入れているが、アムネスティ日本の活動に比べれば足元にも及ばない。

　しかし、宗教界の主導する死刑廃止運動には、自ずと限界があるはずである。死刑執行の停止までは力が発揮できたけれども、廃止までは結びつけない。死刑を最終的に廃止できる国会議員にとって、宗教界は無視できない存在ではあるけれども、最後の「お客」は一般市民であるのである。

　また、死刑廃止に向けた熱気も宗派ごとに温度差が感じられる。プロテスタント、仏教、カトリック、円仏教など、ほぼ全ての宗派が一応死刑廃止運動に加わっているけれども、中身をみるとカトリックが主導し他の宗派はそれに従う形である。

　このように、韓国の死刑運動はいってみれば「市民」のない「神々」の運動である。いかに「市民」を育て、市民団体をつくり、「草の根」レベルの運動を広げることができるか、これからの死刑廃止運動の課題である。

5　司法の判断

　2010年2月25日、憲法裁判所は多数意見で死刑制度を合憲と決定した。死刑制度の違憲・合憲を問う裁判は、憲法裁判所制度が導入される前の大法院

時代にも行われた。

　1983年、大法院は「人道的または宗教的見地から、尊い生命を奪う死刑は避けなければならないのは異論を許さない。しかしその一方、犯罪により侵害されるもう一人の命を無視することはできないし、社会公共の安寧と秩序のために生命刑を存置することも理解できなくもない。これは、すなわちその国の実定法にあらわれる国民的総意として捉えられる…」[10] といって、死刑制度を合憲とした。長さ10行ほどの短い判示で、判決理由という名にはふさわしくないものであった。

　また、1990年の判決では「国家の刑事政策により、秩序維持と公共福利のため、刑法に死刑という刑罰を規定したからといって、これを憲法に違反したものだといえない」[11]、とした。1991年の判決でも、「憲法第12条第1項は刑事処罰に関する規定を法律に委任しているのみで、刑罰の種類を制限していないし、現在わが国の実情と国民の道徳的感情などを考慮して、国家の刑事政策により秩序維持と公共福利のために刑法などに死刑という処罰の種類を定めたからといって、これが憲法に違反であるとはいえない」[12]、と判決した。

　一方、憲法裁判所が発足されてから、死刑制度に対する判断はより慎重になる。1993年、「死刑を宣告した犯罪や被害者の生命の価値を考慮せず、死刑自体が人間の尊厳と価値を否定する刑罰だと断定するのは妥当性がなく、刑罰の本質は応報にもあるといえるので、反社会的犯罪に加えられる社会の道徳的反応の表現である死刑制度は、社会の安定に資するのはもちろん、犯罪被害者および一般人の人間としての尊厳と価値を保護する効果もあるといえる。よって、死刑制度を規定した法律は憲法に違反するとはいえない」[13] と、判決理由で法務部の意見を引用したものの、それなりに死刑制度について分析する態度を示す[14]。

　10　大法院　1983. 3. 8.　宣告　82ド3248　判決
　11　大法院　1990. 04. 24　宣告　90ド319　判決
　12　大法院　1991. 2. 26　宣告　90ド2906　判決
　13　憲法裁判所　1993. 11. 25　89憲マ36、判例集第5巻2集423頁
　14　ちなみに、この裁判で、長く死刑廃止運動に携わってきた李相赫弁護士は、「一人

最高裁判所が死刑制度について本格的に論じるのは1996年の判決である。「死刑が比例原則に従って、少なくとも同じ価値をもつ他の命またはそれに劣らない公共利益を保護するための不可避性が満たされる例外的な場合にのみ適用される限り、たとえそれが命を奪う刑罰であっても憲法に反するといえない」、「人間の生命を否定する犯罪行為に対する不法的効果として、極めて限定的な場合にのみ科される死刑は、死に対する人間の本能的な恐怖心と犯罪に対する応報欲求とが相俟って考案された『必要悪』として不可避的に選択されたものであり、今も依然として機能している点で正当化できる」[15]。死刑制度を合憲としながらも、「必要悪」として捉えたこと、そして二人の裁判官が違憲論を述べたのは、この裁判の特徴である。

　そして、2010年2月25日の合憲決定である。今回の決定は、合憲5対違憲4に意見が分かれ、前回の合憲7対違憲2より、違憲意見が幾分増えた。

　合憲論の主な論旨は以下のとおりである。

（1）　死刑は無期懲役刑や仮釈放のない終身刑よりも、犯罪者に対する法益侵害の程度が大きく最も強力な犯罪抑止力を有しており、極悪な犯罪には適した刑罰である。

（2）　誤判の可能性は司法制度の宿命的限界であり、死刑という刑罰制度そのものの問題だとはいえない。審級制度と再審制度など制度的装置およびその改善を通じて解決すべき問題である。

（3）　裁判官や刑務官が死刑を宣告し執行する過程で自責の念をおぼえるかも知れないが、公益を保護する公的地位にある以上、死刑の適用や執行を受忍すべき義務がある。

　また、合憲論は「死刑制度が違憲であるか否かの問題は憲法裁判所の権限であるが、死刑制度を法律上存置するか廃止するかの問題は立法府が決めるべき立法政策的な問題である」と述べた。死刑問題を立法にゆだねたのは注目すべき特徴である。

　の人間の命は、全地球より重く大切で絶対的であり」と日本最高裁の判決を引用し、死刑の違憲性を主張している。

15　憲法裁判所　1996.11.28、95憲バ1、判例集第8巻2集537頁以下

6　憲法裁判所の合憲論へ問題点

そこで、憲法裁判所の論旨について批判的に考察してみたい。

(1)　犯罪抑止効果の問題

　死刑が犯罪抑止効果を有するかどうかは、死刑存廃の論議において重要なテーマである。そして、犯罪抑止効果は存置論者の強力な拠り所になっている。しかし、少なくとも韓国の状況を見る限り、死刑の犯罪抑止効果は疑わしい。

　ある地方新聞のネット版で、刺激的な記事をみつけた。「死刑を執行しない間に殺人犯罪が38％も増えた」とし、死刑を執行すべきと主張していたのである。

〈表2〉死刑執行者数と殺人件数

年度	死刑執行者数	殺人件数	年度	死刑執行者数	殺人件数
1977	28	506	1993	0	806
1978	0	485	1994	15	705
1979	10	458	1995	19	646
1980	9	536	1996	0	690
1981	0	625	1997	23	789
1982	23	538	1998	0	966
1983	9	518	1999	0	984
1984	0	581	2000	0	964
1985	11	600	2001	0	1,064
1986	13	617	2002	0	983
1987	5	653	2003	0	1,011
1988	0	601	2004	0	1,082
1989	7	578	2005	0	1,091
1990	14	666	2006	0	1,064
1991	9	630	2007	0	1,124
1992	9	615	2008	0	1,120

『犯罪白書』によれば、最後の執行が行われた1997年に789件であった殺人件数が、2007年は1,124件に上っている。殺人件数が急増したという主張は確かなのである。しかし、殺人事件が増えたのは死刑を執行しなかったからだろうか。執行を続けていたら、殺人事件は増えなかっただろうか。

金泳三政権の1997年12月に23人が執行されたとき、法務部は報道資料まで出したし、マスコミも執行の事実を大きく報道した。もし、死刑が犯罪抑止効果を有するならば、大量執行の翌年である1998年には少なくとも殺人事件が減るべきであろう。ところが、結果は正反対であった。1997年に789件だった殺人件数が1998年には966件に達した。何と20％も増えてしまったのである。

犯罪抑止効果の問題点は、死刑を執行し続けていた過去の流れをみてもわかる。たとえば、1977年には506人であったのが、1997年には789件にのぼる。執行を続けていた20年間に、56％も増えたのである。死刑の犯罪抑止効果どころか、むしろ「犯罪促進効果」あるいは「残忍化効果」(brutalization) と呼ぶべきかも知れない。

〈表2〉は、死刑執行者数と殺人件数をあらわしたものである。

(2) 誤判の問題

誤判の問題は存置論にとって大きな弱点であり、憲法裁判所も誤判の可能性を認めている。しかし、それは死刑制度固有の問題点として認めたわけではない。誤判は「神でない以上避けられないし、審級制度や再審制度など訴訟手続きを通じて解決すれば問題ない」とする。

裁判官が神でないのは当たり前である。だから、誤判によって無実な人が殺されるという事態がいつでも生じうる。だから、少なくとも誤判により命が奪われるような悲劇を避けるために、死刑は廃止されるべきである。ところが、憲法裁判所は、誤判の可能性を認めつつ、誤判によって無実な人の命が奪われても仕方がないという。犯罪によって奪われる命は保護する価値はあるけれども、誤判によって奪われる命は保護する価値はない。裁判をやると、それぐらいの過ちは仕方ないという論理である。

「審級制度や再審制度など訴訟手続きを通じて」、無実な命がどのように解

決されるのかもわからない。裁判官の判決による殺人行為は許されて当たり前だという、傲慢と生命に対する差別が感じられる。事件による被害者遺族の感情には感情移入できても、誤判によって無実の命を奪われる遺族の感情はまったく無視する。これは、威張りや開き直りでしかない。

前述した冤罪の「人民革命党事件」について、ソウル中央地裁は2007年1月23日、被告人8人の無罪を宣告した。そして、大法院を含め、国家の不法行為責任を認め、史上最高の637億ウォンの国家賠償を支給することを命令した。事件からすでに32年の歳月が過ぎている。しかし、無実な8人の命は戻らない。

われわれは冤罪の事例を何度も目にしている。それにも拘わらず、未だに誤判の「可能性」を云々する。しかし、命の問題では「誤判」を論じるべきであって、「誤判の可能性」を論じるべきではない。

(3) 仮釈放のない終身刑と死刑廃止法案

死刑廃止について多くの人々は、加害者の赦しだと誤解してしまう。そこで、韓国の廃止論者は「死刑廃止」を言うとき、必ず「終身刑」もセットで紹介するよう努めている。

韓国の廃止論者は、死刑の代替刑として「仮釈放のない終身刑」の導入にほぼ一致しているし、私も積極的に終身刑の導入を訴えてきた。死刑制度に対する国民の厳しい世論と被害者の感情を考え合わせると、彼らを納得させる刑罰は終身刑しかないと思うからである。

ところが、終身刑に対する最初の反応は非常に冷たいものであった。終身刑も死刑と同じく人権を侵害する刑罰だというのである。廃止論者のみならず存置論者の中にも、終身刑は死刑よりも残酷だという理由で、終身刑の導入を反対した者もいた。

終身刑が人権侵害の刑罰であるという考えは、ヨーロッパで以前から提起された問題である。そして、終身刑が残酷な刑罰であることも事実である。しかし、それにも拘わらず死刑の代替刑として終身刑を導入しようと思ったのは、ヨーロッパと我々の状況は全く違うからである。ヨーロッパではすでに死刑が廃止されているので、終身刑の問題を提起してもそれなりに意味が

ある。しかし、韓国では依然として死刑制度が残っており、ヨーロッパと次元が異なる。いつ命が落とされるかわからない厳しい状況で、残酷さを理由に終身刑を反対するのは「贅沢」である。

終身刑は確かに残酷な刑罰である。しかし、この問題は、死刑を廃止してからゆっくり論じても遅くない。終身刑を「一生刑務所にぶち込み、希望のない日々を送らせる、過酷な刑罰」ではなく、「大事な命をつなげる、望みの刑罰」として捉え直す、観点の転換が求められる。

終身刑の導入は国会でも理解を得られている段階である。死刑廃止法案が死刑の代替刑として終身刑を打ち出しているからである。死刑廃止法案が国会に初めて出されたのは1999年であるが、代替刑に関しては全く触れなかった。代替刑は、2001年の廃止法案で初めて提案される。無期刑を宣告する代わり、15年間仮釈放や赦免を禁じる言い渡しをするというのである。しかし、両法案とも法司委員会（日本の法務委員会にあたる）に上程されず廃棄される。無期刑が言い渡されても、15年経てば仮釈放されてしまうかも知れないという悪いイメージが先行したからである。

そこで現れたのが、2004年の死刑廃止法案である。そして、この法案に初めて終身刑が盛り込まれる。提案者である柳寅泰議員は民主化運動で逮捕され、死刑判決が下された元死刑囚であり、赦免により減刑され国会議員になった人物である。この法案は、全体の過半数を超えた議員が賛同したので[16]、廃止の期待も高まったし、法司委員会に上程され、公聴会も開かれた。しかしながら、結局本会議に上程されず廃棄されてしまった。

現在、国会には三人の議員によって四度目の廃止法案が提案されている。いずれも仮釈放のない終身刑を打ち出しているけれども、赦免や減刑を認めない面では前の法案よりも厳しい。国民感情を意識した結果かも知れないが、私は賛成しかねている。終身刑は刑罰制度であるに対し、赦免は政治的制度であり、両者の性格が違う。また、受刑者の老齢化が進みつつある現在、寝たきりの老人を収容する必要があるかは考えものである。

---

[16] 全国会議員299人中、過半数をこえた175人がこの法案に賛同した。

(4) 死刑執行刑務官の苦悩

　帰国して間もない頃、死刑制度が刑務官の人権をどれほど侵害するかについて、刑務官を相手に講演をしたことがある[17]。法的根拠もなくもっぱら命令に従って執行を行わざるを得ない刑務官の苦悩について触れ[18]、侵害される刑務官の人権について指摘した[19]。講演を終えたら、多くの刑務官たちが支持を示してくれた。

　そして、昨年の矯正関連学会で、ある刑務官は死刑執行について「自分たちは力がないので、なかなか意見を出せない。しかし、個人的には死刑が廃止されれば有難い」と述べていた。最近、ある週刊紙は、旧ソウル拘置所の死刑場について紹介する記事のなかで、執行官の苦悩についてもこう書いている。「死刑場の刑務官たちは執行が正当であると自己催眠をかけたでしょうが、多くの人は殺人の悪夢に苛まれアルコール中毒者になったり、辞職願を出して潜ってしまう例も多い」[20]。

　憲法裁判所はこのような刑務官の苦悩などまったく配慮せず、「公益を保護する公的地位にあるから」と片づけてしまう。死刑執行が「公益」であるかは疑わしいけれども、「義務だから受忍しなさい」というのは、「嫌ならば辞めなさい」という脅しである。いくら公務員の仕事とはいえ、人間の命を奪うのを「公益」や「義務」と捉えるのは言いすぎである。「正義の旗をふりかざすあまり、人間の情を失う」愚かさを犯している。

17　講演の内容は、「死刑制度と矯導官の人権」京畿大学『教育論叢』(1999.11) にまとめられている。

18　矯導管職務規則は「死刑執行は上官の指示をうけた正服の矯導官がしなければならない」(同第44条) と定めていた。1963年に制定されたこの法務部の命令が、長い間、刑務官の死刑執行義務の唯一の根拠であったのである。その後、2008年に行刑法を改正した「刑の執行および収容者の処遇に関する法律」は執行の主体を明確にしないまま、「死刑は矯正施設の死刑場で執行する」(同法第91条) とだけ定めている。

19　韓国では刑務官を「矯導官」という。矯導とは受刑者を矯正して社会に導くという意味である。しかし、死刑囚の担当になると、送り先は社会ではなく天国である。

20　「中央サンデー」第134号 (2010.9.19) の記事参照

7　結びに代えて

　死刑存廃論は、中学校と高等学校の討論授業で人気のあるテーマのひとつである。国家人権委員会も彼らのためのテキストを用意し、提供している。ところが、ある中学校の先生によれば、中学生を相手に死刑について世論調査をした結果、廃止が70％で存置が30％であったという。もしこの数字が確かならば、大変な驚きである。一般国民の調査結果と比率が正反対だからである。

　私は、かつて「人間は生まれながら死刑存置派である。教育や省察によって死刑廃止派になって行く」と思っていた。しかし、これは間違いかも知れない。人間は生まれながら死刑廃止派である。ところが、環境や社会によって死刑存置派になっていくのかも知れない。

　残虐な凶悪事件が起こっても、ヨーロッパの人は犯人を殺せとは言わないという。死刑制度がないから、死刑そのものを想像しないのである。それに対して我々は凶悪事件が起こると、「殺せ！」を合唱する。長い間、死刑制度に馴染んだからである。

　死刑とは、そう簡単に想像できる刑罰ではない。もし私たちが暮らしているこの国にも昔から死刑制度がなかったならば、ヨーロッパと同様、死刑について議論しなかったであろう。ところが、生まれてみると、死刑がそこにあった。それで、犯人を死刑に処すことを語り合う。しかし、ちょっと止まって想像してみよう、「死刑のない世界」を。子どもたちに倣って、ヨーロッパに倣って。

（おわり）

［3］台湾における死刑執行の停止と再開：これまでとこれから

謝如媛[1]（国立政治大学法律学系）

（一） 死刑の執行停止と再開

　台湾では、民進党の陳水扁氏が2000年に大統領に当選し、2001年に3年以内に死刑を廃止すると宣言した。死刑減少のための法改正を行い、死刑の執行もその前から明らかに減少してきた。また、実際、2006年から2010年3月までの間に、台湾では死刑が執行されていなかった。

　2009年12月に経済的、社会的及び文化的権利に関する国際規約（社会権規約、A規約と略す）と市民的及び政治的権利に関する国際規約（自由権規約、B規約と略す）の内容を国内法として実施し、さらに、2009年12月法務部は、「死刑を段階的に廃止する政策研究促進会」（以下死刑廃止研究会と略す）を設立し、2010年3月に初回の会議が行われた。その研究会には、学者、弁護士、被害者団体、死刑廃止を主張する民間団体（台灣廢除死刑推動聯盟，廃死連盟と略す）のメンバーなどが集まり、死刑の代替策、刑務所処遇の改善方法、被害者保護措置、治安対策、死刑廃止を促進する広報や教育について議論が進められてきた。

　3年以内に死刑を廃止するという目標は、結局達成されなかったが、すくなくとも「段階的に死刑を廃止する」ことが2010年4月30日の死刑執行再開までの政策の基調とされてきた。

　しかし、2010年2月に、ある国会議員の法務部長への質疑によって、死刑に関する議論が再燃した。就任以来死刑執行を許可していない、かつ在任している限り絶対に死刑の執行を認めないと宣言した当時の王法務部長は、世論の厳しい批判を受け、3月12日に辞任を余儀なくされた。

　その後、新しく就任した曾勇夫法務部長は、最初から「行政は法律の規定に従って行われるべきだ」（つまり確定した死刑判決を執行するべき）と宣言した。

1　Hsieh, Ju-Yuan, Associate Professor of National Cheng-chi University, College of Law, Taiwan.

法務部は早速全国各地で死刑に関する聴聞会を開いたが、会が終わって3日間も経たない4月30日に、4人の死刑囚の死刑を執行した。2011年3月4日に再び5人の死刑囚の処刑を執行した。

（二） 執行再開前後の政府の発言と死刑廃止研究会の決議

死刑に関する議論が起こった当初、法務部は「2011年11月までに死刑を廃止する」という記事に対し、次のようにコメントをした。

A規約とB規約の内容が国内法として規定されたことによって、国内各法が規約内容に適合するかどうかを2011年11月までに検討を行うべきであるが、それまでに死刑を廃止するという意味ではない。法務部は、社会の発展状況、法治観念の成熟、死刑廃止にあわせる必要な措置の提出を考慮しつつ、段階的に死刑を廃止するという立場を改めて強調した[2]。

王元法務部長の辞任前後に、馬英九総統は死刑についてマスコミに問われ、次のような発言をした。「死刑を廃止するか否か、まだ議論が必要だ」、「着実なやり方は死刑の適用を減らすことであり、廃止することではない」、「死刑は法に従って執行されるべきだ」と言い、それまでの死刑執行停止の政策や当時の法務部長の立場と一線を劃した。

このような状況の下で、2010年3月23日に行われた死刑廃止研究会第一回会議では、会議の決議として以下の項目をマスコミに公表した。

一、死刑廃止は最終の目標である。平時の死刑は廃止するが、戦争時の軍事刑法や特別法における死刑規定は認める。

二、死刑について更なる議論が必要なため、死刑廃止についてはタイムリミットを設けない。

三、被害者保護、治安の強化、死刑の減少、死刑の代替方策（無期懲役の仮釈放審査を厳格に行うなど）は、死刑廃止に優先して行われるべきである[3]。

2　法務部、「針對世論誤解『法務部將於100年11月底前完成檢討廢除死刑』、澄清説明新聞稿」2010年2月1日、法務部全球資訊網、http://www.moj.gov.tw/public/Data/02119517447.pdf（last visited June 19, 2011).

3　《台法務部：廢死無時間表　戰時維死刑》、2010-03-23 09：24：37大紀元台灣新聞、大紀元官網、http://www.epochtimes.com/b5/10/3/23/n2854518.htm〈(last visited

(三) 死刑規定の現状
1．絶対的死刑の廃止
　死刑を絶対的（必要的）法定刑とする条文が多くあった。特に戒厳時代に多く適用された特別刑法「懲治盗匪条例」には、絶対的死刑の規定が十条以上もあった。この法律は、2002年に廃止された。その後、絶対的死刑の規定が次々と改正され、2006年に刑法における海賊罪の絶対的死刑が改正されてから、台湾では、絶対的死刑の規定がすべてなくなった。

2．死刑規定の減少
　特に直接に生命を侵害することのない犯罪について、死刑を法定刑から外す動きが明らかである。たとえば、2011年にさらに二つの死刑規定が削除された。ひとつは、「水利法」91条2項、水利に関する建造物その他の設備などを窃盗もしくは毀損し、災害をもたらした者は、その情状が重く、かつ多数の人の生命や財産に損害を与えた場合、もともと死刑または無期懲役もしくは10年以上の有期懲役を科すると規定していたが、2011年の法改正で、死刑の規定は、削除された。

　また、「妨害国幣懲治条例」第3条2項に、行使の意図に基づき、幣券を偽造もしくは変造して、金融秩序を乱し、その情状が重い場合、死刑を科すことができたが、その死刑規定も削除され、法定刑は、無期懲役もしくは10年以上の有期懲役を科することとし、1千万台湾ドルを併科することができるとする。

　上述の改正理由には、B規約に基づいて、最も重大な犯罪でなければ、死刑を科してはならないということがあげられた。

3．現行法における死刑規定
　現在（2011年7月28日まで）、死刑を科しうる規定については、計9部の法律、50条の条文は、死刑を法定刑のひとつとして規定されている。その罪名から規定の内訳をすこし見てみよう。

　June 20, 2011).

（1）刑法において：

内乱に関する罪、外患に関する罪、ハイジャック、航空の安全や設備破壊致死罪、強姦罪や強制わいせつなどの性犯罪で被害者を殺害した罪、公務員が権力を用いて人に特定の薬物の栽培、販売、運搬を行わせる罪、殺人罪、尊属殺人罪、強盗致死、強盗と殺人など（放火、強姦、身代金目的拐取、重傷）の結合犯、海賊罪、海賊と殺人（放火、強姦、身代金目的拐取、重傷）などの結合犯、身代金目的拐取罪、身代金目的拐取致死傷、身代金目的拐取と殺人など（強姦、重傷）の結合犯である。

（2）その他の規定：

刑法典以外に一番死刑の多い法律は、陸海空軍刑法である。現在でも、死刑を法定刑のひとつとする条文が20条もある。

特別法の中には、生命を直接侵害していない行為でも死刑を科しうる罪が数多く存在する。陸海空軍刑法は特にそうである。たとえば、同法20条2項：軍事秘密を敵に漏洩または交付した者は、死刑もしくは無期懲役を科する。

そのほか、薬物の特別刑法である毒品危害防制条例にも、生命法益の侵害のない罪でも死刑を科しうる規定がある。同法4条によると、第一級薬物（ヘロイン、モルヒネ、アヘンなど）を製造、運搬、または販売したものは、死刑または無期懲役を科する。同法6条1項によると、暴行、脅迫、欺罔その他不正の方法で人に第一級薬物を使用した者は、死刑、無期懲役、もしくは十年以上の有期懲役を科する。同法15条（公務員の加重処罰）によると、公務員は、職務上の権力、機会、方法を用いて同法4条2項の犯罪（第二級薬物（大麻、アンフェタミンなど）の製造、運搬、または販売）または第6条1項（暴行、脅迫、欺罔その他不正の方法で人に第一級薬物を使用した者）の犯罪を犯した者には、死刑もしくは無期懲役を科する。

このように、死刑規定の多い特別刑法「懲治盗匪条例」の廃止、各法律における絶対的死刑規定の廃止、生命法益を侵害していない罪について死刑を法定刑から外すなど、法律的には、死刑に関する規定が少しづつ減少してきている。

それでも、死刑を法定刑のひとつとする規定がまだ多い。また、陸海空軍

刑法や毒品危害防制条例のような特別法には、生命法益侵害のない罪でも死刑を科しうる条文が残っている。これらの法律についてさらなる改正が期待できると思われる。

4．無期懲役仮釈放の要件などの改正

司法実務では、死刑を科したくないが、無期懲役が軽すぎるので（2005年法改正以前、刑を執行してから15年が経つと仮釈放が可能となる）、死刑を科すしかない場合があるという声があり、死刑の適用を減少させるために法改正が必要だという意見があった。2005年に改正された刑法では、裁判官に死刑を回避するための選択肢として改正されたといわれる条文がいくつかある。たとえば、64条によると、死刑を減刑した場合、無期懲役を科することとする（もともと、死刑を減刑した場合は、無期懲役もしくは12年以上15年以下の有期懲役を科することとした）。第77条は、仮釈放の要件について規定されているが、改正前は、無期懲役の場合は15年以上の執行が、累犯で無期懲役を科された場合は20年以上の執行が仮釈放の要件とされたが、改正後は、無期懲役では25年以上の執行が、累犯では刑期の3分の2の執行が仮釈放の要件の一つとされる。累犯で無期懲役を科された場合を、初犯で無期懲役を科された場合と特に区別しない理由は、25年の執行が被告人にとって抑止効果がすでに十分であり、それ以上の拘禁が必要であるとすれば、仮釈放を許可しなくてよい、ということである。死刑の減刑が無期懲役と限られ、仮釈放の要件が厳格に改正されたことは、裁判官が死刑を科さない可能性を高めるためだといわれている[4]。

（四） 実務の動向
1．死刑判決からみる犯罪類型と内容

統計によると、2000年から2009年までの十年間の間に、死刑確定判決を受けた人数は、計93人である。この中に、生命法益を侵害していない被告人

---

[4] 朱楠「推動『廢除死刑』之新契機―立法院通過兩國際人權公約施行法之實務分析」法學新論19期、2010年2月、63頁。

は、3人しかいない。この3人は、それぞれ共同連続強盗かつ強姦罪、第一級薬物の販売の連続犯、そして薬物運搬・密輸入罪の連続犯として死刑を科された。そのほかの90人は、すべて殺人罪、または殺人罪とほかの犯罪の結合犯である。

2000年から2009年まで死刑を科された被告人の罪名、条文及びそれぞれの人数は、次の表で示す。

罪名	犯した条文	人数
殺人罪	刑法271条	36
強盗罪と殺人罪の結合犯	刑法332条	19
身代金のための誘拐罪と殺人罪の結合犯	刑法348条	15
強姦罪と殺人罪の結合犯	刑法226条の1	10
強盗罪と殺人罪の結合犯	懲治盗匪条例2条1項6号	9
製造運搬販売第1級薬物罪	煙毒条例	2
尊属殺害罪	刑法272条	1
強盗（連続犯）罪と強姦罪の結合犯	懲治盗匪条例2条1項8号	1

（王兆鵬、台灣死刑實證研究、月旦法學雜誌183期、2010年8月、121頁、表4から翻訳したもの；）

注目に値するのは、2002年以降は、生命法益を侵害せずに死刑を科された被告人がいないことである[5]。

2011年に入ってから8月3日まで、すでに12人の死刑判決が確定された。死刑囚は51人まで増えた[6]。2010年の4人の死刑判決を加えて、計16人の死刑判決が確定した。この16人の犯罪の内容からみると、ほとんどの事件は、2人以上の被害者がいる殺人、強盗殺人、身代金目的拐取殺人、強姦殺人事

5　王兆鵬、台灣死刑實證研究、月旦法學雜誌183期、2010年8月、121頁。

6　http://www.taedp.org.tw/index.php?load=read&id=929 (last visited Oct 3, 20119). この論文を作成している間、死刑判決が次々と確定されたため、何回もこの数字を書き直した。司法の殺伐の雰囲気を感じさせる。また、最近に確定した被告人邱和順の事件（15件目）は、拷問、自白偏重、物的証拠が足りない、被害者の死体は見つからないなど、かなりの疑問点が残っている。

件である。そうでない事件について、（判決時間の序列からして）13件目の事件は、被害者が1人であるし、被害者遺族に600万台湾ドルを賠償したが、最高裁が手段の残虐さ（生き埋め）と被害者遺族が宥恕していないことを理由に、死刑判決を維持した[7]。14件目の事件の被告人は、警察官二人を殺すように知人に教唆した。正犯はすでに1992年に死刑を執行されたが、被告人は15年間逃亡した上で逮捕され、殺人の教唆犯で死刑を科された[8]。

2．量刑に影響する要因

最高裁裁判官の話によると、死刑判決を維持するか否かの原則として、次のような考慮がある。

まず、単純に殺人を行った場合、特に教育の可能性がなく、矯正する見込みがない場合を除いて、被告人に前科がなければ、最高裁は下級審の死刑判決を維持することがあまりない。次に、検察官が無期懲役を求刑し、下級審は検察官の求刑意見に従わずに死刑を科す場合には、その理由を説明しなければ、実務上、最高裁によって死刑判決を破棄されることが多い。最後に、最高裁は、下級審の判決について、量刑が軽いよりは、量刑が重過ぎることで下級審判決を破棄したことが多い[9]。

また、被害者陳述や、被害者と加害者の和解が死刑判決に影響を及ぼすかどうか、すこしみてみたい。

1997年に改正された刑事訴訟法271条2項によると、「審判期日に、被害者もしくはその家族を召喚して意見を陳述する機会を与えるべきである。ただし、合法的に召喚をし、正当な理由がないにもかかわらず被害者が出席しない場合、出席しない意思を明示した場合、あるいは裁判所がその出席を必要でないもしくは適切でないと判断する場合は、この限りではない」とする。また、2003年に改正された同法271条の1によると、被害者は、代理人を依

7 　最高法院刑事判決100年度台上字第3897號。

8 　自由時報電子報、王信福槍殺兩警案　最高法院判死刑確定、2011年7月27、http://iservice.libertytimes.com.tw/liveNews/news.php?no=523029（last visited July 27, 2011）。

9 　王兆鵬、台灣死刑實證研究、月旦法學雜誌183期、2010年8月、124頁。

頼して意見陳述を行うことも可能である。

　ただし、この意見陳述について、その目的とはなにか、被害者の心情の満足を主に考慮するのか、量刑の判断材料に資するのか、量刑においてどう考慮すべきか、立法理由からも実務の運用からも学説の検討からもはっきりとしていない。また、被害者陳述が果たして被害者の回復に役立つか、事実認定や量刑判断に影響を及ぼしているかも十分に議論されていない[10]。

　被害者と加害者の和解は、死刑判決にどんな影響を与えたのか、判決をみるだけでは、和解で刑を減軽するとか、和解していないから刑を重くすることや減軽することができないとか、両方の判決も出ているので、一概にはいえない。

　しかし、最近に出された最高裁判所の死刑確定判決では、被告人が被害者と600万台湾ドルで和解をしたが、最高裁は、和解が成立したけれど、本件の被害者が被告人の刑事責任を許したことは確認できないという理由で、高裁の死刑判決を維持した[11]。また、最近の高等裁判所の死刑判決において、被告人が被害者に相当額の損害賠償を提供しようとしたにもかかわらず、被害者の宥恕をもらえなかったことと被害者の死刑への要望が、無期懲役でなく死刑を科した理由となった[12]。最高裁は、この第二審の死刑判決について、和解が成立しなくても、被告人の賠償への努力を斟酌すべきであると指摘した一方、やはり「被害者遺族の意見をも斟酌し、刑を決めるべきだ」ということを明言した[13]。金銭賠償のほかに被害者の宥恕をも要求すること、また死刑事件の量刑において遺族の意見の斟酌を明言することは、これまでの判決に比べては被害者のことをより重視しているように見受けられる。被害者または遺族の意見はこれから死刑判決にどのような影響を与えるか、注目に値すると思われる。

10　謝如媛、犯罪被害人陳述制度之成效―從英國實證研究成果出發、法學新論30號、2011年6月、13-34頁。
11　最高法院刑事判決100年度台上字第3897號。
12　台灣高等法院99年度上重訴字第60號。
13　最高法院刑事判決100年度台上字第2261號。

3．執行再開の状況

2010年4月執行再開してから、2011年7月まで、9人の死刑囚が執行された。2011年3月4日に5人の死刑囚を処刑した後、法務部は正式コメントで次のような説明を行った。すなわち、この5人は、司法救済の手段が尽きた。また、彼らは強盗殺人、殺人など他人の生命法益を奪うもっとも重大な犯罪を犯し、かつ複数の被害者が犠牲になり、人間性を欠き、許される余地がないと示した[14]。一方、性犯罪者に対する厳しい世論の中で、性犯罪かつ殺人を犯した死刑囚も、優先的に執行される可能性が高い[15]。上述のような基準に従って執行の優先順位を決めるとすれば、現在収容されている死刑囚の多くは、次の執行の対象者になりうる。政治上の必要に応じて、いつ執行があってもおかしくない状況だと思われる。

(五) 死刑廃止論争と被害者問題
1．犯罪不安－死刑と抽象的、潜在的被害者との結び付き

2006年9月、当時の法務部長施茂林は、「部務会議」の中で次の方針を明らかにした。「被害者団体と継続的に意見交流や現地訪問をし、わが国の死刑廃止政策を示し、被害者団体の協力を得て、ともに死刑廃止政策を促進する」こととし、法務部の死刑廃止政策を明示した。

2008年5月、王清峰法務部長が就任するときの記者会見でも、これまでの死刑廃止関連政策の成果、及び犯罪被害者保護業務の成果を検討することを施策の重点としてともに取り上げた[16]。

被害者問題と死刑問題の2つは、政策面においてだけではなく、去年三月以来の死刑論争の世論においても強く結び付けられた。死刑存置であれ、死

---

[14] 法務部新聞稿、2011年3月4日、http://www.moj.gov.tw/ct.asp?xItem=224103&ctNode=27518&mp=001 (last visited July 27, 2011).

[15] 実際、新聞によると、性犯罪を犯した死刑囚を優先的に執行するという法務部のメッセージがあったそうです。Nownews, 2011年3月4日, http://www.nownews.com/2011/03/04/138-2693592.htm (last visited July 27, 2011).

[16] 《法務部舉行部長上任記者會-提出「厲行法治 保障人權」未來各項施政重點》、法務部官網2008/5/21新聞消息-法務部全球資訊網、http://www.moj.gov.tw/ct.asp?xItem=124783&ctNode=27518&mp=001 (last visited June 19, 2011)

刑廃止であれ、段階的な死刑廃止の立場であれば、どちらも被害者の問題に触れており、触れなければならない状況にある。

　しかし、台湾においては、被害者というと、特定の極めて少数な被害者の名前とその被害者のイメージのみを想起させられる。それが意味しているように、実際、台湾では、有名な被害者がいても、強力な被害者団体がないということである。死刑の問題点を指摘し、死刑に反対する被害者団体がないのみか、死刑を強く支持する被害者「団体」といえるほどの社会組織もない。そのため、マスコミで被害者を扱う場合、極めて少数の特定の被害者、およびそれ以外の、抽象的、潜在的な被害者のことを言っている。

　それと同時に、被害者の名で性犯罪者のさらなる厳罰化を求めるキャンペーンが去年から行われている。その影響やマスコミの報道もあり、現行法で規定されている強制治療の保安処分をさらに多くの性犯罪者に適用させ、罪刑法定主義の遡及禁止に違反するような法改正さえも強行させるように、政府に圧力をかけている。現在、関連法案まで提出されている。立法的には、直接に死刑の存廃とは連動していないが、国民の被害者意識を強く煽っている。

　死刑論争は、このような厳罰支持的な雰囲気のなかで取り沙汰されており、死刑廃止論や死刑廃止論者は従来よりも厳しい立場に立たされている。

2．修復的司法の動き－厳罰以外の可能性？

　台湾の被害者問題と死刑の関連では、もうひとつ注目に値することがある。

　それは、修復的司法に関わる議論と政策の提出である。死刑廃止問題で辞任した王元法務部長は、任期内で修復的司法の理念の普及と実践を試み始めた。これまで、対話促進者の研修や全国で八つの地方検察署で修復的司法試行プログラムを行っている。また、中小学校などで修復的司法の理念ややり方を講演、教育プログラムなどを通じて普及させようとしている。

　法務部は、修復的司法の実践を直接に死刑廃止の政策と連結させず、被害者保護政策の一環として行ってきたが、その素材と試行プログラムの内容からみると、まったく関係のないものでもないようである。また、法務部の死

刑廃止研究会でも、修復的司法はひとつ重要なテーマとして取り上げられている[17]。

法務部名義で全国地方検察署に配った修復的司法の素材のひとつとして、「回家」（家に帰ろう）というDVDがある。その中身は、台湾で有名な放火致死（死者16人）事件（神話KTV事件）の死刑囚と被害者遺族の和解プロセスのドキュメンタリーである。また、地方検察署での修復的司法試行プロジェクトでは、軽微な犯罪に限定することなく、被害が重大な犯罪であっても、プロジェクトを適用することが可能であり、実際に殺人事件や強盗致死などの重大事件を対象として、加害者とその遺族との対話を試みているプログラムもある。

修復的司法の理念や実践は、台湾ではまだ認識され始めた段階にあるものだが、上述のような素材だけで、修復的司法は死刑との関連性が果たしてどうなるかも現在でははっきりといえないものだと思われる。そして、コミュニティの支援が十分ではなく、政府主導の修復的司法プログラムは、加害者の任意性を尊重しつつ、個別的被害者のニーズをサポートして満足させることができるか否か、ということを評価するには時期尚早である。ただし、学校での修復的司法の理念の推進や、重大犯罪の被害者への修復と対話の試みを含めて、このような動向は、被害者と加害者を激しく対立させようという世論と、また被害者の刑事手続における権利を確立させ、加害者と対峙させるような動きとは対照的になってきている。私は、修復的司法の考え方を通じて、現在は厳罰を求めている社会が、異なる視点で死刑の問題をみられるようになる、という一縷の望みを抱いている。それは、被害者が加害者を宥恕することへの期待ではなく、むしろ、修復的司法の視点と実践を通じ、より多くの市民が犯罪の原因やその改善に関心を持って理解し、加害者のことも被害者のことも抽象的な分類としてではなく、一人一人生身の人間として認めることへの期待である。

17　内部資料、未公開。

(六) 結びに代えて

　政府の方針として、「最終的に」死刑を廃止するという目標はまだ掲げられている。問題は、「いつ」廃止するかということである。陳水扁政府の時に、三年以内に死刑を廃止すると明示したこと（実現しなかったが）とは対照的に、タイムリミットがないことを極めて強調するようになった。その意味は、実質的に死刑廃止の立場の後退だと考えられる。

　また、刑法や特別刑法の改正や廃止の動きからみると、死刑の規定が少しづつ減少している。これから、特に生命法益を侵害していない法規定の改正によって、さらに死刑規定を削減することが期待できると思われる。ただし、法改正には限界がある。死刑規定が存続している限り、もともと生命法益の侵害を前提にして死刑判決を下し続ける司法実務には、上述のような法改正は、特に大きな影響をもたらさないと予想できる。

　そして、死刑囚の刑の執行について、前述のように、曾勇夫法務部長は、最初から「行政は法律の規定に従って行われるべきだ」（つまり確定した死刑判決を執行するべき）と宣言した。法務部の公開意見でも、「死刑執行」は「死刑廃止」の問題と区別するべき、法律において死刑が廃止されない限り死刑が執行されるべきだ、ということが示されている[18]。この立場は、これからも死刑執行の基調として維持されると思われる。

　死刑廃止のタイミングについて、政治情勢は重要な要素だと思うが、被害者問題や国民の被害者意識も重要な鍵だと思う。台湾では、何人か個別の被害者がマスコミでの発言権を握っているが、影響力のある被害者団体がまだ現れていない。また、被害者調査や被害者関連研究もまだ不十分である。そのため、被害者政策は、ほとんど政府の主導によるものであり、政治情勢に影響されやすいし、「被害者のために厳罰が必要だ」という理由は世論に利用されやすいのである。

　被害者保護を優先的に行うことや、被害者保護が完備するまで死刑を廃止できないという議論は、結局被害者の保護と刑罰の合理化が両立できないと

18　法務部、有關報載國際特赦組織批評臺灣執行死刑、人權倒退、法務部説明、2011年5月13日、http://www.moj.gov.tw/public/Attachment/151317265922.pdf　(last visited　July 28, 2011).

いう印象を作り上げ、死刑が被害者にとって必要不可欠だという意識を強化してしまう。政府が、死刑を廃止する課題を被害者対策と強く連結させることは、被害者の利益の促進や世論の要請に好意的に応えているようにみえるが、実際の被害者対策については十分な資源を与え、被害の実情を理解し、対策の実現を図るというまでに至らず、まだかなりの改善余地がある。

　因みに、2011年度の被害者補償の予算は、2010年度より大幅に削減された[19]。ほかに被害者に対する精神的支援や、福祉的措置を完備させることもまだまだ不十分である。この状況は、民間の支援が盛んではない台湾の被害者にとって、大変厳しい状況だと思われる。

　台湾の政府が、被害者対策の重要性を掲げていながら、実際にそれに相応する行動を行っていないことは、被害者の不満や世論の被害者への同情を呼び、死刑存続の正当性や死刑執行への支持を求めているのではないか、死刑という手段で簡単に被害者問題を始末してしまおうと図っていないか、と疑問を感じずにはいられない。

19　中央社「7成反廢死　法務部：加強對話」2011年03月25日、http://tw.nextmedia.com/rnews/article/SecID/102/art_id/21233/IssueID/20110325（last visited June 20, 2011）.

[4] 中国はどのようにその死刑制度を改善しているのか

王雲海（一橋大学大学院法学研究科）

はじめに

中国では、死刑判決の件数も死刑執行の人数も世界で最も多いであろう。死刑執行の人数に関して、アムネスティ・インターナショナルが最近の数年間その数字を年毎に発表している。それによると、最も少ない年では470人（2007年）で、最も多い年は3400人（2004年）であるという。これに対して、そのような数字は実際に執行された人数のわずか一部でしかなく、本当の執行人数は2000人から1万5000人の間ではないかという指摘もある[1]。実際はどうであろうか。これに関して、中国政府はその数字を公表しないどころか、それを最高の国家秘密の一つとしてその漏洩を厳しく処罰している。なぜ死刑に関する情報をそこまで隠そうとするのであろうか。その直接で最大の理由は、死刑判決もその執行も人々を驚かすほどあまりにも多いことで、それを公表したら大きな批判を引き起こすからであろう。公表しないこと自体は死刑が公表できないほど多いことを物語っているのである。

一 死刑多用がどうして可能なのか

なぜ中国では死刑がこれほど多くて、中国の法律がいかにしてそれを可能にしているのであろうか。

（一） 刑法上死刑罪名が多いこと

従来の刑法が定めていた死刑罪名は極めて多くて、広範囲に及んだものであった。中国の刑法は総則と各則に分けられており、その各則には10の章があり、1つの章は1つの犯罪類型として、その下で具体的罪名が定められている。この10の章のうち、第9章の「瀆職罪」を除けば、すべての章には死

---

[1] David T. Johnson & Franklin E. Zimring, *The Next Frontier: National Development, Political Change, and the Death Penalty in Asia*, Oxford University Press, 2009, p. 225.

刑罪名が含まれており、死刑罪名は合わせて68個もあった[2]。死刑罪名の多い順、罪名数、全死刑罪名に占めるパーセンテージ、具体的死刑罪名は次の通りである。第3章の「社会主義経済秩序破壊罪」は死刑罪名の最も多い章であって、16個の死刑罪名があり、死刑罪名全体の約25％にあたる。16個の罪名は、偽薬品生産販売罪、有毒有害食品生産販売罪、武器弾薬密輸罪、核材料密輸罪、偽貨幣密輸罪、文化財密輸罪、貴重金属密輸罪、貴重動物及び製品密輸罪、普通貨物物品密輸罪、通貨偽造罪、集資詐欺罪、手形詐欺罪、金融証書詐欺罪、信用証書詐欺罪、付加価値税納税証書不正作成及び使用罪、付加価値税納税証書不正製造及び販売罪である。第2章の「公共安全危害罪」は二番目で、14個の死刑罪名があり、全体の約22％にあたる。14個の罪名は、放火罪、溢水罪、爆発罪、毒物投与罪、危険方法による公共安全危害罪、交通道具破壊罪、交通設備破壊罪、易燃易爆設備破壊罪、電力設備破壊罪、航空機ハイジャック罪、銃弾薬爆発物の違法製造売買運輸郵送貯蓄罪、核材料違法売買運輸罪、銃弾薬爆発物窃盗略奪罪、銃弾薬爆発物強盗罪である。第10章の「軍人職責違反罪」は三番目で、12個の死刑罪名があり、全体の約18％にあたる。12個の罪名は、戦時命令違反拒否罪、軍事情報隠匿虚偽報告罪、軍事命令伝達拒否及び虚偽伝達罪、投降罪、戦時離脱逃走罪、軍事職務執行妨害罪、軍人逃走又逆罪、軍事秘密違法収集買収提供罪、戦時風説伝播罪、軍用物質武器装備窃盗強盗罪、武器違法売買譲渡罪、戦時住民残害及び財産略奪罪である。第6章の「社会秩序管理妨害罪」は四番目で、8個の死刑罪名があり、全体の約13％にあたる。8個の罪名は、犯罪方法伝播罪、暴動脱獄罪、集団暴力監獄ハイジャック罪、古文化遺跡古墳盗掘罪、古人類化石盗掘罪、麻薬密輸販売運輸製造罪、売春組織罪、売春強制罪である。第1章の「国家安全危害罪」は五番目で、7個の死刑罪名があり、全体

---

2 詳細は、王雲海『死刑の比較研究―中国、米国、日本―』（成文堂、2005）、第8頁以下を参照。なお、中国刑法上の死刑罪名の数に関して、強姦罪と少女姦淫罪とは同じ罪名か否かに対する理解の違いにより、同じ罪名とする「68個説」と、違う罪名とする「69個説」とがあり、筆者を含む一部の学者は「69個説」が正しいと指摘していたが、全国人民代表大会や最高人民法院などの中国の公的機関はいずれも「68個説」を唱えている。本文は刑法改正を扱うものであるので、一応「68個説」に従う。

の約10％にあたる。7個の罪名は、祖国反逆罪、国家分裂罪、武装反乱暴乱罪、敵投降罪、スパイ罪、境外のために国家秘密情報の違法窃取探索買収提供罪、敵援助罪である。第4章の「公民人身民主権利侵害罪」は六番目で、5個の死刑罪名があり、全体の約8％にあたる。6個の罪名は、故意殺人罪、故意傷害罪、強姦罪、誘拐致死罪、婦女児童誘拐売買罪である。第8章の「横領賄賂罪」は七番目で、2個の死刑罪名があり、全体の約3％にあたる。2個の罪名は、横領罪と収賄罪である。第7章の「国防利益危害罪」は同じく七番目で、2個の死刑罪名があり、全体の約3％にあたる。2個の罪名は、武器装備軍事施設軍事通信破壊罪と欠陥武器装備軍事施設故意提供罪である。第5章の「財産侵害罪」は同じく七番目で、2個の死刑罪名があり、全体の約3％にあたる。2個の罪名は、強盗罪と窃盗罪である。

(二) 刑事手続が死刑を容易にしていること

　従来、刑事訴訟法は、死刑の刑事手続を相対的に容易にしていた。中国では、死刑事件に関して、その第一審は中級人民法院レベル以上の人民法院で行われること（中国の裁判所は県の基層人民法院、市の中級人民法院、省・直轄市・自治区の高級人民法院、全国の最高人民法院という四級に分けられている）、被告人は弁護人をつけていないときには人民法院が被告人のためにつけなければならないこと、および、「二審終審制」が実施されているが、死刑事件の場合、通常の審判手続きが終了した後に、新たに「確認許可手続」に付することが定められていたが、それ以外には、証拠則、訴追手続、審判構造などの面において通常の刑事事件とは全く同じである。通常、刑事事件についてその手続の時間的上限が設けられている。被疑者・被告人は身柄が拘束されてから計算し始めて、捜査は2ヶ月以内、起訴は1ヶ月以内、第一審は1ヶ月以内、終審たる第二審は1ヶ月以内において、それぞれ完了しなければならない。死刑事件であっても、通常の場合、長くとも5ヶ月以内に判決が確定されなければならず（例外的に一定の手続を経て処理期間を延長することもありうる）、極めて早く判決が確定されるのである。しかも、第二審は法廷を開く必要がなく、書面審理だけで判決などが言い渡される。死刑事件の第二審も同じである。また、死刑事件の場合は、判決が確定された後に、「確認許可手続」が

予定されているが、この手続を行うのは刑事訴訟法上最高人民法院であると規定されていたにもかかわらず、1983年9月から司法解釈により、殺人罪などの凶悪犯罪について高級人民法院にその権限が授与されてしまった。それにより、死刑判決に対する確認許可が大変容易になり、時間的にもかなり早くなった。さらに、中国の死刑には「即時執行死刑」と「2年執行猶予つき死刑」との二種類がある。前者の場合、確認許可手続を経て許可されれば、すぐ死刑執行命令が出されて、一週間以内に死刑囚を実際に死なせなければならず、死刑判決が確定しながら長い間執行されない状況は存在しえない。後者の場合だけは2年間の猶予期間を与えて、その間、死刑囚は刑務所で強制労働して、2年後に、故意犯罪がなければ無期懲役刑に、さらに重大な立功の状があれば15年以上20年までの有期懲役刑に減軽される。実際上も、約99％の2年執行猶予つき死刑の死刑囚は最終的に減軽されている[3]。しかし、実際上、あくまでも「即時執行死刑」は基本であって、「2年執行猶予つき死刑」は例外であるとされているので、「2年執行猶予つき死刑」があっても、多数の死刑囚は迅速的で即時的に執行されるのを妨げていない。

(三) 刑事法の適用様式が死刑多用を認めていること

従来の刑事法の適用は死刑をより多く生み出すようなものであった。死刑の適用基準に関して、刑法の規定そのものと人民法院の死刑選択との間で相反する二つのパターンがある。一つは、刑法が死刑の適用基準自体をはっきりと定めて、人民法院に裁量の余地を与えないもの（いわば「絶対的死刑」）であって、人民法院は被告人の行為が当該死刑罪名に該当すると判断すれば、ほぼ例外なく死刑を言い渡す。もう一つは、刑法自体が法定刑として死刑だけでなく、死刑を含む複数の法定刑を設けて、実際に死刑を言い渡すか否かは完全に人民法院の裁量に任せるもの（いわば「相対的死刑」）である。この二つのパターンのいずれも中国での死刑多用に寄与している。というのは、中

---

[3] 王雲海「中国の『死刑制限論』と『二年執行猶予つき死刑』」、『法律時報』第75巻11号（2003年）、89頁を参照。

国での刑事法適用に当たっては、判例制度はまだないので、「絶対的死刑」のように、法律の規定自体が死刑の適用を排他的に要求していれば、人民法院の判決はほぼ例外なく死刑を言い渡す。逆に、法律の規定自体は死刑適用の基準を具体的に定めておらず、人民法院の裁量に委ねていれば、それは本当に各人民法院と各裁判官の日ごろの裁量にかかるようになる。そこで、このような「日ごろの裁量」を実際上強く左右するのは、「厳打キャンペーン」と呼ばれる刑事法適用様式と、「殺人償命（人を殺した者は命で償え）」と言ったような民間的報復感情である。前者は、政治指導者が治安などに対する自分達の判断に基づいて、犯罪者をより重くより早く（中国語では「従重従快」）懲罰するために、司法機関ないし全社会を動員して展開する政治運動的な法適用である。このようなキャンペーンに際して、人民法院とその裁判官はその裁量権を、犯罪者をより重くより早く懲罰できるように行使し、通常の法適用では死刑にならない事件でも死刑を言い渡すようになる。後者は、規範としての法にはまだ合理化されていない一般民衆の生の感情または常識である。これらも長い間不文の基準として生きており、人民法院とその裁判官は、法律上の基準もなく政治からの干渉もなく、完全に自由裁量できるときには、それに従って「裁量」を行う場合が多い。これも中国刑罰全体の厳格さ、特に死刑適用の多さを引き起こしている。

二　死刑多用への批判に対してどのような政策の転換が図られるのか

　死刑を極めて多用していることに対して、中国内外からの批判はかつてから強かった。国際的には、1980年代に入ってから、国連を中心に死刑の廃止やその執行の停止を求める動きが活発になった。これは国連の常任理事国としての中国にとってかなり大きなプレシャーになった。また、同じ時期に、近辺のアジア諸国を含む多くの国々が死刑の廃止や執行停止に踏み切って、死刑廃止の国際的流れができたことも、中国にとって無形な圧力となった。国内的には、中国政府は1997年10月に「経済的、社会的及び文化的権利に関する国際規約（社会権規約・A規約）」、1998年10月に「市民的及び政治的権利に関する国際規約（自由権規約・B規約）」にそれぞれ署名し、2001年2月にA規約を批准したことなどにより、国内での死刑多用に対する疑問や批判は、

国際社会での批判と同調することができて、従来少数の法律家による非公式的なものから社会全体を巻き込む公式的なものにまで発展した。また、その時期は政治指導者の新旧交代にあたって、新たに政治指導者になった人々の多くは、法律を直接勉強したことがある者か、法治主義の意識をもった者であるために、死刑多用に対する政治一辺倒という従来の発想とは違って、その問題性をも認めるようになった。このような背景の下で展開された死刑多用への批判・反省の結果として、「存置、制限、廃止」という公式とも言えるような「三段論」的死刑方針が1990年代後半から事実上形成された。つまり、いまの中国では、死刑をすぐ廃止することは無理ではあるが、その適用を徐々に制限し、最終的にその廃止を実現するという[4]。実際上、1990年代後半から、中国はまさにこのような方針のもとで死刑制限をはかろうとして、死刑制度を変更し始めたのである。

三　死刑制度がどのように改善されているのか
（一）　死刑罪名の減少

中華人民共和国は1949年の成立から今日まで二つの刑法典があった。1979年に制定された最初の刑法典のなかには死刑罪名は28個であったが、1997年に制定された刑法典には68個があった。このように、約20年間40個の死刑罪名も増やされたが、そのすべては、全国人民代表大会が、一時的な治安情勢、政治雰囲気、特に経済政策の実施状況との関連で、それらに対する直接的政治反応として、「特別刑法」という形で導入されたものであって、一種の「政策立法」または「ムード立法」による死刑罪名の新設である。1997年刑法典の68個の死刑罪名は制定時の1997年までに随時に制定された特別刑法の中ですでにあった死刑罪名をただそのまま継承しただけである。このように、死刑罪名の新設を含む特別刑法が制定されるかどうかは死刑罪名の動向を大いに左右するのである。従来とは違って、1997年刑法典が制定されてからは、死刑を制限しようとして、死刑罪名の新設を含むような特別立法は一切採択されなくなったのである。

4　趙秉志等編著『穿越迷霧：死刑問題新観察』、（中国法制出版社、2009）、第86頁。

特に、2010年2月に、刑法に対する改正が行われて、死刑について次のような重要な改正内容があった。つまり、刑法上の68の死刑罪名から次の13の罪名から死刑を外して、死刑罪名を55個に減らした。つまり、文化財密輸罪、貴重金属密輸罪、貴重動物及び製品密輸罪、普通貨物物品密輸罪、手形詐欺罪、金融証書詐欺罪、信用証書詐欺罪、付加価値税納税証書不正作成及び使用罪、付加価値税納税証書不正製造及び販売罪、犯罪方法伝播罪、古文化遺跡古墳盗掘罪、古人類化石盗掘罪、窃盗罪である。

また、中国には「矜老恤幼」（高齢者に配慮を配り、子供に思いやりする）伝統文化があるし、高齢者の被告人には再犯の危険性が少ないといった理由で、一部の論者は、かねてから、18歳未満の少年に対して死刑を適用しないと同様に、一定の高齢者に対しても死刑を適用しないようにすべきであると主張していた。今回の改正はこのような主張に一定の配慮し、75歳以上の高齢者被告人に対して、特に残忍な手段で殺人した場合を除いて、死刑を適用しないことを決定した。

(二) 死刑適用基準の厳格化

公務員横領収賄犯罪、麻薬犯罪、経済犯罪などに対して、中国刑法自体は死刑を設けているだけでなく、死刑適用の金額的または重量的要件をも定めている。例えば、刑法規定自体からすると、公務員横領収賄犯罪の場合、横領、収受した金額が10万元であると、死刑になる。また、麻薬犯罪の場合、密輸、販売、運搬、製造したヘロインが50グラム以上であると、死刑になる。しかし、これらの犯罪はあまりにも多いので、本当にこのような法定死刑要件を適用すると、年間数万人ないし10数万人の被告人を死刑にせざるをえない。このような極端な局面を避けて、死刑の適用を制限しようとして、最高人民法院は、2000年以後、随時、「通達」という形で、司法解釈を地方の人民法院に公布し、死刑適用の法定要件を絶えず引き上げてきている。そして、各地方の人民法院は最高人民法院の適用要件をさらに引き上げたうえで死刑を実際に適用している。2012年5月現在、地方によりばらつきがあるものの、公務員横領収賄犯罪の死刑適用要件はほぼ法定金額の10万元の約100倍に、麻薬犯罪のそれは法定量の約10倍以上にそれぞれなっている。ま

た、即時執行死刑と2年執行猶予つき死刑の実際的適用状況に対して、2002年以来、最高人民法院は、「即時執行死刑が原則で、2年執行猶予つき死刑が例外である」という従来の主従関係を徐々に転換させて、死刑判決のなかでの即時執行死刑判決の比例を適用基準の厳格化を通じて抑制し、代わりにその分を2年執行猶予つき死刑判決のほうに回すような死刑運用を図ってきている。その結果、2010年7月の時点で、2年執行猶予つき死刑の件数は即時執行死刑の件数をはじめて上回り、この逆転により実際上の死刑適用がかなり制限されるようになったそうである。

(三) 死刑手続の整備による死刑適用制限

先にも述べたように、中国での死刑多用を可能にしている要素の一つはその手続の容易さと迅速さである。そこで、2000年代に入ってから、死刑事件の「質」を確保し、その適用を制限しようとして、最高人民法院を中心に手続面からの工夫がされるようになった。①従来、「二審終審制」が実施されたものの、死刑事件を含むすべての事件の二審（控訴審）は書面審理だけであるのを改めて、2006年9月から、死刑事件（即時執行死刑事件のすべて、新しい証拠が提出された2年執行猶予つき死刑事件）はその二審が第一審と同じように法廷公開審理に切り替えられて、死刑事件に対するより充実した審理が可能になった。②判決が確定された後の「確認許可手続」について、1983年9月に殺人罪などの凶悪犯罪についてその権限が地方の各高級人民法院に委ねられていたが、2007年1月からその委任が改められて、すべて刑事訴法の規定したとおりに最高人民法院はこれを遂行、行使するようになった。従来、最高人民法院による「確認許可手続」を行った場合の死刑不許可率が約15％であったので、この許可権の最高人民法院への取り戻しにより、死刑事件が約15％の減少が見込まれると言われている[5]。③最高人民法院などは2010年6月に「死刑事件における証拠審査判断に関する若干規定」を公布し、同年7月1日から実施するようにした。それにより、従来は死刑事件の証拠則、挙

5　楊宇冠主編『死刑案件的程序控制』、（中国人民公安大学出版社、2010）、第306頁。
6　中国における死刑多用の本質などについて、王雲海『日本の刑罰は重い軽いか』、（集英社新書、2008）、197頁以下を参照。

証責任、証明程度は一般刑事事件のそれと全く同じであることが改められて、死刑事件における証拠則が一層の規範化を図られて、特に構成要件事実についての、及び、死刑量刑事由についての厳格証明責任などが要求されるようになった。これも死刑適用の制限につながると期待されている。

三 今後への展望

これまで見たように、中国はいろいろな方策を通じてその死刑制度を改善し、死刑多用の状況を変えようとしている。しかし、これまでの改革は十分なものとはまだいえない。特に、死刑の多用を問題として意識し、それを改善しようとする場合は、何よりも重要なのは、死刑判決の件数やその執行人数を今のように国家機密として固く隠すのをやめて、それを事実通りに公表して、中国での死刑とその多用の是非を議論するための基礎にする、ということであろう。

〔テーマ・セッション〕

日本版ドラッグ・コート構想

石塚伸一（龍谷大学：京都）＝丸山泰弘（立正大学：埼玉）

1　企画の趣旨——処罰からハーム・リダクションへ——

石塚　伸一（龍谷大学）

　わたしたちは、アメリカ合衆国の「ドラッグ・コート（Drug Court）」をモデルとする薬物依存症者たちの回復プログラムを研究してきた。その核心的要素は、薬物関連犯罪について有罪答弁をし、かつ、社会復帰プログラムへの参加に同意した場合、裁判所は量刑判決の言渡しを延期し、当該プログラムを取消されることなく終了すれば、そのときには、なんらの処罰をされずに自由になることができる、というスキームである。これは、ある種のダイバージョン・システムである。現在、アメリカでは、2300以上のドラッグ・コートがあり、12万人以上の薬物依存症者がなんらかのプログラムに参加している。

　日本では、多くの人が、違法薬物使用者は犯罪者であり、彼らは処罰されるべきであると信じている。ほとんどの依存症者は、医療機関による治療も、福祉関係者による支援も受けるチャンスが与えられていない。その結果、彼らは、薬物乱用を繰り返し、再び刑務所に戻ってくる。わたしたちの「日本版ドラッグ・コート」構想は、すでに過剰負担となっているこのような懲罰的政策を、司法、医療および福祉の3つのアプローチのバランスのとれた薬物政策に改革し、その結果として、具体的には、みずから処遇プログラムに参加する意志のある多くの依存症者を刑事司法システムからダイバートすることを提案するものである。

　わたしたちは、同時に、効果的かつ効率的な処遇を開発してきたと思っている。わたしたちは、この大胆なダイバージョンを「日本版ドラッグ・コート（Japanese Drug Court）」と呼び、「処罰から治療へ」をスローガンとしてきた。

〔キーワード〕日本版ドラッグ・コート、ハーム・リダクション、薬物政策、薬物依存症

今回の世界大会では、2011年8月7日にテーマ・セッション「日本版ドラッグ・コート構想～処罰からハーム・リダクションへ～ "The Concept of Japanese Drug Court: from punishment to harm-reduction"」とラウンドテーブル・ディスカッション「薬物政策について語り合いましょう "Talk a Lot about What Contemporary Situation of Drug Policy"」を主催した。

まず、第1部では、まず、本企画の趣旨の説明と「日本版ドラッグ・コート」構想について紹介があり（石塚伸一・龍谷大学）、「日本の薬物問題の現状」（丸山泰弘・立正大学）「米国のドラッグ・コートの現在」（森村たまき・国士舘大学）および日本における薬物依存症者の自助グループである「ダルクの25年のあゆみ」（近藤恒夫・日本ダルク）について紹介があり、ディスカッションに入った。

第2部では、ダルクの研究期間であるアパリ（アジア太平洋地域アディクション研究所）の活動とアジアにおける役割について包括的な紹介があり（尾田真言・アパリ事務局長）、フィリピンにおける具体的展開であるJICAにおけるダルクの活動について紹介があった（三浦陽二・沖縄ダルク）。

つぎに、アジアからのメッセージとして、レオナルド・エスタシオ（フィリピン大学）が「フィリピンにおける薬物対策」について、趙越南（国立釜金精神病院）が「韓国における薬物対策」について報告した。

ラウンドテーブル・ディスカッションでは「薬物政策について語り合いましょう "Talk a Lot about What is Contemporary Situation of Drug Policy"」を合言葉に、薬物問題ついて、さまざまな立場からの発言を受け、意見交換を行った。

市川岳仁（三重ダルク）、加藤武士（京都ダルク）および矢澤裕史（奈良ダルク）、金尚均（龍谷大学）、野村佳絵子（京都橘大学）、西念奈津江（精神保健福祉士）などが、話題提供者となった。

2 報 告

［1］日本の薬物問題の現在
――刑事司法における直接強制および間接強制による薬物プログラム――

丸山　泰弘（立正大学）

キーワード：日本の薬物政策、刑事司法における新たな取組み、直接的強制、間接的強制。

1．はじめに

　これまで多くの論者が指摘してきたように、刑事司法手続において薬物依存症者に対し「薬物乱用」、「薬物依存」および「薬物中毒」の違いに目を向けずに、ただ刑罰を科すという政策を採ってきたことで、様々な問題が生じている。しかしながら、ここ数年、刑事司法手続の中で、治療的視点を取り込んだ政策が動き始めたという事実もある。従来の薬物使用の害悪を教育し、乱用者には徹底した処罰を用いてきたものから、トリートメントを重視した認知行動療法的な処遇が行われつつある。そこでは、参加者に対し様ざまな形態で介入ないし干渉が行われている。
　そこで、本報告は、現在の日本の刑事司法が抱えている薬物問題を概観し、新たに行われるようになった政策の意義と問題点を検討することを目的とする。

2．日本の刑事司法手続における薬物問題の処理
――厳罰化の中での薬物問題――

　日本の刑事司法における薬物犯罪の検挙人員の数をみると、「覚せい剤」が中心的な問題である。また、営利犯を除いた単純自己使用罪者数および単純所持罪者数だけで、検挙人員の約9割を占めていることから末端使用者の問題解決が喫緊の課題であるといえる。
　また、矯正施設の年末受刑者を罪名別で見た人員の割合は、窃盗と覚せい剤取締法違反者がほとんどで、その両罪で全体の約3分の1を占めているのが現状となっている。覚せい剤取締法違反についての科刑分布の推移を見ると1980年ごろまでは第一審で有罪判決が出た者の約70％が1年未満の実刑であったものが、年々1年未満の実刑は減少し、対照的に2年未満、3年未満の実刑判決の言渡しが急激に増加している。さらに、薬物事犯者は矯正施設への再入率が高く、現在では覚せい剤受

刑者が新規受刑者の約5分の1、年末在所受刑者の約4分の1を占めるようになっているのが現状である。

3．新たな処遇の導入とその問題点

(1) 新しい処遇と意義

　日本の刑事司法における薬物対策は、これまで単純自己使用者および単純所持者に偏った政策を行い、また言渡し刑期が長期化するといった一種の厳罰化といえる政策を採ってきている。しかし、これまでの反省を促す処罰から、早い時期にダイバートし、薬物検査を用いて、カウンセリングなどを取り入れた認知行動療法的な方法を採る政策も始まりつつある。たとえば、①「即決裁判手続を活用した方法」、②「裁判段階から更生保護段階を活用した方法」、③「矯正段階での特別改善処遇を活用した方法」および④「保護観察所での簡易薬物検査を活用した方法」などが挙げられる。

(2) 新しい処遇の問題点

　このように、ただ反省を促す処罰だけでなく、少しでも回復に目を向けた制度が運用され始められたことには大きな意義があるが、より治療的な観点を進めた制度にも、いくつかの問題が残されている。

　これらのほとんどが本人の同意を前提としておらず、薬物プログラムが義務化されることで本人の同意とは関係なく行われるようになる。一部では、「義務化」されているとまではいえないとする説も存在するが、たとえ義務化ではないことが認められ任意による参加が実務で運用されようとも、参加しないことが処遇上不利益になるということが容易に予想されうる。そういう意味では本報告でいう「間接的な強制」が懸念される。

　以上のように刑事司法手続で治療的処遇が行われるようになってきているが、治療的であることだけを根拠に自由への介入があることには、まだ疑念が残る。その治療の目的が社会防衛的な根拠になるのであれば、保安処分の問題が再浮上するからである。さらに、介入の程度が軽微であることや、治療的であるからというものでは、これまで対象とされてこなかった人々にまで介入の手が広がることへのネットワイドニングとしての問題も考慮する必要があると思われる。

4．報告のまとめと若干の考察

　上述してきたように、厳罰によって反省を促すだけの手続から、より治療的なプ

ログラムが提供される必要があり、その方向に向けてわずかではあるが、進みだしていることが確認された。ただし、その治療プログラムは、更生保護法で義務化したように直接的な強制としてプログラムに参加させることを含んだ状態である。そこから司法だけの問題ではなく、医療だけの問題でもない薬物犯罪の問題を考察する際には、どこまでの治療的処遇が行えるのかを明確にすることが困難である。少なくとも医療的な行為がかかわる以上、インフォームド・コンセントは重要な概念であり、本人の自己決定に基づかない治療はありえないと考える。そういった面から、刑事司法手続の中で行われる治療的なプログラムも「同意」を前提としたものに比重を置くことになる。国際レベルの取組みがその方向に向っている。しかし、その「同意」を前提とした制度においても、「間接的強制」としての問題点が示されていることも事実である。

［2］米国ドラッグ・コートの現在

森村たまき（国士舘大学）

1．ドラッグ・コートとは何か？

　1989年にフロリダ州マイアミ＝デード・カウンティに開設されたドラッグ・コートは、薬物事犯者に拘禁ではなく治療を提供し、刑罰の「回転ドア」を停止させることで「世界のコカイン首都」の刑務所の過剰拘禁を削減するためにはじめて登場した。20年後の2009年現在、アメリカ国内には2459カ所のドラッグ・コートが存在し、ドメスティック・バイオレンス・コート、メンタル・ヘルス・コートといったドラッグ・コート型の「問題解決裁判所」も1189カ所に存在する。

　各ドラッグ・コートのスタイルはそれぞれ独特であるが、それらに共通するのは、薬物依存症の薬物事犯者に、拘禁の代わりに裁判所が監督する治療を提供する点である。そこでは薬物依存症は病気と考えられ、薬物依存症者は犯罪者というよりも患者と見なされる。ドラッグ・コートは薬物依存症という病気を抱えた犯罪者に、刑事告訴、有罪判決、刑務所収容の恐怖によって治療を強制し、ケアと援助を提供する。

　効果あるドラッグ・コートの共通要素をまとめた10キーコンポーネントが1997年に発表されている。

　ドラッグ・コートは対審構造をとらない、コラボレイティヴな裁判所である。すなわち裁判官、検察官、弁護人（警察官、トリートメント・プロヴァイダー、プロベーション・オフィサー、ソーシャル・ワーカーらも）らがみな「チーム」としてクライアントの最善の利益のために協働する。

　ドラッグ・コートのチームリーダーは裁判官であり、きわめて活動的な役割を果たす。プログラム開始初期には毎週持たれることもある「ステイタス・ヒアリング」において、裁判官はクライアントと直接治療の進捗状況やNAミーティングへの出席状況、薬物検査の結果などについて会話する。もし成績が良好であれば裁判官はクライアントに賛辞を送り、コーヒーマグや映画のチケットをプレゼントしたりヒアリングや薬物検査の頻度を減らすなどの褒賞を与える。

　他方、尿検査で陽性が出たり、NAミーティングやヒアリングに欠席するなどすると、裁判官はクライアントを口頭で叱責し、出廷回数を増やす、コミュニティー・サーヴィスを命令する、あるいは刑務所への数日間の収容を行うなどの制裁的処置がとられる。しかし、再使用（リラプス）は回復への必然的過程と見なされて

いるため、一回スリップしたからと言ってプログラムが打ち切られたり、収監されることはない。

　ほとんどのドラッグ・コートの期間は12カ月から18カ月であるが、もっと長期にわたる場合もある。ドラッグ・コートを「卒業」するためにはクライアントは一定期間クリーンでなければならず、その他の要件を満たさねばならない。卒業式には家族や友人たちが集まってクライアントの努力と成功を讃え、地元の政治家や有名人が招待されるなどして盛大に祝われる。

2．ドラッグ・コートのモデル

　ドラッグ・コートは答弁前と答弁後の二つのタイプに分けられる。答弁後のタイプは判決前と判決後の二つに分けられる。答弁前モデルでは、被告人は有罪答弁を行うことなくドラッグ・コート手続きが開始され、ドラッグ・コートのプログラムを終了すると起訴が取り下げられ、犯歴は残らない。答弁後の判決前モデルでは被告人は有罪答弁を行うもののドラッグ・コート参加中その効力は停止し、プログラム修了と共に起訴は取り下げられる。ドラッグ・コートのプログラムを終了できなかった場合、有罪答弁に基づき有罪判決が下されて刑が科されることになる。答弁後の判決後モデルは、裁判官の監督するプロベーションにより近い性格のものである。ドラッグ・コートのプログラム修了に失敗したクライアントは、停止されていた刑の執行が開始され、収監されることになる。

　初期のドラッグ・コートは基本的に有罪答弁前／公判前ダイバージョン・モデルをとっていたが、次第に答弁後モデルに移行している。2009年12月31日現在、成人ドラッグ・コートの58％が答弁後モデルをとっている。答弁前モデルは12％に過ぎず、20％が双方の混合型である。起訴留保型から判決留保型に移行したニューヨークのDTAP（Drug Treatment Alternative to Prison）プログラムのように、失敗した場合に刑罰が科されることが確実であればあるほど、プログラム保持率が高くなると認識されているためである。

3．ドラッグ・コートの有効性

　ドラッグ・コートの効果に関する評価研究は大量に存在する。全米ドラッグ・コート専門家協会（NADCP）は、ドラッグ・コートは他のどのプログラムよりも効果が高いと主張する。NADCPはまた、ドラッグ・コートは刑務所収容よりも安価であり有効な税金の使い道だと主張する。また必要とする人々すべてに利用してもらえるには、ドラッグ・コートの数はまだまだ少なく、一層の拡大が必要だと主

張してもいる。

4．最近のドラッグ・コート批判

　創設以来ドラッグ・コートは多くの注目を集め、つねに毀誉褒貶の喧しい存在である。

　最近では全国刑事弁護士協会（NACDL）、薬物政策連合（DPA）司法政策協会（JPI）が、ドラッグ・コートに対する大規模な批判を行っている。すなわち、司法制度を通じた治療が他の治療と比べて特別有効であるわけではない。ドラッグ・コートが公共の安全を向上させるための最善の方策であるわけではない。ドラッグ・コートは最もコスト・エフェクティヴであるわけでもない。ドラッグ・コートは統制の網を拡大する。ドラッグ・コートはとりわけ黒人を平等に取り扱っていない。ドラッグ・コートに関する研究はしばしば信頼できない。ドラッグ・コートの存在が、他の効果の証明されたトリートメントへのアクセスを制約している。ドラッグ・コートは拘禁を削減するわけではない。

5．NADCP の対応

　NADCP はこうした批判にただちに反論し、ドラッグ・コートは人の命を救い、コストを削減するがゆえに、薬物事犯非犯罪化勢力の攻撃を受けるのだと主張している。NADCP によれば、DPA と JPI の研究はドラッグ・コートに支離滅裂な批判を投げつけるもので、科学への尊敬を欠き、不公正きわまりないという。

結論

　日本の薬物政策は長らく規制薬物の使用を犯罪として取り締まってきた。薬物依存症が治療を必要とする病気であるという視点は、日本の薬物政策にはまったく存在しない。それゆえ裁判所が裁判過程においてトリートメントを監督するドラッグ・コートの実践は衝撃的であったし、魅力的でもあった。

　ドラッグ・コートは急激な増加とともに、初期の答弁前／公判前ダイバージョン・モデルから答弁後モデルへと変化しており、裁判官の監督するプロベーションと言えるものに性格を変えている。

　ドラッグ・コートに関する評価研究、理論研究は数多く、評価もまちまちである。DPA と JPI による最近の批判だけが唯一の批判ではない。とはいえ、薬物事犯者に対する治療の必要性が常識となっていない日本の薬物政策がドラッグ・コートの実践から学ぶべきものは依然多い。

［3］ ダルク25年のあゆみ

近藤　恒夫（日本ダルク）

はじめに

　薬物依存対策のためにわたしが取り組んできたことを2つに分けてお話します。まず、わたしがダルクを立ち上げた経緯とダルクの歴史について、つぎに、現在ダルクが薬物依存対策のために考えていることや実践していることなどを紹介します。

1．ダルクの歴史
（1）ロイ神父との出会い

　わたし自身、かつて覚せい剤依存症でした。覚せい剤に手を出したのは、歯の痛みという些細なものでしたが、その後どっぷりとその世界にはまってしまいました。わたしは、「シャブ」のために、家族をないがしろにし、借金を重ねて瞬く間に堕ちていきました。

　その間、精神病院に一時入院していたときに、後にわたしの人生を大きく変えることになったロイ・アッセンハイマー神父と出会いました。当時、わたしは、シャブをやめられず、とうとう逮捕されてしまいました。拘置所に面会に来てくれたのは、ロイ神父だけでした。彼は、神父でありながら、アルコール中毒で、一風変わった人物でした。わたしは、だんだん彼に心を開いていくようになりました。

　わたしは、ロイ神父に連れられてAA（アルコホーリック・アノニマス）のミーティングに通うようになりました。劣等感にさいなまれていたわたしにとって、どうにか顔を上げて話すことができる場は、ミーティングしかなかったのです。毎日、休むことなく通い続けました。わたしは、判決で1年半の通院治療と自助グループへの参加を言い渡されていましたので、この間はなかなか忙しい日々でした。

　そんな中、AAの仲間たちが、わたしのクリーン1か月を祝ってくれました。しかし、わたしのシャブへの欲求は、なくなってはいませんでした。このころ、「ジャスト・フォー・トゥデイ（今日一日のことだけ考えて生きよう。）」というAAの仲間たちの合言葉の意味を理解することになりました。「今日一日、今日一日だけクスリを我慢する。そして、明日も今日一日だけ我慢する…」と考えればいいのだということに気づいたのです。

（2） ダルク開設

　やがて、わたしは、MAC（メリノール・アルコール・センター）のスタッフになり、ロイさんの仕事を手伝うようになりました。当時、ロイさんは、札幌にマックを作ろうと奔走しており、わたしも、資金調達などの手伝いをしました。こうして、札幌マックができたわけですが、なんと、わたしが初代所長に任命されたのでした。札幌マックは、大盛況で、わたしは、一生懸命活動しました。

　こうした活動の中で、わたしは、AAの回復プログラムは薬物依存症者の回復にも効果があると確信しました。そこで、AAとは違う薬物依存症者のための施設を作ろうと考え始めたのです。

　そして、マック創始者のミーニー神父に薬物依存症の施設を作りたいといったところ、「薬物依存症者に回復はありえない」と言われてしまいました。いろいろな人に相談しましたが、みんな否定的でした。しかし、そういわれると、わたし自身が否定されてしまうことになります。わたしはあきらめず、さまざまなミーティングやセミナーに出席して自分の体験談を話すうちに、自然とわたしの周辺に薬物依存症者が集まってきたのです。そして、4年間の執行猶予期間をクリーンで満了したわたしは、次第に薬物依存症者をマックに入寮させてもらうようになりました。

　ところがそのうちにトラブルが起こり、わたしは、薬物依存症者の回復施設を作る決心を固めました。そして、NA（ナルコティクス・アノニマス）の仲間たちと部屋探しをはじめ、荒川区東日暮里に一軒家をみつけました。でも、そこを借りる金がなかったわたしは、心臓発作で苦しむロイさん──そのとき、わたしは発作のことに気づいていませんでしたが──に72万円を借りて、そのボロボロの一軒家に住むことになりました。

　1985年7月1日、これが民間初の薬物依存症者の社会復帰を応援するリハビリ施設、「ダルク」の出発でした。昨年ダルクは25周年を迎えましたので、それ以来26年、わたしは、ダルクの活動を続けてきたことになります。

　ダルク（DARC）のネーミングはドラッグのD、アディクションのA、リハビリテーションのR、センターのCを取ってつけました。ジャンヌダルクは、フランスを救った愛国の女性の名前です。後に知ったのですが、聖書の「ノアの箱舟」は「ダルク・ド・ノア」というそうで、わたしは大きな力に導かれたようにいい名前をつけることができたと思っています。

2．最近のダルクの活動
――非犯罪化・ダイバージョン・社会内処遇――
（1） 非犯罪化

　最近、オーストラリアのテレビ・コマーシャルで、おもしろいものが手に入りました。「クラブで踊る3人の若者のうち1人がMDMAを使ってショック状態に陥る。2人の仲間は逮捕を恐れて救急車を呼ぶかどうか迷いますが、結局、通報して友人は助かる」という内容で、まさに「押尾に学べ」というタイムリーなテーマでした。もう1つ入手したビデオでは、マイアミのドラッグ・コートが紹介されています。ドラッグ・コートとは、判事も検事も弁護士も1つのチームになって、薬物依存症患者に薬物を再乱用させないためにどうしたらいいのかを、みんなで話し合い、決定していくという裁判です。

　わたしは、薬物事案をダイバージョン・非犯罪化に持って行く方向性に興味があります。つまり、警察の段階で起訴猶予にするかわりに課題を出し、それをしない場合には裁判に上げる、という方法もあり得るのではないかと考えているのです。

　わたしたちは、スピード違反や駐車違反で捕まって、点数がなくなると講習を受けることになります。罰金を支払って、印紙を買って、何時間も見たくもない交通事故のビデオを見せられる。その方が、裁判に上げるよりもずっと厳しいです。このような制度を薬物にも適用して、いわば薬物講習会のようなものができればいいと考えています。司法において裁判に上がってしまうと、私たちにはなかなか介入することができません。しかし、警察の段階なら地域社会を巻き込んでいろいろなことができる可能性があります。地域社会の中で、刑務所に行かせないようにフォローアップしていくというシステムができるのが理想的だし、それは実現可能なことです。

（2） ダイバージョン

　警察の段階であれば、1週間程度は親が死んだとか、冠婚葬祭などと嘘をついても会社をクビになることはありません。ところが、たとえば刑務所に3年間入ってしまうと、家族崩壊や離婚問題が待っています。そして、仕事も生活の基盤も帰るところもなく、全部崩壊してしまうことってしまう。それは無論、薬を使ったためにそうなっているわけですが、国家的に考えるとマイナスにしかなりません。

　初犯の段階で再犯させないためにできることはたくさんあります。ここで、「制度がないからやらない」というのではなく、手始めにモデルケースで何か新しいことを実践してみればいいのです。

　2010（平成22）年度には、東京で初犯の執行猶予がついている人たちに検査を受

けてもらう企画をしました。その検査は「アイスクリーン」という、おしっこではなく、唾液で薬物反応が陽性か陰性かを調べるキットです。検査が終わってから、ダルクの当事者たちが自分の経験を話すのを聞く、というセッションを2時間ほど行ないました。

　それは、残念ながら1年で打ち切られましたが、こうした取り組みが飛び火して、これからいろいろな都道府県で始まればいいと思っています。それはたぶん、再犯をして刑務所に行かせないための抑止にはなりますし、会社を休む必要もなく参加できます。毎週土曜日の午後から始まることにすれば、執行猶予はついていても、仕事も失わず、家庭も崩壊しないで、今までどおり仕事ができます。つまり、社会内で処遇されることになるのです。

　執行猶予で出てくる人たちは、東京都だけで年間1,000人ほどいます。つまり、この1,000人が野放しということです。「執行猶予だから儲かった」と思っている人が大半ですが、この人たちが再犯をすれば今度は実刑で刑務所に行くことになります。わたしたち市民はそれを何とか食い止めていかなければなりません。現状では、個人も地域も社会も警察にまったくすべてを依存している状態です。このような状況下で、わたしたちは、自分たちでできることを見つけていかなくてはなりません。

（3）社会内処遇

　ダルクの活動の中心は、社会の中で当事者が当事者をサポートすることです。ダルクに来るのは本当に困っており、どこにも行き場のない人たちなので、彼らがまた再犯を繰り返すリスクは非常に高いものです。彼らは何も失うものがないほど失っているのに、まだ薬への欲求が強い人たちなので、薬をやめるように説得しても、彼らは何千回も同じような話を聞いているので効果がありません。そんなわけで、私はもう彼らに薬をやめさせようなどとは思わないことにしました。

　20年間薬をやめても20年後に再発することがあるし、数年間薬をやめても社会に戻ればまた再発する。つまり薬物依存症は、医療用語でいう慢性病のようなものです。ところが、日本の社会の仕組み、あるいは行政の仕組みはこの事実に沿っていないのです。慢性疾患に対する療法は、どのように病気と仲良くつきあっていくかということであって、治療はそれしかないのです。

　それなのに、刑務所から3か月の仮釈放をもらって、保護観察3か月といった保護観察の制度があります。これでは仮釈放で出てきた人も、保護観察が切れたらもう制度とは関係なくなってしまうのです。

　このような制度は依存症にとってあまり役に立ちません。依存症の人たちはいわ

ば、ゴールのないマラソンのようなことをやっているのです。毎日毎日、「今日1日、今日だけ薬をやめていこう」と頑張っている人たちなのです。それに対して、区切りのある制度、つまりここからここまでは面倒を見るが後は知らないよ、というような制度は、実際には役に立たない。たとえばそれは、学校の制度に似ていて、学校は卒業すれば学校とは無関係になってしまうし、退学になればなおさらですね。

　彼らはこうしたハイリスクの人たちなので再発は当然あります。依存症の人たちは、だいたい14歳で薬物に関わり、逮捕されるのが27歳ぐらい、そしてダルクに来るのが30歳前後です。今では平均年齢が34歳ほどになっています。それは、刑務所からダルクに来る人たちが多くなったからです。以前20代後半でダルクに来ていた人たちが、いまや40代になり高齢化しています。

（4）「ダメ。ゼッタイ。」だけではダメ

　薬物乱用防止県民大会や都民大会に私やダルクのメンバーたちが呼ばれて話をすることがよくありますが、県民大会はどこも「ダメ。ゼッタイ。」の標語通りのことをやっていて、参加者たちの中には薬物を使っている人は一人もいません。

　これに対して、「乱用防止」や「再乱用防止」というテーマで大会があれば、ちょっと覗いてみようかという気になる人たちがいるかも知れないでしょう？県民大会は、薬を使っている人は絶対に来られない場所になっている。それをもう少し考え直した方がいい。問題を持った人が来られるようなシステムを作るべきなのです。

　まずは、彼らを孤立化させないということが大切です。薬物依存症は孤立化すると必然的に犯罪化、沈殿化して、どんどん地下に潜っていく。だから、薬物依存症を浮き彫りにさせるための施策が必要なのです。そのために私たちダルクは活動してきました。

　逮捕される心配のないダルクのような場所で、一緒に問題を持った人たちや、ハイリスクの少年たち、あるいはこのままでは覚せい剤や大麻やMDMAに関わってしまうような人たちが集まって、相談できることが必要なのです。

　薬物依存症者は、自分が悪いことをしているという意識が強いので、相談するという能力が、家族にも本人にもないことが多い。だから、相談などしたらもう逮捕されるしかない、という図式が本人や家族の中にできあがっています。わたしが薬を使って問題行動を起こしていたときに、わたしの家族が精神保健センターに連絡したそうですが、精神保健センターと警察は全部つながっているという回路が頭の中にできてしまっていたので、「行政はすべてつながっている」という被害妄想が

あってなかなか相談に行くことができませんでした。

そのような意味で、彼らを援助する相談窓口を増やして、いかに治療へとダイバージョンさせていくか、ということを考える時期にきているのではないかと思います。覚せい剤乱用防止の県民大会や都民大会に出席できないこのような人たちに、何か新しい回路を作ってあげることが、わたしの一番の願いです。

3．むすびにかえて
――ダルクの曖昧さ――

ダルクは26年間継続してきましたが、ここまで続けられたのにはいくつかの理由があります。

第1に、ダルクがあまり組織化していないという点です。現在日本におよそ60のダルク施設があります。東京に日本ダルク本部という名称の施設はありますが、ここはダルク全体の統括をしているところではありません。各ダルクはアメーバ状に全国へ広がり、それぞれ生き残りの方法を模索しています。あるところはNPO法人として、またあるところは企業や個人からの寄付を集めて活動しています。いわば、ダルクは独立採算制なのです。

第2番目に、関係省庁から一定の距離を保ってきたという点が挙げられます。このために、わたしたちは、政府の要求を強制されることなどなくやってくることができました。政府から資金をもらえない代わりに、私たちはいかなる圧力団体からも制約を受けることがありませんでした。

3番目に、ダルクが去る者を追わず、戻ってくる者を拒まなかったことがあります。このような姿勢でやってきたことで、利用者にとってダルクは第2の家となり、大きなトラブルも起こらなかったのです。

こうした状況において、わたしたちには曖昧さを保つことが必要になります。区別や選別の姿勢は依存症のリハビリテーションにはなじまないのです。依存症者には彼らの行動に対して大らかに許容してくれる環境が必要なのです。このような曖昧さを抱える能力のおかげで、今日のダルクがあるのです。

[4] NPO法人アパリ

尾田　真言（アパリ事務局長）

はじめに

　日本の薬物政策の現状を分析しながら、アパリの日本における活動について検討したい。

1　アパリの活動

　日本では薬物乱用者は病人としてではなく犯罪者として処遇されている。また、量刑は、年々重罰化している。しかし、刑事司法制度における薬物依存症回復プログラムは5年前にはじまったばかりである。このような状況下で、アパリは、この11年間刑事司法手続きの各段階にいる薬物依存症者に回復の道筋をコーディネートしてきた。

　ところで取締り処分側機関とリハビリ施設や病院などの援助側機関との最大の違いは何であろうか。答は薬物依存症者に対して何をしたらよいかを義務付ける強制力があるかないかである。刑事司法手続は薬物依存症者を刑務所に入れたり、保護観察付執行猶予に付したり、仮釈放後に保護観察に付したりする強制力を持っている。しかし援助側機関は治療を求める本人に対してしか援助することができない。このためアパリでは取締り処分側機関が持っている事実上の一種の強制力を利用して、社会内で薬物依存症回復プログラムに参加させるようにしむけている。すなわち、保釈と仮釈放の場合には、制限住居と帰住地をあらかじめ定めておくことで勝手にそこから離れるとそれらが取り消されるという事実上の強制力が働くので、治療機関に居住しなければいけなくなる。

　日本には6つの薬物規制法がある。ちなみに日本では覚せい剤を使用すれば、たとえ所持していなくても犯罪となる。つまり自己の尿中から覚せい剤が検出されれば逮捕され有罪とされることになる。このように厳しい規制をしていても検挙者数は先進諸国の中では奇跡的に少ない。

2　覚せい剤事犯の動向

　つぎに、覚せい剤の発明について言及したい。誰が覚せい剤を発明したのか。日本では覚せい剤のことをシャブ、かつてはヒロポンと呼んでいた。覚せい剤は1893年に日本人の薬物学者である長井長義博士が喘息の治療薬を製造する過程でエフェ

ドリンから合成した。その後、覚せい剤は薬局で目を覚ます薬として覚せい剤取締法が1951年に施行されるまで販売されていた。

2009年の犯罪統計によると、日本で最も検挙人員の多い規制薬物は覚せい剤であり、2009年現在約1万5000が覚せい剤取締法違反で服役している。また近時、約1万2000人が覚せい剤取締法違反で検挙されている。2番目に検挙人員が多いのは大麻取締法違反、3番目に検挙人員が多いのはシンナーあるいはトルエンである。アヘン類の検挙者はほとんど日本にはいない。MDMAやコカインの検挙人員も非常に少ないが、大麻に関する犯罪は比較的多くなっている。

量刑についてみてみると、薬物事犯者は定型的に処理されている。日本の判事には法定刑の範囲内で大きな裁量がある。典型的なケースを紹介すると、覚せい剤の法定刑は1月以上10年以下の懲役であるが、初犯者は懲役1年6月執行猶予3年に処せられている。執行猶予が取り消されることなく執行猶予期間が満了すると刑の言い渡しの効力がなくなる。2犯目の場合は、懲役2年実刑となる。これが普通の量刑である。

毒劇法違反の場合、法定刑は1月以上1年以下の懲役または50万円以下の罰金である。USドル換算なら約5000ドル以下の罰金ということになる。初犯者は罰金。2犯目も罰金。3犯目で懲役6月執行猶予3年、4犯目でやっと懲役1年実刑となる。

大麻取締法違反の場合は、大麻の所持についての法定刑が1月以上5年以下の懲役であるが、初犯者は懲役6月執行猶予3年、2犯目で懲役1年実刑となる。

2006年5月24日に監獄法が受刑者処遇法に改正されたことにより、すべての刑務所では薬物依存症者に対して薬物依存症回復プログラムを特別改善指導として実施することが義務付けられた。交通刑務所を除くすべての刑務所ではダルクのスタッフを民間協力者として非常に安い給料で招いている。しかし刑務所には1回50分で12回の標準プログラムが数年に及ぶ刑務所生活の中で実施されるにとどまっている。

3 薬物依存症の治療

このように、刑事司法手続きの中ではほとんど薬物依存症治療は行われていないことになる。また公立の薬物依存症者のためのリハビリ施設は存在せず、いくつかの民間の薬物依存症者のためのリハビリ施設があるだけである。もっとも有名なのがダルクであり、ピアカウンセラーが12ステップの回復プログラムを用いている。ダルクは1985年に東京で近藤恒夫という覚せい剤の元乱用者であり今では30年間ク

リーンを続けている男によって創設された。30年前の日本にはNAはなかった。そこで近藤はAAのミーティングに毎日4年通った後に日本で最初の薬物依存症者のためのリハビリ施設、ダルクを26年前に創設した。ダルクは民間の薬物依存症者のリハビリ施設であり、現在では沖縄から北海道まで全国59施設ある。すべてのダルク・スタッフは回復者が務めている。

4　アパリとダルク

　ダルクとアパリの違いは何か。アパリは2000年にダルクを支援するためのシンクタンクとして設立されたダルクとは独立したNPO法人である。アパリでは設立年の2000年から保釈中の刑事被告人、執行猶予付執行猶予者および刑務所からの仮釈放者・満期釈放者に対して積極的に回復の道筋をコーディネートしてきた。アパリは現在では全国のダルクと密接に連携して、刑事司法手続の各段階にいる薬物依存症者に焦点を合わせて具体的な回復の道筋を次の2つの方法でコーディネートしている。

　1つめは、保釈中の刑事被告人に対する薬物依存層回復プログラムをダルクや病院で受けてもらうこと、2つ目は薬物事犯で受刑中の受刑者の引受人としてダルクの施設長をあっせんし、仮釈放のその日からダルクで受け入れるということをしている。実際にアパリでは群馬県藤岡市という東京から約100キロ離れた場所にある自然の豊かな山の中にリハビリ施設を用意してダルクに運営してもらっている。

[5] JICAにおけるダルクの活動

三浦　陽二（沖縄ダルク）

　JICAとの連携の下進められている「フィリピン貧困層の薬物依存症に対する支援」についてお話しします。

　このプロジェクトは2004年に、ダルクと縁あり、親しくさせていただいている、ある保護観察官がフィリピンの薬物問題の状況について報告してくれたことからはじまりました。その時以来、わたしたちは、ダルクのシンクタンクの一つであるアパリと協力してこのプロジェクトを進めてきました。

　2004年の12月から数回にわたり、フィリピンの薬物依存症の状況に関する調査をしました。わたしたちの調査は、最初はミンダナオに焦点を絞っていました。ところが、日本のJICAからテロ関連の危険を指摘され、ミンダナオでの調査を中止せざるを得ないことになってしまいました。そういうわけで、わたしたちは、2009年から今度はマニラに焦点を当てた調査を再開しました。わたしたちは、①フィリピンで中核となるメンバーを訓練し、②ARM（APARI Recovery Meeting）と呼ばれる、12ステップに基づいたミーティングを決まった場所で決まった間隔で行ない、③ARMを私たちのサポートが終わったあとも継続することに注力しました。

　フィリピンでは富裕層の薬物依存症者たちのリハビリ・プログラムは素晴らしいものです。わたしたちの仕事は、富裕層の注意を喚起して貧困層との橋渡しをすることでした。フィリピンでの活動中に、懐かしい人たちとの再会もありました。ダルク代表者である近藤恒夫とわたしは、1999年にフィリピンのNAの代表者であるリッチ・コスティバル氏と出会いました。彼は、フィリピンの薬物依存症のリハビリ・センターを開設し、このプロジェクトの重要な役割を担ってくれました。彼が参加してくれたおかげで、私たちのプロジェクトは加速しました。フィリピンのNAミーティングに参加しているメンバーの中から最低月1回、ARMを維持してくれる中核メンバーを選出することができました。彼らは、ある程度、薬物依存症についての基礎知識があります。

　フィリピンの貧困層の子供たちは、食べるものがなく、空腹を紛らわすために「ラグビー（シンナー）」を吸引しています。日々の糧を得るために薬物を売る人た

ちもいます。ダルクはこれまで26年間、薬物依存症者が依存症から回復する手伝いをしてきました。それでも、わたしたちは、生活保護法のないフィリピンにおいて、貧困問題をも同時に解決していかなくてはならず、少なからず困難を感じました。

　現在、私たちはまた今回と同じような活動をしようと、JICAに働きかけているところです。たとえば工場のようなものを作って雇用を創出し、将来NAプログラムを設立することを考えています。

［6］フィリピンの現況と課題：法規制と依存症の治療への取り組み

レオナルド・エスタシオ Jr.（フィリピン大学）

　まず、フィリピンについてご説明します。フィリピンの島々・フィリピン共和国は南北1840キロにまたがる、大小7107の島々から成り立っています。3つの主な島として、ルソン島、ビサヤス島、ミンダナオ島があり、当初、ミンダナオ島でダルクとアパリによるプロジェクトが行われる予定でしたが、安全上の問題などがあり、マニラに活動の場所を移しました。

　最も小さな行政区分として42,000の村（バランガイ）があり、人口は9,000万人、宗教は80%がカソリック、15%がプロテスタント、その他、イスラム教徒などです。この講演は次のような内容です。①概要　②フィリピンの薬物問題（薬物乱用と流通、法規制）　③法規制とその役割（国レベルとコミュニティレベル）　④法の適用と依存症の治療　⑤まとめです。薬物対策の力学（ダイナミクス）、薬物問題を使用、流通、法律という面から、国家レベル、コミュニティレベルに分けて分析した上で、次のステップではフィリピンの薬物問題を考える上で何が行われるべきかを考えていきます。

　まず概要ですが、フィリピンでは、古いものも最新のものも、薬物に関する法規制は多様な政策ではなく刑罰によって行われるとみられています。これはエビデンスに基づいて政策を決定するというプロセスを欠いているからだと考えられます。この講演では、国内の最近の薬物事情について概観するため、コミュニティを基盤としたアプローチを検討します。社会の底辺にいて支援の届かない依存症者のコミュニティに焦点をあて、最近の薬物対策はその日常生活にどのような影響を及ぼしているかを検討します。また、NGOやNPOによる地域での取り組みやアパリのような海外の組織も分析の対象にします。そして最後に、薬物に抵抗しうるコミュニティ作りのために政策を決定する、より折衷的なアプローチ（様々な検討を加えてアプローチを選ぶこと）について議論します。

　フィリピンの薬物の使用状況は次の通りです。政府の2004年調査では、人口9,000万人中、現在の規制薬物使用者が約700万人、使用歴のある人が約1,100万人、その平均年齢は26歳、男性、独身、高校卒業、都市在住が平均的ということが分かっています。シャブ、マリファナ、シンナー、咳止め、エクスタシーなどが主で、UNODC（国連薬物犯罪局）の2009年のリポートでは、われわれの国はアジアで最も覚せい剤の使用者が多いということです。

薬物の流通については国内と海外のシンジケートが関わっていて、小さな島々にも及んでいます。東アジアや東南アジア、さらにオセアニアに向けての覚せい剤の供給地となっているほか、最近では覚せい剤、ヘロイン、コカイン流通の中継地点ともなっています。覚せい剤の製造工場やマリファナの栽培地があるため、国内の使用者も多く、さらに警察は押収した薬物を横流ししているといわれています。薬物対策法として、1972年には共和国法6425号が、2002年には共和国法9165号「包括的薬物規制法」が作られました。後者の法律では、薬物に関するいかなる行為も犯罪として扱われます。フィリピンでは死刑は廃止されているので、最高刑は終身刑になりますが、所持、製造、売買、栽培の場合には終身刑が科されます。また、車の免許を持っている人や銃火器の所有者、学生や労働者、兵士、警察、議員や大統領などへ立候補する者には薬物検査が義務付けられています。日本と同様、薬物の使用は犯罪となり、初犯の場合は6か月のリハビリ、再犯は6年から12年の自由刑で5万から20万ペソの罰金、3度目は12年から20年の自由刑で5万から20万ペソです。また、この法律によってDDB（危険薬物委員会）が設置されました。これは政策や対策を決定する機関で、実行機関としてPDEA（フィリピン薬物統制局）が作られました。2010年にPDEAが作成した法執行に関する報告書によると、使用者、売人など約8,000人が逮捕され、うち69人が外国人でした。覚せい剤の製造工場が7ヵ所見つかりました。48億ペソ相当の覚せい剤が押収されたほか、207ケ所のマリファナ畑なども見つかりました。その当時はマフィアやシンジケートに関する情報が求められ、その提供者には830万ペソの報奨金が与えられました。そのほか、1万回以上のアドボカシーキャンペーンを行いました。
　一方、驚くことに治療についての情報は無く、私の持っているデータは2003年〜2005年と古いのですが、使用者700万人のうち、2万4千人のみが治療を受けたとあります。私の疑問はなぜ、たった2万4千人しか治療を受けていないかということです。裕福な人はリハビリ施設にアクセスして治療を受けることが出来るほかは、政府が運営する施設は不足し、人員が過剰になって長い順番待ちとなっています。貧しい依存症者はほんの一部しか治療を受けられていません。最も重要なのは、政府は治療よりも逮捕、訴追などの取り締まりを重視している点です。典型的な民間の治療施設では、最低でも1か月400ドル、国立の治療施設でも本人かその家族が月に100ドル払う必要があります。ここまでのまとめとして、新たな法規制は供給を減らすことには特筆すべき成果を上げましたが、次の3つの点で失敗していると言えます。
　つまり、トップレベルのシンジケートや麻薬王を逮捕したり、罰則を科すことが

できていない点、薬物使用の拡大を防げていない点、数十万人にのぼる薬物使用者の治療を失敗している点です。どんな法規制が有効であるかを示す最適な指針とは、薬物の供給・入手のし易さが減り、使用者の拡大が抑えられているかどうかということです。

また、これらを把握するには、薬物の蔓延している地域で使用・流通・法規制がどのような関連をもっているかを詳細に調べることが最適な方法です。薬物が蔓延している地域の研究とは、生活の場をその対象にすることで、確実で地に足の着いた個別の観察、分析を可能にします。

また、総合的、全体的、多面的なアプローチをとることで、使用者やほかのアクターの日常生活に薬物規制法がどのような影響を及ぼしているかを検討します。私はホープ村という地域で調査をしました。この地域はケソン市にある142の村の一つで、1万2千世帯、9万人が生活しています。広さは96ヘクタールで7つの居住区に分かれています。この地域では9万人のうち2万7千人、つまり30％が薬物を使用しています。これは国全体のレベル（10％）よりも高い。覚せい剤やマリファナ、シンナーが主流で、治療を受けているのは、全体の約20％だけです。入手経路は友人、親族、売人などで、地域自体がマリファナや覚せい剤、シンナーの取引所となっています。売人は増加しています。家族の誰かが使っていたり、売っているために人々にとって薬物が身近で、蔓延しやすい状況になっていることに加え、クスリを売ることが収入源となっています。

国内全体の状況と比べると、警察の存在感は薄く、取り締まりも逮捕も活発ではなく、学校などでの薬物乱用防止教育も公には存在していません。われわれのデータでは、初めて使ったのは男性で13歳、女性で15歳と、とても早く、16歳から25歳の青年層に使用者が多く、無職で独身というのが典型的なほか、使用歴が20年以上で、50歳になっても使用している人もいます。

コミュニティレベルの政策を見ていくと、3つの活動主体が考えられます。①村議会　②警察（司法関係者）　③教会や学校です。村議会は明らかに薬物対策に失敗し、依存症者に治療やリハビリについて説明したり、実行させることもできませんでした。②警察は薬物事犯者の取り締まりに失敗し、国際的なデータでは、押収した薬物を転売するという例も指摘されています。③教会や学校は薬物の危険性と、使用は犯罪であることを伝える役割を期待されていますが、その役割を果たしておらず、関係者がそういった勉強会へ参加することもありませんでした。

別の主体として、地域の人々の連携やNGOの存在が考えられます。つまり、需要と供給や危害が加わることを抑えるための直接的な取り組みを行うのです。例え

ば、2000年にはアディクタス・フィリピンというNGOとKKPCというNPOがホープ村で地域を基盤とした薬物対策プログラムを実施しました。"House to House Drug Campaign"というキャンペーンで、家庭を訪問して薬物問題への取り組みを促したり、人々の創作意欲を活かして薬物乱用防止のポスターを作り、そのポスターを薬物問題を訴えるのに使用したりしました。能力開発では、子どもたちに薬物の危険性や薬物に近づかないよう伝え、薬物問題を話し合うセミナーを開いたりして、薬物の蔓延からコミュニティを守る方法を学びました。

2000年以降、この活動はUNODCやILO、WHOなどから支援を受けて行われています。また、2009年からはアパリがJICA草の根支援の資金を得て、ファミリー・ウェルネス・センターと組み、薬物使用者の治療におけるサポートをしてくれています。彼らは12ステッププログラムを中心としたARM（アディクション・リカバリー・ミーティング）というミーティングを試験的に導入し、10〜15人の依存症者を集めました。このARMは低所得者向けのミーティングです。APARI-JICAプロジェクトの現在までの暫定的な効果として、10人から15人がミーティングに参加するようになり、40％が薬物の使用をやめ、60％が以前よりも使わなくなったということです。2011年からは月に2回程度ミーティングが行われています。

アディクタス・フィリピンとKKPCとAPARI-JICAプロジェクトによる依存症者の治療が意味することは、コミュニティを基盤とした治療モデルであり、低コストで治療・介入を行うという自助グループ（AA、NA等）の意義を伝えるものです。さらに施設で行われる既存の治療に勝る治療センター、従来の心理セラピーを超える治療介入を目指しています。生活や健康管理を含むより折衷的なアプローチを目指しています。われわれはこのプロジェクトがさらに大きく広がることを望んでいます。従来の組織は、その役割を果たしておらず、関係者がそういった勉強会へ参加することもありませんでした。

この発表では薬物に関わる「使用」「流通」「法規制」のダイナミクスを国レベル、コミュニティレベルに分けて説明し、これまで何が行われてきたかを説明しました。

最近、フィリピンのビナイ副大統領は、「警察の仕事で最も重要な仕事は達成されていない。我々は警察の仕事以上のものをしなくてはならない。我々には、包括的な薬物対策が必要だ」と発言しました。

私には、この「包括的な薬物対策」の具体的な内容はまだわかりません。フィリピンの薬物対策はパラダイムシフトが必要です。つまり、司法においては、刑罰重視ではなく、更生保護や修復的司法のアプローチを生かし、またコミュニティを基

盤とするアプローチでは、需要と供給、そして薬物によって生じる危険を減らすこと（ハーム・リダクション）、地域を発展させること、それぞれを組み合わせた折衷的アプローチを用いることで、薬物に負けないコミュニティができるのだと考えます。

［7］韓国の薬物依存症の現状と対策

チョウ・ソンナム（釜谷国立病院）

　私は韓国の釜谷国立病院で働くチョウ・ソンナムと申します。私の病院は韓国では唯一、精神科で薬物依存症に対する治療プログラムを行っています。まず、韓国の薬物乱用の歴史について説明します。1950～60年代はアヘンとヘロインが主流で、1957年に麻薬取締法が作られました。1970年代はメタドン、バルビツール、マリファナが主流で、1970年に依存性薬物取締法、1976年に大麻取締法が作られました。この時期は歌手や俳優の間で大麻が流行り、多くの芸能人が大麻使用で逮捕されました。1980年代に入ると、覚せい剤、鎮痛剤、シンナーや接着剤、ガソリンなどの化学物質が主流となり、1980年に向精神薬取締法、毒物取締法が作られました。そして、1990～2000年代には、コカイン、ヘロイン、エクスタシーが主流となりました。2000年に作られた麻薬及び乱用薬物取締法はこれまでの麻薬、向精神薬、大麻に関する取締法を一元化したもので、病院で治療を受けている薬物依存症患者について医師に課せられていた通報義務がなくなりました。自主的に治療することを促進するためです。

　薬物乱用の現状を説明しますと、1999年以降、薬物事犯は毎年1万人を超えています。政治家の多くは韓国を「安全な国」と考えていましたが、薬物に関しては「安全な国」から「危険な国」に姿を変えたと言えます。使用者も増加していて、国外からエクスタシーやLSDなどいわゆるクラブドラッグといった新たな依存性薬物が流れ込んできています。また、使用者層も拡大していて、ビジネスマン、主婦、青少年などにまで広がっているほか、プロポフォールを乱用する医療関係者も増加しています。国外への旅行の増加に伴って密輸も増え、インターネットで取引をするケースも増加しています。覚せい剤が最もよく使用されていて、特に労働者層に広まっています。薬物事犯のグラフを見ると、麻薬ではアヘン使用について「薬物乱用」ではなく文化だと考えている高齢者層が大多数を占めています。地方では祭りなどでアヘンを使うことが多く、彼らは違法だとは知らなかったのです。向精神薬で最も多いのは覚せい剤で中国からの密輸が大半を占めています。2003～2006年の間は総数が減少していますが、これは韓国でマフィアの取り締まりが行われた上、SARSの流行に対する警戒で中国からの密輸が激減したためで、2007年には再び総数は増加しています。

　薬物事犯の特徴についてみてみると、19歳以下はアヘン使用はゼロで、向精神薬

と大麻が多い一方、アヘン使用は60歳以上が6割を占めています。全体としては常習犯が40％以上で、全体の37％は無職、87％の人々の教育レベルは低く、男女比は6対1となっています。治療や保護を受けている依存症者についてみると、2002年を境に司法機関からの送致は減少傾向にありますが、自主的な入院は増加しています。2005年に突然司法機関からの送致が増えますが、治療ではなく、保護としての要請で、その後は減少しました。

国内には依存症者を受け入れる病院が11ヶ所ありますが、特別な病棟はありません。釜谷国立病院は韓国で唯一薬物依存症治療の為の病棟（200床）がある病院です。依存症患者のうちおよそ90％が釜谷で治療を受けました。

2010年の司法機関からの送致は激減しています。司法関係者が逮捕・起訴を優先しているためと見られますが、治療効果はない、病院は使用者をかくまっている、犯罪者を隠しているなどネガティブに捉えていて、治療につなげるのが難しい状況です。我々も話し合いはしていますが、覚せい剤使用者のうち、精神病者は、そうでない人に比べて薬物の使用開始時期が早く、27.1歳と22.7歳という違いがあります。また、使用が止まるまで、精神病者は11.1年。そうでない人は10.3年という違いもあります。

多くの薬物乱用者は治療を受けていません。薬物使用については疾病調査がないため、これはわれわれの推計ですが、国内に30〜100万人の使用者がいると見られます。薬物事犯で逮捕される人は年に1万3千人以上で、そのうち70％は薬物の使用者です。刑務所には3500人の依存症患者がおり、これは入所者の約7％を占めますが、特別な治療施設はありません。私の推測ですが、治療を受ける薬物依存症患者というのは年に400〜2000人の間、つまり使用者の0.1％に過ぎません。治療につながるルートとして少なくとも3パターンがあり、保護としての治療の要請が年に300〜400人、治療および身柄拘束の命令が50人、40〜50時間の講習への参加命令が1000人ほどです。そのほか、どの医者が治療を行っているか把握していませんが、民間のクリニックで年に1000人かそれ以下の人が治療を受けていると思われます。

政府による治療類型には、「医学的な治療と保護」「医学的な治療と身柄拘束」「講習への参加」があります。「医学的な治療と保護」とは、自主的な委託が基本ですが、自首してきた場合などに検察官が起訴猶予して治療を行わせる場合や、本人やその家族が治療に来る場合があります。期間としては約1ヶ月の診断と、2ヶ月以下の治療を行います。私の病院も含めて政府による治療は無料で、12の病院がこのような治療を行っています。

次に、「医学的な治療と身柄拘束」についてですが、これは医療観察法という法

律があり、裁判所の命令で薬物使用の刑事被告人に適用されます。期間は3か月以上、国立の医療観察法病棟のある病院で行われます。病院は精神病や薬物依存症の刑法犯向けで、法務省が管掌しています。私は五年ほどここで働きましたが、この病院で始めて薬物依存症の問題を知りました。「講習への参加命令」というのは、裁判所か検察官が命じるもので、刑の執行や訴追が猶予されます。講習は薬物依存症についてで、40〜50時間にわたります。不定期の尿検査も行われます。講習は主として動機付けを目的としています。

　韓国のNAについては、私は医療観察法病棟のある病院に勤めているときに患者を通じて知ったのですが、1996年の時点では、月に1回、毎週第2火曜日にその病院に入所している依存症患者がミーティングを行っていました。2004年「NA KOREA」として発足し、毎週火曜午後7時に50人ほどの依存症患者が参加していました。そして2005年、正式にNAに登録しました。2006年に「第1回NAコンベンション・日韓合同大会」が釜山で行われました。キャッチフレーズは「It's OK」、韓国からはNAメンバー100人、日本からは50人が参加しました。2007年には第2回がソウルで開かれ、キャッチフレーズは「Not Alone, All Together」。韓国からは150人が、日本からは40人が参加しました。2008年と2009年はコンベンションが開かれませんでした。なぜならNAのリーダーがリラプスで逮捕されてしまったからなんですが、2010年11月6日・7日に第3回がソウルで開かれました。その時のキャッチフレーズは「Just For Today」でした。

　現在、韓国には5つのNAがあります。ソウル、仁川（インチョン）、楊州（ヤンジュ）、釜山（プサン）と釜谷国立病院です。

　われわれは薬物依存症の脳への影響などについてこれまで調査研究を行い、4つの論文を発表しています。ここまでの結論として、まず疫学的な調査の必要性があげられます。薬物依存に関する疫学的な調査が無い為に、われわれは韓国に依存症の患者がどのくらいいるのかを把握していません。その為、韓国政府は薬物汚染の深刻さを理解していませんし、治療やリハビリのための取り組みを行っていないのです。また、ドラッグ・コートも必要です。薬物依存症の治療とリハビリに関し、法システムと医療システム間の協議やミーティングは行われていません。ですので、治療に関する政策は限定されています。

　検察側は治療より逮捕や刑務所内処遇を好みます。我々は治療の効果についてもっと話し合うべきで、裁判所が治療を受けるよう命じるという手続きも必要だと考えています。裁判所命令であれば公正さを保てます。さらに、刑務所内での治療プログラムも必要です。今年、刑務所での治療プログラムは8か所の刑務所で試験的

に週1度2時間の授業を3ヶ月行う、という形でスタートしましたが、期間は延長すると思われます。ほかの刑務所にも広がるでしょう。刑務所内にもシステム化された治療プログラム、例えばTC（セラピューティック・コミュニティ）など、治療のための設備が必要です。このほか、NAやハーフウェイハウスもさらに必要です。現在、韓国にはNAのグループが5つ、ハーフウェイハウスは1か所しかありません。NAの役割は今後さらに拡大するでしょうし、DARCのようなリハビリ施設も必要とされています。来年にも釜山にDARCを作ろうとする動きがあると聞いています。

最後に、薬物依存症について学ぶ国立の研究機関が必要です。私は今年の9月から大学の社会福祉学部に移り、薬物依存症のリハビリなどについて講義を行う予定で、大学病院でも患者の治療にあたります。また、国立病院では薬物依存症者専用のベッド200床を改装中で、今後2～3ヶ月で再開する予定で、薬物依存症に関する教育を受けた職員、特にリハビリの専門家を配置する予定です。

私はNAなど第三の存在が重要だと考えていますし、ハーフウェイハウスも数を増やすべきだと考えます。もっと日本で行われている活動についてできる限りあなた方から学びたいと思っています。

［8］支援の際の基本的価値とスタッフ教育の重要性について

市川　岳仁（NPO法人三重ダルク常務理事/精神保健福祉士）

はじめに

本稿は、2011年8月、神戸において開催された国際犯罪学会での報告に加筆したものである。

1　三重ダルクについて―支援の基本的価値とスタッフ教育について―

ダルクは、依存症経験のある当事者同士が、お互いをサポートする回復コミュニティとして始まった。現在、日本中に49か所（65施設）ほどある（2012年現在）ダルクのなかで、三重ダルク[1]は17番目に誕生した、比較的初期にできた施設である。

（1）三重ダルクの特徴

三重ダルクの特徴は、地域に密着した取り組みを行っていることである。単なる断薬だけでなく[2]、地域コミュニティのメンバーとして尊厳を取り戻していくことを目標にしたプログラム提供を行なっている。さらに、精神保健福祉士や介護福祉士などの専門資格をもつスタッフもおり、経験からくるサポートに専門知識をプラスした、新しいタイプのサポートを行っている。

その他にも、地域の人々と関わりを持ち、一緒になって作業をしながら依存症を回復していくという新しい試みに取り組んでいる[3]。

当事者だけでなく、いろいろな人たちと関係を持ちながら、依存症からの回復を目指す―。三重ダルクはそんな新しい形のコミュニティとして活動を続けている。

（2）三重ダルクの基本プログラム

三重ダルクの場合、基本的に3段階の回復プログラムとなっている。（図）

ステップ1では、解毒と個別課題の把握を行い、その後に続くリハビリのプランを作成する。

1　NPO法人三重ダルクホームページ　http://www.miedarc.com
2　ダルクの目的はただ一つ、「薬物をやめたい仲間の手助けをすることだけである」とされている。
3　三重ダルクは東紀州地域において、農家や漁業関係者との連携で農業・漁業・林業に従事することもできる。

DARC プログラムの流れ

STEP 1　トリートメント	
解毒・身体ケア 薬をやめる・からだの健康	個別課題の把握 私の問題はなんだろう？

STEP 2　リハビリテーション	
依存症のケア 心の健康 （ミーティングやワーク）	社会スキル訓練 コミュニケーションのとりかた、パソコン、調理など

STEP 3　労働/地域生活移行期	
自助グループ活動 自助グループ活動	学業/就労　支援 勉強/資格/仕事　など

　ステップ2では、依存症のケアと社会スキルの訓練を行う。

　ステップ3では、希望者に学業復帰[4]や資格取得[5]の支援をしている。また、地域で仕事を探したり、東紀州での農業・漁業・林業に従事する事もできる。

　さらに、アディクション以外の重複障がいを持つクライアントの支援に力を入れており、特に発達障がい（知的障がい、アスペルガー症候群、ADHDなど）を持つクライアントの支援を得意としている。非言語コミュニケーション、ビジュアルを使ったプログラム進行など、彼らの障がい特性をふまえた支援内容となっている。

（3）スタッフの教育について

　ダルクそのものは専門的なリハビリ施設ではなく[6]、またそれが「良さ」でもあるのだが、クライアント時期から一定の期間を経てスタッフとして従事しているメンバーが、ダルク内での"内向きの貢献"で終わることなく「社会的存在となる」

4　高校・大学などが中心。

5　介護ヘルパー、介護福祉士、宅建主任、精神保健福祉士などをすでに取得、あるいは現在資格取得に向けて努力している。

6　ダルク創設者である近藤恒夫は、著書『薬物依存を越えて』（海拓舎、2000）の中で、「自らは決して専門家ではないし、強い信念があるわけではないが、かつて自分が苦労した問題を今日抱えている人を見て、放っておけないから手を差し伸べているだけである」と語っている。

ために（さらには、回復者カウンセラー以外の道を選ぶことができるようになるために）、三重ダルクでは、スタッフは仲間のサポートに従事しながら、同時に各自大学などに在籍してそれぞれの専門性を高める勉強[7]をしている。また、こうしたスタッフの努力を支援するために、三重ダルクでは大学でのスクーリングなども職員研修として認定するなど、学びやすい環境を整え援助している。

2　回復者カウンセラーへの意識調査から

　こうしたスタッフ教育を行っている背景には、日本の当事者カウンセラーが抱える課題状況がある。

　今回の国際犯罪学会での発表にあたり、回復者カウンセラーの意識調査を行った。調査は2011年6月の第一週に行われ、ダルク14か所、277名（入寮者190名、スタッフ87名、うち責任者17名）に対して実施された。調査にあたっては茨城ダルクの岩井喜代仁代表に多大なご協力をいただいた。心より深く感謝申し上げる。

（1）　ダルクスタッフとクリーン

　スタッフになった人の81.6％が、クリーン0～2年でスタッフの立場に、責任者になった人の88.2％が、2～7年で責任者の立場に就いていた。当事者AからBになるための敷居がとても低いといえる。

　スタッフになった理由は、「スタッフや責任者に言われて」がもっとも多く（64.3％）、責任者（17名）の前職はすべてダルクスタッフであった。

　また、2000年までの時期に開設されたダルクでは、開設時の責任者のクリーン（断薬期間）が2年まで、2000から2009年までの時期に開設のダルクでは、責任者のクリーンが3年から6年、2010以降に開設されたダルクでは、責任者のクリーンが7年以上となっており、近年になるほど開設時の責任者の断薬期間が長くなってきているのが特徴的である。

　茨城ダルク代表の岩井氏は、こうした「スタッフになる基準」について、「入寮し、健康状態と人間性およびクリーン（断薬期間）を作り、その結果、5年以上茨城ダルクにて生活をした上で再度、本人の希望を聞く。スタッフになる基準とするのは概ねクリーン3年以上、5年未満。また、施設の責任者にし、その後、独立した施設長となれるのは、その施設が開設されてから2年以上責任者の立場をやっていただいた上で決めています」と語っている。

---

[7]　多くは保健福祉系大学の通信課程。

（2） 自らの回復とダルクスタッフであること

94.2％のスタッフ、100％の責任者が、"ダルクの職員であること"は「自らの回復に役立つ」と答えた。

反面、少し気になるのは、「あなたにとって『回復』とはどのようなことを指すか？」という問いに対して、利用者の93％、スタッフの97％、責任者の89％が、個人的事柄に関する記述をするに留まり、「自らの存在の公共性」について述べているのは、わずかに留まったことである。つまり、「クスリを使わなくなった」とか、「朝起きられるようになった」といった内容にはじまる個人的な事柄に関しては、ずいぶん変化が起こったと答えている反面、自分の公共性について触れられた答えが少なかったのが特徴的である。

例えば「私は今、社会のとても大事なメンバーの一人である」などといった、自らの公共性に関する記述が少なかった。このことからは、ダルクのスタッフであること＝社会的存在であること（の意識）ではない事が窺われる。

（3） 考 察

今回の調査結果は、過去の筆者の研究[8]を裏付けるものとなった。
ダルクで「社会復帰」という言葉を聞くことが多い。筆者はその言葉を聞くたびに、「ああ、この人は、自分が社会不在だと感じている。社会にいないと感じているんだな」と思う。それを裏付けるような数字が出ていることは気になる。

たしかに薬物依存症の回復者、特に資格を取ったとか勉強したというわけでもなく、経験で支えている人たちの社会的な価値は、今も全く定義されていない。外から見れば、ダルクのスタッフも患者扱いになりかねない。回復者（ピア）カウンセラーとしての役割が社会で定義されないまま今日まできていることが、この数字になっていると思う。

社会が回復者を資源として使っていくのであれば、「この人たちはこういう役割、こういう価値を持ったリソース・パーソン＝（資源）である」という、基本的な価値づけを一旦しないと、社会も彼らを使えないのではないか。ただ「ダルク」という場を彼ら自身で作り、その家族なり支援者に支えられて、その場を維持することが出来たとしても、これではまだ、社会的な存在として成立することは出来ていないのではないか。

---

[8] 詳しくは、市川岳仁「薬物依存からの回復における当事者性の意義と課題～ＮＰＯとしてのダルクの活動を素材に～」龍谷大学大学院法学研究、第12号、2010を参照願いたい。

3　回復者カウンセラーの意義と課題

　以上のことから、ダルクのシステムは非常に優秀であるが、しかし、いくつかの課題もあると言えるのではないか。

（1）　回復者カウンセラーの課題──ピアの旬と役割喪失の問題──

　身体障がいなどのピア＝当事者と、薬物依存症の当事者というのはちょっと違う。薬物依存症の場合、かつての経験はあるが、それは今も…ということとは違う。薬物を使った期間より使わない期間の方が長くなった時、10年も20年も回復した時に、今まさにクスリの問題で目の前にいる人と本当に同じだと言えるのか。これは深刻な問題である。

　ピアカウンセラーという意味で言えば、10年も20年もやめている人よりも、3年ぐらい止めている人の方が優秀であると考えると、古くなった人たちは、それなりに役割喪失を経験していくだろう。（ここ数年に渡って、長期間回復していた人が、鬱になったり亡くなってしまった。）だから、古くなった人は次の立ち位置が本当は必要なのだろう。

　しかし、問題は、後ろを振り返った時に"ダルクでスタッフをしてきたこと"が、社会のキャリアとして認められないことだろう。入寮者として10年いようが、スタッフとして10年いようがキャリアにならない。この部分に対する当面の解決として、筆者の場合は勉強をして、精神保健福祉士の資格を取った。

　薬物依存症の回復には、ピアサポーターが絶対に必要だろう。やはり仲間でなければ出来ないことがある。当事者性は絶対に必要な部分である。ただ、自分の仕事としての意識と、自分の治療の意識がゴチャゴチャになっている。このことが今回のデータに反映されているのではないかと思う。

　ダルクのスタッフであるから、社会的存在だと感じられるわけではない。私たちのような援助職者を定義する資格が必要だろうと思う。しかし、ダルクの良いところはダルク以前の経歴が不問なところである。これは失くしてはいけない。これがあるからこそ皆が可能性を感じられる、希望があると思える大事なところである。ダルクが希望のないところになったら意味がないので、この「前歴不問」というのは、ぜひこれからも守っていきたい。

　そういう底辺の価値というか、懐の広さみたいなものは、絶対になくすべきではない。ただ、それを社会が我々を認知して、一緒に働けるようになるための価値のようなものを一緒に創っていかなければならない。そのための基本的価値と（この経験則を有してることをもって）十分働くことのできる人だということを、どこかで証明していけるような認証の仕方を探る必要があるだろう。

（2） 組織（NPO）としてのダルクの課題

　古くなった人たちが、当事者ピアカウンセラーとしての役割を次に渡していき、より積極的かつ、直接的な資源構築を担うのが理想である。しかし、この時に注意せねばならないのは、今ある制度上の役割を下請けで引き受けさせられて、安いお金で利用されるような扱われ方ではなく、自分達がこれまで創ってきたものを活かすような形で資源を作っていくことである。

　これはダルクだけでなく、様々なNPOが抱えている問題点でもある。今ある国の仕事を、非常に安価に、下請け的に受けさせられる。

　例えば法務省による更生緊急保護、自立準備ホーム[9]。新しい受け皿として、ダルクがある部分期待をされている。ただ問題は、そこで起こった色々な問題が、ダルクの問題として責任を負わされる可能性がある[10]。さらに、このシステムを使って入寮者を受けた場合、ダルクのある自治体とのトラブルも予想される。

　例えば、自立準備ホームの制度を使って仮出所者を受けた場合、数か月後には法務省からの経済的支援が切れてしまう。その時に、もう数か月間もダルクでの生活実績が残ってしまったこの人を、どうするのか。国（法務省）の代わりにダルクが自治体と喧嘩させられるということになりかねない。

　こういう問題がこれまでも頻繁に起こっている。たとえば生活保護である。生活保護費は本人の権利の問題としての受給であり、ダルクの入寮費ではない。本人が生活に困窮している場合に、基本的な国民の権利として受給する。しかし、本人は手続きの仕方も分らず、一人では申請も出来ないことが多い。精神病院では、この手続きをソーシャルワーカーがする。ダルクの場合も、スタッフが申請手続きを援助しなければならない現状がある。そして、本来は本人と自治体の問題であるはずのところにダルクが巻き込まれることになる。

　だから、本当はダルクではないところのソーシャルワーカーが、（ダルクに行く人に関しても）きちんとケースワークをして、手続きを済ませて、ダルクに繋げてあげた方が良いのではないか。矯正施設からの受け皿にダルクをという流れの中では、これを専門に担えるワーカーがいた方がよい。それで筆者は、地域生活定着支援センターで働いている。

　たまたま、私は定着支援センターが設置される時期に資格が取れていたので、センターに関わることが出来た。そこで働く意味は、ダルクのスタッフの負担を軽減

9　法務省ホームページ http://www.moj.go.jp/hogo1/souma/hogo02_00029.html
10　たとえば、再使用者の通報義務など。

することにある。ダルクのスタッフの本当の仕事は、そんなところではないと思っているからである。

おわりに

　回復者を活かすようなシステムを社会の中で創っていけるかどうかが、日本の回復者が今後もさらに継続して回復していくためのキーワードだろう。

　いま世の中が一気に動いている。社会が急速に動きを変えている。この時に、私たちを取り巻く環境が、また専門家優位の、ダルクが登場する以前の、ある種の専門家支配的な、当事者のエンパワーがない状態のネットワークに戻るのか。いよいよ国が乗り出してくる。国が乗り出してきた時に、回復者がまた「患者のアイデンティティー」に戻されるのか、あるいはある種の援助者として、資源としてきちんと認知されていくかの瀬戸際である。

　さらに、これまでの経験則、つまり知的財産を奪われずに、これを守っていけるかどうか。そういう形で次の時代を築いて行けるのならば、非常に希望があるし、もっとたくさんの薬物依存症者が回復していくことになるだろう。また、専門家による薬物依存症者の治療的アプローチが色を強めて、患者の立ち位置で扱われることになれば、ダルクが生まれる前の状態に戻りかねない。そんなことになれば、せっかくここまで回復してきたたくさんの、何百人、何千人という数の薬物依存症者の回復すら危ないと危惧している。

　過去の経歴に関係なく、自らの体験（当事者性）を活かした貢献ができるという敷居の低さを守りつつ、さらにそこからステップアップしていけるようなシステムの構築が急がれるのではないだろうか。

[9] 薬物依存症と向き合うダルク——正義ではなく許しと寛容——

加藤　武士（NPO法人京都DARC）

はじめに

　DARC（ダルク）では日々、薬物をやめたい仲間を手助けしている。DARCはDrug Addiction Rehabilitation Center の略で薬物依存症回復施設である。足を骨折した人がリハビリを行うことと同じように、薬物を手放し素面で生きるためには病んだ心身のリハビリが必要である。人は、薬物を使うことで、感情や金銭のコントロールを失い、生活が困難になっていく。ダルクは、もう一度素面の生き方を取り戻して社会で有用な一員として暮らすための回復と成長の場である。ダルクは、25年前に近藤恒夫氏と彼の支援者によって創設された。ダルクの活動はシンナー依存症者や元ヤクザの覚醒剤依存症者がダルクの玄関先に置いていかれるようにして始まった。現在、全国49か所（65施設）のダルクとその関連施設が活動するまでに成長した。京都ダルクは常勤スタッフ6名と非常勤スタッフ5名で運営している。2009年度には延べ3,400人の利用があった。

　　京都ダルクの活動は以下のとおり
　　・共同生活援助事業
　　・共同生活介護事業
　　・自立訓練（生活訓練）事業

　　また、我々は年間を通して外部における特別講演をおこなっている。
　　・刑務所への薬物離脱指導　年150回以上
　　・家族向けメンタルプログラム　年36回
　　・各種講演活動　年44回

　我々は回復可能であるというメッセージを運び続けている。薬物依存症に関して、「ダメ。ゼッタイ。」に偏った施策だけではなく、さらなる精神科医療・福祉行政の対応を望んでいる。
　それには、隔離された場所で行うのではなく、地域社会のなかで取り組むことが重要である。我々は、日常生活における様々な困難を乗り越えるための道案内をする。

ダルクでの回復率を指摘されることがあるが、大切なことは誰でも利用できることである。

日本における最近の薬物問題

薬を使うきっかけは、薬物を使う好奇心だけでなく様々な理由がある。その多くが彼らの友人や悪い仲間からの誘いを断ることができずに薬を使う。一度薬を使い始めると、その快楽を求め続け、止めることが難しくなっている。また、疲れや苦悩を失くすという理由で彼の仕事のために覚醒剤を使う人もいる。

若者への薬物汚染の社会問題としての要因を以下のように推察する。

それらはニュースやメディアによって世間に知られるようになっている。薬物の種類が多様化している。例えば、シンナー、ガス、覚醒剤、大麻、MDMA、向精神薬、その他の合法ドラッグである。誤った知識によって罪の意識が失われている。彼らはインターネットを通して多くの情報が得やすくなっており、誰にも知られずに薬物を購入する事さえできる。

日本の行政における薬物政策

国際的診断基準は ICD-10（WHO）、DSM-4（USA）として存在する。

日本政府は1999年の法改正によって精神障がい者として依存症者を認定した。この改正によって薬物依存症者は医療・福祉の援助を受けることが可能になっている。

ダルクにおける利用者の傾向

当初、人間関係を失った利用者の多くがダルクに助けを求めた。彼らは離婚を経験していたり、刑務所に行っていたり、精神病院の患者であった。

けれども、最近はすべてを失っていない利用者が増えてきている。また、発達障がい、アスペルガー症候群・注意欠陥多動性障がい・ギャンブル依存症・異性依存症などの様々な問題を抱えた人間もダルクに来ている。我々はアディクト達が社会で他の人々のように働くことができるように我々のプログラムに参加できる環境を創設することを目的とする。

ミーティングの効果

様々な理由からミーティングを必要としている。我々はそれぞれの経験を分かち合うためにミーティングに出席する。

我々は新しいメンバーを中心に輪になって座りミーティングを行う。
　司会者は、その日のテーマを提供して、参加者自身の話を導くようにする。ディスカッションや論争はしない。言いっぱなし聞きっぱなしで経験を分かち合う。最後に、希望を持って、参加者達は自信を与えられ、再び人生をスタートする望みを取り戻すのである。
　ミーティングは回復を分かち合うのに重要な場所である。ミーティングは我々がかつてどうだったのかこれからどうなれるのか、ということでも、「みな同じだという、一体感」が示される。その一体感がなかったら、我々はどうすることも、どこに行き着くこともできない。だから我々はミーティングに足を運び続けている。

渇望のための工夫

　我々のスローガンは「今日だけ薬物をやめておこう」という意味である"今日だけ"である。これは、"もう二度と使わない"というのに比べて、受け入れやすく、容易なことである。また、渇望をコントロールする手段として、薬物の手助けなしに生活を楽しむ方法を見つけることを提案している。内的な引き金（気分、感情、思考など）と同じように自分自身の外的な引き金（人、場所、物、時間、状況など）を理解することは重要であり、渇望をコントロールするのに大いに役に立つ。クリーンタイムがより長くなると、薬がないことから生ずる動揺が少なくなる。我々の回復には時間と新しい経験が必要であり、どのように生活を楽しむかを見つけ、やがて薬物依存症から開放されていくのである。

スポンサーシップとスピリチュアリティー

　スポンサーシップとはこの場合においては資金的なスポンサーという意味ではない。長期間プログラムを積み重ねてきた者は新しく来た仲間の信頼のおける相談相手としての行動をする。スポンサーシップにより、彼らはお互いにプラス思考の影響を与えながら自己の充実感を成長させていくことができる。花の素朴な美しさは我々より偉大な力が我々の周囲で働いていることを教えてくれる。

家族との関係

　嘗て、私は母親に「親でもない、子でもない」と言われた。結婚をして、薬を使わない素面で3年が過ぎた頃、私は母親に会いに行った。しかし、母は私を拒絶した。玄関の扉を閉じたまま、私に家に帰れと言った。私がダルクで10年間クリーンタイムを保ち続けた時、ようやく母親は私が来る事を受けいれてくれた。

家族との関係では、否定的な感情―不満、後悔、恨み、不寛容などを手放し、新しい関係を築きあげていくために　誠実さ、感謝、思いやり、愛が大切なことである。

おわりに

　ダルクは万能ではない。

　家族、友人、医療、福祉、司法やその他の地域の協力などの外部からの支援が必要不可欠である。薬物を取り除いた新しい生活を始める依存症者のために、より良い環境を創出する手段として、あらゆる関係機関の情報と活動を合同化して、縦割りではなく横に広がりを持って薬物依存症に向き合わなければならない。

[10] 刑事法研究者の立場から
―― ドイツの非刑罰化・非犯罪化政策 ――

金　尚均（龍谷大学）

はじめに

ここでは、ドイツの非犯罪化・非刑罰化政策との対比で、日本の厳罰政策や米国のドラッグ・コートを考えてみることにする。

一　ドイツの非犯罪化・非刑罰化政策

ドイツには「少量」の薬物所持は起訴しないことができるという法律がある。その考え方は、日本の厳罰政策とはまったく違うし、ドラッグ・コートとも異なる。ドラッグ・コートは、いったん起訴するが、ドイツでは起訴前にダイバージョンする。また、ドイツでは検察官による起訴猶予の可能性も認められている。

ドイツでは、「少量」のマリファナ単純所持の規制の合憲・違憲が問題になり、1994年、連邦憲法裁判所は、マリファナの単純所持の規制は、原則として、合憲であると判示した。しかし、例外的に、自己使用目的の少量所持等について検察官が起訴しないことを許容すると判示した。なお、『ドイツ麻薬剤法』第31条ａは「自己使用目的での少量の違法薬物の所持など」について、起訴猶予の可能性を認めているが、「少量」の定義については各州の「少量」に関するガイドラインに委ねている。

そもそも、マリファナは違法薬物に該当しないのではとの疑念について、上記の憲法裁判所の判決は、違法薬物であることを肯定し、規制は憲法適合的であると判示した。爾来、他のヨーロッパ諸国でも、ソフトドラッグとハードドラックの区別が問題となった。

二　連邦諸州の規制状況

ドイツは連邦制なので、州ごとに定義が異なる。マリファナについては、15グラムまで処罰しない州もあれば、30グラムまでは処罰しない州もある。たとえば、ハノーバーでは6グラムまでを少量とする。6グラム以下の所持は起訴しない。15グラム以下は検察の裁量で起訴しないことができる。現在、連邦各州においては、マリファナなどのカンナビスについてはおおむね6グラムを少量するとの点で一致が見られる。なお、少量とは、1週間で3回の使用を目安としている。

ヘロイン、コカイン、アンフェタミンなどは1グラム以下なら単純所持は処罰しない。これらは、州のガイドラインで示されている。治療の過程で再使用することがある。通報を義務化しないためには、起訴の可否をあらかじめ区別しておくことには意味がある。少量の定義は、再犯者のためのものだ、ともいわれる。すべての州に類似の規定があり、再犯者のために用いられており、実務上、少量の所持は起訴されない。

三　フランクフルトの実態調査

　2年前に訪問したフランクフルトでは、重度のヘロイン中毒者に市当局が患者にあわせた純度のヘロインを与えていた。健康保険制度の下で依存症者を保護していこうという政策である。ドイツの政策は、ドラッグ・コートとは異なる考え方に基づいている。フランクフルトには注射針を提供するプログラムがある。患者は、違法に購入した薬物を注射器に入れて打つ。職員は、打ってはくれない。他人に打つのは違法だからだ。これは治療への入り口として機能している。エイズの感染を防止することが最初の目的だった。そのシェルターには「ヘルスルーム」と呼ばれる注射を打つ部屋がある。最近、保険制度を使ってヘロインそのものをくれるようになった。評価は分かれるが新しい道だ。

おわりに〜質疑の内容〜

　つぎのような議論があった。
（1）日本にも、同じような制度を導入できないだろうか。プログラム参加の意志を持つ者が、再使用してしまうと犯罪者になってしまう。医療や福祉の支援が必要な人を刑務所に入れてしまうとプログラムは十分に機能しない。再使用に気付いた家族が、警察に通報すると刑務所に入れられてしまう。家族を刑務所に入れられるのが嫌だということで、ただ困って見ているというようなこともある。
　健康被害を可及的に縮減しようとする「ハーム・リダクション」の考え方からすれば、「底をつく」前のもっと早い段階でプログラムを提供する方策を講ずべきことになる。

（2）10年前、ボンにも「ヘルスルーム」のようなところがあり、そこでは針だけではなくヘロインそのものも与えていた。エイズの感染を防ぐための政策だった。
　その当時、8つの都市で実験的にヘロインを提供していた。この実験は2001年から2007年まで行われ、その成果について、肯定的な評価が優勢だったことから、

2008年に重度の中毒患者に薬物を交付する立法がなされた。したがって、適正な手続きに基づくヘロインの提供は、合法である。

[11] 精神科ソーシャル・ワーカーの立場から

西念奈津江（精神科ソーシャル・ワーカー）

　2010年末まで北陸の地方都市にある精神科病院のソーシャル・ワーカー（精神保健福祉士）として、依存症からの回復支援に携わってきた。現在は、北陸地方にある2か所の刑務所で処遇カウンセラー（薬物担当）として薬物依存離脱指導を担当している。

　精神科病院では主にアルコール依存症の回復支援に携わってきた。精神科病院でのアルコール依存症者との関わりでは、「自分の金で好きな酒を飲んで何が悪い」「誰にも迷惑かけていない」「飲酒は罪じゃないだろ」「だから酒をやめる気はない」といった、彼らの依存症に対する「否認」に向き合っていた。ところが刑務所での薬物依存離脱指導では参加者の多くが「覚せい剤は犯罪だからもう使いません」「もっと意志を強くして、心を入れ替えて頑張ります」と背筋を伸ばして宣言する。それならやる気があっていいじゃないか、というものではない。合法だから何が悪い、というアルコール依存症者と、違法だからやめます、という違法薬物の依存症者。飲むか飲まないか、使うか使わないか、そして合法か違法か、といった対立軸に囚われているという意味において、両者に大きな違いはない。

　依存症の専門医療機関を除けば、多くの精神科医療機関においては未だ、違法薬物依存症（乱用）の問題は医療ではなく司法が扱うものとの認識が根強く、薬物依存症からの回復支援には消極的だ。またアルコール依存症の治療やプログラムの目標は「断酒」に置かれていることが多い。同様に、刑務所でのプログラムの目標も「断薬」に置かれている。つまり回復支援に携わる者もまた、違法か合法か、医療か司法か、飲むか飲まないか、使うか使わないか、といった対立軸に囚われている。果たしてその先に依存症者の回復はあるのだろうか。

　依存症からの回復は終わりの無いマラソンと例えられる。依存症者が依存対象に対する無力を認め、慢性疾患である依存症と付き合いながら、新しい生き方を模索し、ありのままの自分を赦し、またそこに価値を認め、そのままでいい、そのままがいいと思えるようになる。そんな「その人らしさ」の本質を追い求める気の長いプロセスそのものが回復なのだと私は理解している。そのプロセスは、言うまでも

なく病院や刑務所、あるいは回復施設での一時的な関わりで完結するものでもなければ、対立軸を行き来することでもない。依存症からの回復における最も大きな舞台は、彼らが、そして私たちが暮らすこの地域社会そのものである。そこで彼らはその人らしく生きているだろうか？　私は今、私らしく生きているだろうか？　制度、政策の早く大きな流れの渦の中で、その視点を見失ってはいないだろうか。薬物依存症の人たちとの関わりを通して、わたしは、改めて、ソーシャル・ワーカーとしての原点に立ったように思う。

[12] 依存症とジェンダー

野村佳絵子（京都橘大学）

　私は、社会学という立場から、摂食障がいの自助グループをフィールドとして研究活動を行っています。本稿では、依存症とジェンダーに着目して、若干のコメントをします。
　まず、摂食障がいにある種の「依存性」があると仮定した場合、つまり頑として食べない（拒食症）、食べては吐く（過食症）、を繰り返すことによって食べ物のことが片時も忘れられない状態を依存と考えた場合、摂食障がいと薬物依存症を並列して考えることができます。摂食障がいの治療において、「にわかに食べ吐きを中断するように指導すべきである」と「断つ」ことが強調されますが、当事者の声を詳細に聞いてみると、禁止だけに焦点をあてた治療プログラムは推奨できないことは明らかです。なぜなら、たとえ拒食や過食の症状を断ったとしても、根本の問題が解決しなければ、食べ物から男性（あるいは子ども）へ、食べ物からアルコール（あるいは薬物）へ、といったふうに、次から次へと依存対象が移っていく例も少なくないからです。
　当事者の考える「回復」とは何でしょうか？　これまでの研究成果から、自分と向きあい、他の人とのやりとりを通して、これからの生き方を模索する、そういった一連のプロセスが「回復」である、ということができます。さらに、症状があろうがなかろうが、自分自身の摂食障がいについて、懸命に試行錯誤している人は、プロセスという「回復」の実践者である、ともいえます。それゆえ、摂食障がいは、「食に対する病」ではなく、一人の人間の「生き方追求の手段」とみることができます。したがって、摂食障がいの場合、「症状と共生する」道も選択肢としてあり得ます。薬物依存症の治療にあたっても、「断薬ありき」以外の選択肢を考えることも可能ではないでしょうか？
　また、私が摂食障がいのフィールドで出会う当事者の多くは女性であり、既存研究においても90%以上が女性であることが指摘されています。一方、（私の経験がまだ浅いものの）薬物依存症のフィールドで出会う当事者の多くは男性であり、既存研究においても、アルコール依存症などと同様、薬物依存症は「男性の病」であるかのように考えられています。そのせいか、これまでは、摂食障がいの治療施設や治療プログラム、さらには自助グループまでもが、女性を中心に作られたものが多く、薬物依存症やアルコール依存症のそれは、男性中心であったという見方もでき

ます。もちろん、そのプログラムにのって奏功した例もあるでしょう。しかしその逆もあります。とりわけ、女性の依存症者には、性的虐待など女性独自の問題が多数存在し、「寂しさ」や「悔しさ」など心の葛藤を持つ者が圧倒的に多いことが指摘されています。回復や治療のためであるといえども、男性集団の中に女性が加わったり、男性プログラムを女性が実施したりすれば、別の「問題」が引き起こされる可能性があります。それゆえ、女性が大多数を占めるといわれている摂食障がいを通じて、薬物依存症やアルコール依存症を考えるという応用力が、今後問われてくるでしょう。すでに、女性の依存症者らに対しては、周囲の人たちが「その人の人生に関心を持つだけでよい」、彼女らの回復とは「自分の考えや感情を言葉で表現できるようになること」であるともいわれています。

　しかしながら、次の点を考慮する必要もあります。それは、女性の薬物依存症者は、同じ女性の依存症者の中でもマイノリティにあたる、つまり、女性集団の中での競い合い、という現実です。「摂食（障がい）やアルコール（依存症）はまだかわいらしいが、薬物（依存症）だけにはなりたくない」「薬物（依存症）の女性と一緒にしないでほしい」という女性たちの声に、同じ女性として、どう向き合っていけばよいのでしょうか？　果てしなくつづくパワーゲームから、降りる／脱却する道はあるのでしょうか？

　一般的・普遍的な回復プログラムの構築とともに、個別・具体的な対処法もまた、必要になってきます。社会学の役割の一つとして、マクロとミクロ、両方の視点を持って、相対的に観ていくことが大切だと考えています。

[Special Issue: RYUKOKU Programs 2011]

"Ryukoku Programs" at 16th World Congress (ISC) in Kobe

RYUKOKU Programs

We would like to propose "Ryukoku Programs" to mark the renewal of our institute to provide chances by which we will discuss with a number of scholars and practitioners as our guests on some themes concerning to criminal policies and rehabilitation of ex-criminals. We are going to organize sessions and roundtable discussions in the 16th World Congress of the ISC between 5. and 9. August 2011 as follows:

6101 Plenary 1: Global Econimic Crisis and Criminology (Ishizuka, S.)
7108 The Concept of Japanese Drug Court: from Punishment to Harm-Reduction
(Ishizuka, S & Maruyama, Y.)
7118 Talk a lot about What Is Contemporary Situation of Drug Policy
(Ishizuka, S.; Maruyama, Y.; Kim, S.)
8111 The Death Penalty in East Asia and the United States
(Ishizuka, S.; Johnson, D.; Fuse, Y.; Hamai, K.)
8122 Death Penalty from Worldwide Perspective
(Ishizuka, S.; Johnson, D.; Fuse, Y.; Hamai, K.)
8132 Integrated System of Teaching Criminology and Criminal Justice
(Fukushima, I.)
9102 The New Survey Module of "Trust in Justice" in the European Social Survey: Measuring Penal Populism (Hamai, K. & N. Tsushima.)
9114 Beyond Punishment: Collaboration between Criminal Justice and Social Welfare (Hamai, K.)
5101 consideration of openness and security at school: focusing on security for children in the school property (Hamai, K.)

[Symposium]

Death Penalty in East Asia and the United States

Ryukoku University Corrections and Rehabilitation Center[i] (CRC) proposed **"Ryukoku Programs"** to mark the renewal of our institute to provide chances by which we will discuss with a number of scholars and practitioners as our guests on some themes concerning to criminal policies and the rehabilitation of excriminals. We are going to organize sessions and roundtable discussions in the 16th World Congress of the ISC between 5. and 9. August 2011, as follows:

[Symposium]

The Death Penalty in East Asia and the United States[ii]

Death Penalty from Worldwide Perspective[iii]

[Coordinators]
Ishizuka, Shinichi (Ryukoku University : Kyoto)
Johnson, David (University of Hawaii : Manoa)

[Presentations]
(1) Japan
Ishizuka, Shinichi (Ryukoku University : Kyoto)
Fuse, Yusuke (Ryukoku University : Kyoto)
(2) Korea
Park, Byungsick (Dongguk University, South Korea)
(3) Taiwan
Hsieh, Ju-Yuan (National Chengchi University)
Lee, Chia-Wen (National Cheng Kung University : Taiwan)
(4) China
Wang, Yunhai (Hitotsubashi University : Tokyo)

(5) USA

[Comments]
Zimring, Franklin E. (California University : Berkeley)
Hamai, Koichi (Ryukoku Yuniversity : Kyoto)
Scherdin, Lill (Oslo University : Norway)
Klapake, Jay (Ritsumeikan University)

1. JAPAN

Capital punishment is legal for 18 crimes (homicide, treason etc.) The death penalty is ordinarily imposed in cases of multiple murders involving aggravating factors. Executions are carried out by hanging. The prisoner's family and legal representatives are not informed until after the execution. Since December 7, 2007, the authorities have been releasing the names, the nature of the crimes, and the ages of executed prisoners. Since the end of World War II, courts have sentenced 824 people to death, and 668 of them have been executed. At the end of 2010, 111 people lived on death row. Between 2001 and 2008, local district courts have sentenced many defendants to death in the first instance, totaling 119. Ministers of Justice executed 9 people in 2007, 15 in 2008, and 7 in 2009, even though the average number of executions from 1990 to 2006 was only 3. We can call this time "Monsieur Verdoux" ("one murder makes a villain ; millions a hero ; numbers sanctify"). After the change in ruling political party in August 2008 and the introduction of a new trial system, the "SAIBANIN SEIDO", which consists of 3 professional and 6 lay judges, we have had only 8 death sentences and 2 executions. We want to show the contemporary situation and analyze some changes in the political context. We also hope to propose perspectives to abolish the death penalty in Japan.

2. SOUTH KOREA

Capital punishment is legal and still handed down. A murderer who killed ten people was convicted on April 2009 and sentenced to death. However, the country's last execution took place on 31 December 1997. We can tell you that no executions have been carried out since the late President Kim Dae-jung came to power in February 1998. After brutal and spectacular crimes happened recently, the Highest Court upheld in February 2010 the death penalty in a 5 to 4 decision, and then in March of that year the Minister of Justice suggested that the execution of death row inmates will continue, breaking the virtual 13-year moratorium. After that, however, the Ministry of Justice has announced that perhaps the death penalty should be replaced by life imprisonment without parole. Korea's National Human Rights Commission recommended that capital punishment be abolished too. Because UN Secretary-General Ban Ki-moon came from South Korea, we expect that the government cannot resume such a barbarous punishment.

3. TAIWAN (Republic of China)

Capital punishment is legal. Before 2000, the Taiwan Area had a relatively high execution rate when some strict laws were still in effect in the harsh political environment. However after some controversial cases during the 1990s plus some officials' attitudes shifting towards abolition, the number of executions dropped significantly since 1998, with only three executions in 2005 and none between 2006 and 2009. Execution resumed in 2010 after strong pro-capital punishment activities burst out earlier that year. President Chen Shui-bian announced his intention to abolish the death penalty in May 2001. Although the right to abolish the death penalty is held by the Legislative branch of government, which is dominated by the conservative party, the Pan-blue coalition. The Minister of Justice, a member of the Democratic Progressive Party, did not sign death warrants except for serious and noncontroversial cases. As a result, the number of executions have reduced significantly since 2002. These conditions remained in effect until Chen Shui-bian's tenure expired on May 20, 2008. We even named Taiwan as a moratorium state. In May 2008, the new President, Ma Ying-jeou, nominated Wang Ching-feng as the Minister of Justice. As Wang also held an anti-capital punishment standpoint, she delayed signature to allow executions until March 2010. Her attitude caused controversy and social pressure, which influenced her position. In March 2010, a new Minister, Tseng Yung-fu, promised to resume executions, and on April 30, 2010, he gave orders to carry out 4 executions, thereby ending the 52-month moratorium.

4. CHINA (People's Republic of China)

Capital punishment is legal. The majority of executions are for cases of either aggravated murder or large-scale drug trafficking. China executes the highest number of people annually. China's criminal code explicitly forbids the death penalty for young offenders under the age of 18 at the time of the crime. The Dui

Hua Foundation estimates that China executed between 5,000 and 6,000 people in 2007, down from 10,000 in 2005. In 2009, Amnesty International estimated 1718 executions during 2008. The methods of execution are by firing squad and lethal injection. This is the same three-drug cocktail used in the United States. On 6 April 2010, China executed a Japanese national who was caught illegally carrying more than 1.5 kg of stimulants at the airport, by lethal injection. After 3 days, three more Japanese were executed. Pressure placed on local and regional bureaucracies under the auspices of the "strike hard" campaigns has led to the streamlining of capital cases: cases are investigated, cases and appeals are heard, and sentences are carried out at rates much more rapidly than in other states. After a first trial conducted by an Intermediate People's Court concludes with a death sentence, a double appeals process must follow. The first appeal is conducted by a High People's Court if the condemned appealed to it. Since 2007, another appeal is conducted automatically (even if the condemned opposed the first appeal) by the Supreme People's Court in Beijing. If the sentence is upheld, the execution is carried out shortly thereafter. As a result of its reforms, the Supreme People's Court overturned about 15 percent of the death sentences handed down by high courts in the first half of 2008. Before the Beijing Olympics, international public opinion influenced the Chinese government to reduce executions and forbid public executions, starting in 2007.

5. USA

Capital punishment in the United States varies by jurisdiction. In practice it applies only for aggravated murder and felony-murder. Capital punishment existed in the colonies that predated the United States and that were later annexed to the United States under the laws of their mother countries and continued to have effect in the states and territories they became. The methods of execution and the crimes subject to the penalty vary by jurisdiction and have varied widely throughout time. Some jurisdictions have banned it, others have suspended its use, and others are trying to expand its applicability. There were 37 executions in the United States in 2008, the lowest number since 1994 (largely due to lethal injection litigation). There were 52 executions in 2009, 51 by lethal injection, and one by electric chair (in Virginia). There were 46 executions in 2010, 44 by lethal injection, one by electric chair (Virginia), and one by firing squad (Utah). Capital punishment has often been a contentious social issue in the United States. Historically, public opinion was frequently supportive of the

death penalty, but Americans have become more divided on the issue in recent years. A 2010 Gallup poll showed that 64% of Americans favored capital punishment in cases of murder, and 29% opposed it. However, when given a choice between the death penalty and life imprisonment without parole in the 2010 poll, the disparity narrowed, with 49% favoring the death penalty and 46% favoring life imprisonment. The highest level of support recorded was 80% in 1994 (16% opposed), and the lowest recorded support was 42% in 1966 (47% opposed).
http://en.wikipedia.org/wiki/Capital_punishment_in_the_United_States

6. AMNESTY International Report on 2009

Amnesty International today challenged the Chinese authorities to reveal how many people they execute and sentence to death, as the organization published its world overview of the death penalty for 2009. In Asia, thousands of executions were likely to have taken place in China, where information on the death penalty remains a state secret. Only seven other countries were known to have carried out executions: Bangladesh, Japan, North Korea, Malaysia, Singapore, Thailand, and Viet Nam (with 26 executions known to have taken place). Afghanistan, Indonesia, Mongolia, and Pakistan did not carry out executions in 2009, the first execution-free year in those countries in recent times. Across the Americas, the USA was the only country to carry out executions in 2009.

Known Executions in 2009:
Bangladesh (3), Botswana (1), China (+), Egypt (at least 5), Iran (at least 388), Iraq (at least 120), **Japan (7)**, Libya (at least 4), Malaysia (+), North Korea (+), Saudi Arabia (at least 69), Singapore (1), Sudan (at least 9), Syria (at least 8), Thailand (2), **USA (52)**, Viet Nam (at least 9), Yemen (at least 30).
**Methods used included hanging, shooting, beheading, stoning, electrocution and lethal injection.

Death Sentences in 2009:
At least 2001 people were sentenced to death in 56 countries in 2009: the true number is much higher:
 Afghanistan (at least 133), Algeria (at least 100), Bahamas (at least 2), Bangladesh (at least 64), Belarus (2), Benin (at least 5), Botswana (2), Burkina Faso (at least 6), Chad (+), **China** (+), Democratic Republic of Congo (+), Egypt (at

least 269), Ethiopia (at least 11), Gambia (at least 1), Ghana (at least 7), Guyana (3), India (at least 50), Indonesia (1), Iran (+), Iraq (at least 366), Jamaica (2), **Japan (34)**, Jordan (at least 12), Kenya (+), Kuwait (at least 3), Liberia (3), Libya (+), Malaysia (at least 68), Mali (at least 10), Mauritania (at least 1), Morocco/Western Sahara (13), Myanmar (at least 2), Nigeria (58), North Korea (+), Pakistan (276), Palestinian Authority (17), Qatar (at least 3), Saudi Arabia (at least 11), Sierra Leone (at least 1), Singapore (at least 6), Somalia (12, six of which in Puntland and six within the jurisdiction of the Transitional Federal Government), South Korea (at least 5), Sri Lanka (108), Sudan (at least 60), Syria (at least 7), Taiwan (7), Tanzania (+), Thailand (+), Trinidad and Tobago (at least 11), Tunisia (at least 2), Uganda (+), United Arab Emirates (at least 3), **USA (at least 105)**, Viet Nam (at least 59), Yemen (at least 53), Zimbabwe (at least 7)

---

i . *Ryukoku University Corrections and Rehabilitation Center*
67 Tsukamoto-cho, Fukakusa,Fushimi-ku, Kyoto 612-857 Japan
Tel : +81-(0)75-645-2040 / Fax : +81-(0)75-645-2632

Since our establishment in 1639, Ryukoku University has tried to contribute to support social minorities and excluded people, based on the spirit of Shin Buddhism (Jodo Shinshu). Criminals and juvenile delinquents belong to these groups, too. We founded at first the Corrections and Rehabilitation Course (CRC) as an educational program on these fields in 1977, and secondly the Corrections and Rehabilitation Research Center (CRRC) as a research institute in 2001. Finally we have established the Corrections and Rehabilitation Center, which is going to integrate these two facilities and other additional social functions in April 2010.

ii . About 70 percent of the countries in the world have abolished capital punishment, but the United States and several East Asian nations retain it. The papers in this session will describe and analyze death penalty policy and practice in these two regions.

In Japan, the government has used capital punishment more often since about 2000. South Korea became an abolitionist de facto state in 2008. Executions and death sentences in Taiwan declined dramatically after the country started to democratize in the late 1980s. China carries out more executions than the rest of the countries in the world combined. And in the United States, 34 states and the federal system retain capital punishment, but executions are concentrated in only a handful of southern states.

This session will present current information about capital punishment in these five countries. Professor Franklin E. Zimring (University of California at Berkeley) and Professor Koichi Hamai (Ryukoku University) will serve as commentators. The papers will address several common questions, including these :

(1) The current situation of capital punishment in each country.
(2) The connection between capital punishment and social and political contexts.
(3) The relevance of international movements and human rights norms.
(4) Local opinion about abolition and retention.

iii. We are going to hold Symposium 4, on Monday August 8th 2011, (13 : 15-16 : 30, in room 301). The title is "The Death Penalty in East Asia and The United States", in which we focus on only East Asia and the U.S.. Though these societies have already developed enough to abolish death penalty from the viewpoints of industrial, cultural, and civil development, the governments retain this penalty. In the world today there is no doubt that this punishment has become rare and unusual. Following the Symposium, we will discuss the same theme from worldwide perspectives. Each participant will engage the four questions above.

[1] The Death Penalty in Japan

Yusuke Fuse (Ryukoku University)

Introduction

It is safe to say that recent situation in Japan concerning the death penalty, far from improving, has deteriorated. Such circumstances will be clearly understood in comparison with Korea, Taiwan, China, and the USA. It is noteworthy that Japan has been isolated amongst industrialized democracies and kept the death penalty system unquestioned. There has been no remarkable movement toward abolition or reform of capital punishment regardless of the global trends. Neither substantial research nor discussion has been conducted as to whether the death penalty is truly needed and hanging is constitutionally accepted.

1. Changes Relevant to the Death Penalty

(1) Lay Judge System

It started in May 2009. Six lay judges randomly selected amongst constituents and three professional judges deliberate, decide whether the defendant is guilty, and sentence. Thus, the new system directly involves the nation in the court procedure including trials of capital cases. Prosecutors sought death sentence in eleven cases until July 2011, among which eight defendants were actually sentenced to death.

(2) "Historic" Regime Change

The Democratic Party of Japan (DPJ) came to power at the general election in August 2009 when the Liberal Democratic Party of Japan (LDP) lost after it ruled almost continuously since 1955.

In spite of the DPJ's election manifesto that it will consider the introduction of life imprisonment without parole, the Minister of Justice, Keiko Chiba, ordered the executions of two inmates on July 28, 2010. On the other hand, the present Minister (as of August 8, 2011), Satsuki Eda, stated that capital punishment has various flows. No execution has been carried out since Mrs.Chiba ordered the last.

(3) Wrongful Prosecutions and Convictions

A man sentenced to life imprisonment for the 1990 kidnapping and killing of a 4-year-old girl (the Ashikaga Case) was acquitted in a retrial in March 2010 due to the new DNA tests. Two other men also sentenced to life imprisonment for the 1967 murdering on the occasion of robbery (the Fukawa Case) were also acquitted in a retrial in June 2011 on the grounds that they were possibly misled by investigators under interrogation and forced to admit the suspicion. Besides, a high-ranking government official was charged with drafting and executing a false official document but finally acquitted in September 2010. In relation to her case, a public prosecutor was found guilty of altering the evidence. These cases mentioned above are not capital ones but severely shook the trust in criminal justice system.

2. *The Rise and Fall in Death Sentences*

According to the annual report of judicial statistics, the number of Japanese death sentences given in the first instance was in single figures (between 1 and 8) every year from 1991 to 1999, except in 1995 ($n=11$). The number rose to two digits (between 10 and 18) in 2000-2007 and then fell again to single figures (between 4 and 9) in 2008-2010. Judging from the statistics published by the National Police Agency of Japan, such rise and fall can be partly attributed to the increase and decrease of murderers who were arrested and charged around this period.

3. *Leadership from the Front*

No execution was carried out in 1990-1992 and the number of executions was in single figures (between 1 and 9) every year from 1993 to 2010, except in 2008 ($n=15$).

The then Minister of Justice, Kunio Hatoyama (LDP), approved of his subordinate officers executing three inmates in February, four in April, and three in June, 2008. Given the unprecedentedly short interval, he was criticized for the arbitrariness by some opponents.

The DPJ fought the general election in 2009 under the banner of 'Leadership from the front' and pledged that the party will facilitate wide-ranging discussions about capital punishment. The election manifesto said:

> It is only the USA and Japan amongst developed countries that retain the death penalty. While paying attention to the international trends, the DPJ promises to deliberate on as to whether Japan should retain or abolish the death penalty, moratorium on executions, prior notification of execution,

executing methods and so on.

Although workshops have been held within the Ministry of Justice since the summer of 2010 when Mrs Chiba approved the executions, it is apparent that political leadership has still been dominated by bureaucratic control in the Ministry.

4. *Lay Judge System and Constitutionality of Hanging*

Hanging has been the only method of execution in Japan since 1882 while the USA changed the means from hanging to electrocution, lethal gas, and lethal injection searching for more 'humane' way. In April 1955, the Supreme Court of Japan upheld the constitutionality of hanging : "Hanging adopted by this country cannot be considered inhumanely crueler than other methods." Thus, in Japan, cruelty of hanging has never been profoundly questioned for more than half a century.

The death penalty system including the constitutionality of the executing method should have been elaborately re-examined before the lay judge system started. The Ministry of Justice needs to deal with these issues by setting up an external Commission, not by leaving them to the internal workshops.

[2] Capital Punishment in Korea and Abolition Movement Against It

Dr. Park, Byungsick (Dongguk University)

Introduction

Korea has recognized the capital punishment under statute. Yet, Korea became 'de facto' moratorium country on death penalty having not practiced it for the last thirteen years since December 1997. Although the opinion poll shows more pros than cons on this issue and the Constitutional Court of Korea rendered a 5-4 decision for it, people do not seem to believe that there will be an execution in the near future.

In Korea, there have been 900 executions from 1948 through 1997 which includes political prisoners as well as hideous criminals. Under the circumstances, I strongly believe that death penalty should be abolished and, for this reason, I myself have actively joined the movement against it.

Hereafter, I would like to introduce the capital punishment system in Korea and current movement against it.

1. Capital punishment in Korea
(1) Constitutional basis for capital punishment

The Korean Constitution does not prescribe the capital punishment. It simply states in the Article 110(4) that "Military trials under an extraordinary martial law may not be appealed in case of crimes of soldiers and employees of the military ; military espionage; and crimes as defined by Act in regard to sentinels, sentry posts, supply of harmful foods and beverages, and prisoners of war, except in the case of a death sentence." The Constitutional Court decided that "this article should be interpreted to allow death penalty indirectly."[1] Yet, it should be noted that this article was added into the Constitution during the Amendment of 1962 in order to regulate special crimes through military tribunal under the wartime and martial law situation.[2] Therefore, the proviso, "except in

---

1 The Constitutional Court, November 28, 1996, 95 Hun-Ba 1, 8KCCR 2, 537, 544 ~545 ; The Constitutional Court, February 25, 2010, 2008 Hun-Ga 23, KCCR 161, 421
2 The Constitutional Court, February 25, 2010, 2008 Hun-Ga 23, KCCR 161, 440

the case of a death sentence," was also added to allow the appeal from the trial court's death sentence even under the national emergency. In other words, the privisio of the Article 110(4) does not justify death penalty but discourage death penalty to guarantee the right to life.

As such, the Korean Constitution does not have any written provision to recognize the death penalty. Therefore, the issue of unconstitutionality of death penalty should be determined by the constitutional interpretation of the right to life, the goal of penal system and the human value and dignity.

(2) Crimes to be punishable by death penalty

Crimes to be punishable by the death penalty under the Criminal Act are as follows: Rebellion; Invasion of foreign enemy; Use of explosives; Death by arson; Murder; Rape and murder; Hostage and murder; Robbery and murder; and Maritime robbery and murder. However, in addition to the Criminal Act, there are over 20 other laws and 100 articles which regulate death penalty.

The laws that regulate death penalty are as follows: (the elements of each crime are omitted).

- The Act on special crimes and aggravated punishment
- The Act on punishment of battery
- The Special Act on punishment of sexual crimes
- The national security Act
- The narcotics and controlled substance Act
- The Special Act on illegal drug dealing
- The Special Act on health crimes enforcement
- The Act on organ transplant
- The Act on the protection of cultural property
- The Act on crimes under the jurisdiction of international criminal court
- The Korea Minting & Security Printing Corporation Act
- The aviation Act
- The Act on aviation safety and security
- The Act on punishment of Harmful act on ships and maritime structures
- The atomic energy act
- The Act on protection of atomic energy facility and prevention of radio-

activity
- The Act on control of radioactive waste
- The Act on prohibition of chemical and biological weapon, manufacture of certain chemicals and biological agents, import and export
- The Act on use of conventional weapons such as landmine and its transfer
- The Act on combat police unit
- The military criminal Act

As observed above, death penalty is prescribed by many laws which are strange to the public and even the legal experts. Especially, the military criminal Act, having only 42 Articles, punishes 62 different acts of crimes. It may be called "law of death penalty," indeed. Given this reality, one may possibly be sentenced to death under an unknown law. Although the Ministry of Justice claims that death penalty is applied only to brutal criminals such as serial killers or rapist killers who relinquished their humanity, death penalty is applied to many crimes without hideous natures.

2. Execution in Korea

There have been a total of 902 executions for the last 50 years from the establishment of the South Korean government in 1948 through the year of 1997 when the last execution was made. Among them, around 40 percent of executions are for the violation of the National Security Law (former Anti-Communism Law), which depicts the sad history of a Korea divided by ideologies. Although executions from the violation of the National Security Law significantly diminished, nobody can be sure that there will be no more execution for ideological issues as long as two Koreas exist.

In 1954, immediately after the Korean War, the highest number of executions (68) was made and, among the number, 38 executions were for the violation of the National Security Law and the National Emergency Act. Under the former President Park Jung-Hee's regime, 58 people were killed with the death sentence and 19 of them were convicted for espionage. In the "People's Revolutionary Party" case, a student movement leader was executed with the finding of guilty for being a North Korean spy. Shockingly, the execution was made within 20 hours after the Supreme Court affirmed the conviction and this incident created the international criticism under the name of "judicial killing."

Executions have been made not only under the military dictatorship but also under the so called "civilian regime" of the former President, Kim Young-Sam on a frequent basis. There were 15 executions in 1994 when heinous crimes was committed by organized gangs; 19 in 1995; and 23 in 1997 by the end of the presidential term. The execution of 1997 has been the last execution so far.

The succeeding President Kim, Dae-Jung, who was once a death-row inmate as a political prisoner, proclaimed himself as human rights President. Not surprisingly, there was no execution during his Presidency. Neither was any execution under the succeeding President Roh, Moo-Hyun. As Korea has 5 years of a presidential tenure, Kim Dae-Jung and Roh Moo-Hyun administration together stopped the execution for 10 years. Practically, Korea became the defacto abolition country on death penalty. There has been no execution under the current Present Lee, Myung-Bak. Yet, there have been isolated attempts to reinitiate the execution whenever hideous crimes occurred such as a serial killer was arrested in February 2009.

According to the Criminal Procedure Act in Korea, the Minister of Justice should deliver an execution order within six months after Court makes a final judgment, and upon receipt of the order, there should be an execution within five days (Article 456, Article 466). Theoretically, President retains no right to interfere with execution. Nevertheless, the execution rate is analyzed according to each different President because it is practically impossible for Minister of Justice to deliver the execution order independently. Procedurally, the Minister of Justice makes the political and social justification for an execution and proposes it to President. Upon President's permission, the Minister delivers the execution order. This shows that the capital punishment in Korea is closely related to politics.

Although Korea became a de facto abolition country on death sentence, the sentencing of death penalty continues even now. Table 1 shows the number of death sentence and actual executions since 1980. While there have been around 20 to 30 death sentences in a year in the past, the number decreased into less than 10 since 2002. This decreasing number explains the long term moratorium on death penalty. Currently, there are 59 death row inmates in Korea.

⟨Table 1⟩ Number of criminals confirmed death penalty and executions

Year	Confirmed to Death Penalty	Executions	Year	Confirmed to Death Penalty	Executions
1980	32	9	1995	19	19
1981	33	0	1996	23	0
1982	35	23	1997	10	23
1983	19	9	1998	14	0
1984	18	0	1999	20	0
1985	25	11	2000	20	0
1986	8	13	2001	12	0
1987	18	5	2002	7	0
1988	15	0	2003	5	0
1989	17	7	2004	8	0
1990	36	14	2005	6	0
1991	35	9	2006	6	0
1992	26	9	2007	0	0
1993	21	0	2008	3	0
1994	35	15	2009	6	0

3. Death penalty abolition movement and its limitation

The history of movement against death penalty in Korea is not long. Among several organizations against the death penalty, there is "the Council for the Death Penalty Abolition" and "the Interfaith Union for the Abolition of Death Penalty." The former was organized in response to "the International Agreement to Abolish the Death Penalty by United Nations" and "the Declaration of the Year of Death Penalty Abolition by Amnesty," in 1989. It was also originated from a religious organization to rehabilitate the inmates in the Seoul Correction Center named "Seoul Correction Center Rehabilitation Committee." The latter group was launched in 2004 by religious organizations from Catholic, Protestant and Buddhism as a major force of the movement. Although Amnesty International Korea puts a substantial amount of efforts on this issue, the influence is insignificant. Therefore, it is fair to say that death penalty abolition movement in Korea is led by religious organizations.

The religious organizations are very powerful in Korea. Most Koreans declare their religions identity and, therefore, politicians cannot ignore the demand of religious organizations in fear of losing votes in election. Separation of church and the state, thus, cannot be an issue in death penalty abolition movement in Korea.

Yet, there is also a limitation in the movement led by religious organizations. Although religious organizations showed the power to stop the execution, the power did not reach to pass a bill to abolish the death penalty. It is because the lawmakers fear citizens but not the religious leaders.

Therefore, it is a remaining task for death penalty abolition movement in Korea to raise the public awareness on this issue and to organize the movement led by those awakened citizens.

4. Court's Decisions

There has been several constitutional review of death penalty law in Korea. Before the Constitutional Court of Korea was established, the Supreme Court of Korea reviewed cases on this issue. For instance, in a decision made in 1983, the Court said that "there is no argument that we should avoid death penalty which deprives a person's dignified life from the perspective of humanity and religion. Yet, we cannot ignore the value of victim's life and the public welfare and order."[3] In a decision made in 1990, the Court said that "we cannot find the death penalty law unconstitutional because the state has the public interest to maintain order and public welfare through criminal justice system."[4] In a decision made in 1991, the Court also found the death penalty law constitutional because "the law is to keep the public order and welfare based on people's moral sentiment and national circumstances."[5]

However, the Supreme Court's decisions were only about ten lines long and did not extensively discuss the constitutionality of death penalty law. The

---

3 The Supreme Court of Korea, March 8, 1983, 82 Do 3248
4 The Supreme Court of Korea, April 24, 1990, 90 Do 319
5 The Supreme Court of Korea, February 26, 1991, 90 Do 2906

situation gradually changed after the Constitutional Court appeared. For the first time in 1993, the Constitutional Court, in its opinion, quoted both the opinion of the ministry of justice for the constitutionality of death penalty and the opinion of the petitioner for unconstitutionality.[6] Further, in an opinion rendered in 1996, the Court extensively discussed this issue by stating that "death penalty can be justified as an inevitable "necessary evil" composed of instinctive horror and retribution. It is applied to extremely limited cases as illegal effects to crimes in its nature of negating human life and yet it still functions."[7] This ruling has its significance as it negatively evaluations the death penalty by naming it "necessary evil" although it found the law constitutional. Further, it was a 7 to 2 decision and, therefore, the minority opinion for unconstitutionality by two Justices stand.

The most recent case was decided on February 25, 2010. Although the death penalty was still found constitution by a 5 to 4 decision, the number of votes for unconstitutionality increased. Further, it should be noted that the Court said that "although it is the Constitutional Court's task to decide whether the death penalty law is unconstitutional, it is the Legislator's task to decide whether to abolish this law."

5. Problems with the Constitutional Court's Decisions

The grounds of constitutionally of death penalty found by the Court are as follows:

(1) Death penalty violates a person's legal interest more severely than lifetime sentence or lifetime without parole and therefore is appropriate for hideous crime with the most effective deference power.
(2) Possibility of misjudgment is the inherent limitation of judicial system and not the independent problem of death penalty. The problem should be solved by improvement of the system such as the appeal or the retrial system.
(3) Even though the judge and prison officers may feel guilty for execution, it is their duty as public officials to protect the public interest.

---

6 The Constitutional Court, November 25, 1993, 89 Hun-Ma 36, 5KCCR 2, 423

7 The Constitutional Court, November 28, 1996, 95 Hun-Ba 1, 8KCCR 2, 537

The Court's reasoning has the following falsities.

(1) Whether death penalty deters crimes

A newspaper claimed that the execution should be resumed in a report that "a number of murder cases have increased by 38% for the past 10 years without death penalty execution". According to the statistics report on crime, 789 murder cases in 1997 increased to 1,124 cases in 2007. However, is this increase due to no execution? If there have been continuing executions, would there be no increase of murder case? Does death penalty really deter crimes?

Even without considering foreign cases, the Korean case with no execution for 13 years explains that death penalty has little deterrent effect to crimes. During the execution on December 23, 1997, the Ministry of Justice promoted the justification of capital punishment and the media reported it widely. Given the message clearly delivered, people should have feared punishment and should have not committed murders. However, 789 murder cases in 1997 increased to 966 cases in 1998. This statistics proves no deterrent effect of capital punishment. For instance, 506 murder cases in 1977 rose to 789 in 1997 only to prove that the increase was made by 56% during the execution of death penalty. The death penalty may have a brutalization effects rather than deterrent effect. Table 2 shows number of executions and the number of murder cases.

(2) The issue of misjudgment

Constitutional Court acknowledges the possibility of misjudgment. Yet the Court argues that misjudgment may occur as people are not God and such mistakes may be solved by legal procedures such as the appeal or the retrial system. This argument justifies the situation where such a mistake may be done during a trial.

However, a life taken away by a crime and a life taken away by a misjudgment are both innocent deaths. As the act of murder by the criminal cannot be forgiven, there is no reason to acknowledge the act of murder by court with misjudgment. Such an argument is discriminatory against life and the arrogance of judgeship.

On January 23, 2007, the Seoul Central District Court rendered a not-guilty

<Table 2> Number of executions and homicide

Year	Executions	Murder	Year	Executions	Murder
1977	28	506	1994	15	705
1978	0	485	1995	19	646
1979	10	458	1996	0	690
1980	9	536	1997	23	789
1981	0	625	1998	0	966
1982	23	538	1999	0	984
1983	9	518	2000	0	964
1984	0	581	2001	0	1,064
1985	11	600	2002	0	983
1986	13	617	2003	0	1,011
1987	5	653	2004	0	1,082
1988	0	601	2005	0	1,091
1989	7	578	2006	0	1,064
1990	14	666	2007	0	1,124
1991	9	630	2008	0	1,120
1992	9	615	2009	0	1,390
1993	0	806			

verdict to 8 defendants in the retrial for People's Revolutionary Party Case and ordered to pay 63.7 billion won to surviving family members after finding the misconduct of the state as well as the Supreme Court. I wonder what the Justices of Constitutional Court would think about those 8 people who lost their lives from the misjudgment. Misjudgment is not a "possibility" but the "reality" we face.

(3) **Agony of executioners**

People understand the agony of a prison officer who executes the death penalty. A magazine recently interviewed the agony of a prison officer who said "prison officers put themselves under self-hypnosis with the belief that the execution is justifiable act and yet most of them suffer from nightmare. They either become alcoholics or vanish after resignation."[8]

A prison officer spoke at a correction conference that "officers like me do not have such power to speak out. Personally, however, I would appreciate it if death penalty is abolished."

The Prison Office Work Manual of 1963 prescribes that "the execution of death penalty should be done by a prison officer in uniform upon receipt of order from senior officials." This is the only ground that prison officers should execute the death penalty. The Constitutional Court instructs that prison officers should take this agony because they are public officers to protect the public interest while ignoring their agony during the execution done with the order of the Minister of Justice not a statute. Can we call it 'public interest' to kill people regardless of what kind of justice it is?

"Tolerance may be excessive but justice becomes cruelty if it is excessive." The philosopher and a poet, Su Dongpo from Northern Sung Dynasty said.

6. Substitution of death penalty and act of abolishing death penalty

As the public opinion against penalty abolition grows, a bill to abolish death penalty was also submitted. Currently, a bill containing "lifetime imprisonment without parole" has been submitted to the National Assembly.

In 1999, the first bill to abolish death penalty was submitted to the National Assembly but it did not mention the substituting penalty to death penalty. It was the bill of 2001 when the substituting penalty was brought into attention. This bill suggests that the Court exclude the possibility of parole for 15 years if it opts to sentence lifetime instead of death penalty. Yet these two bills were not even discussed in the standing committee.

In 2004, a bill to replace death penalty with lifetime imprisonment was introduced. Representative, Yoo In-tae, who was once sentenced to death for democracy campaign himself, proposed the bill. At the time, the majority of the Legislative agreed (175/299), and the expectation was high. However, this bill

---

8 "The Korea Central Sunday," Vol. 24 September 19, 2010

was not even adopted as an agenda at the General Assembly. The most recent bill submitted to the National Assembly contains provisions that absolutely prohibit parole or commutation.

Some argue that lifetime imprisonment is more cruel than death penalty by violating human rights. I agree that the lifetime imprisonment without parole is a punishment without hope and violates human rights. Nevertheless, I have strongly proposed lifetime imprisonment and worked for it to be included in a bill to abolish death penalty because it was the only persuasive alternative for the people in this country under the circumstances where the majority of people still oppose the abolition of death penalty.

It is reasonable to discuss the problem of lifetime imprisonment in a country where the lifetime imprisonment substituted the death penalty. Yet it is luxury to insist upon the complete abolition of death penalty when death row inmates' lives are at stake under the current death penalty system. The problem of lifetime imprisonment may well be discussed after death penalty is abolished. The problem of lifetime imprisonment needs to be approached from the view of "hopeful punishment that saves precious lives" rather than "harsh punishment that imprisons people in the prison forever without hope." Most of the Korean activists against death penalty are in agreement to propose the lifetime imprisonment.

Conclusion

I have an interesting story. My son told me that he had an interesting debate on "internet user identification with real name" and "death penalty" at his junior high school class. During the debate on death penalty, my son said, that the teacher showed students the result of a survey from junior high school students on death penalty issue. The survey showed that 70 percent of respondents favored the abolition of death penalty while 30% favored the existence of the death penalty. This result is the exact opposite to that of adults.

Is a human born to be pro-death penalty or anti-death penalty? I used to believe that "people are born to be pro-death penalty and yet learn anti-death penalty as they grow." After I heard the story about survey from my son, however, I thought that perhaps people are born to know nothing about death penalty but learn it as they grow up.

If death penalty does not exist, people would not think of it even if brutal crimes are committed because people would not be able to imagine it without an institution. Let us throw away the familiar system of death penalty and imagine the world without it. It is not difficult. It has been achieved by the majority of countries in the world.

[3] Taiwan's Anti-Death Penalty Movement in The Local-Global Dynamics

Chia-Wen Lee
National Cheng-Kung University, Taiwan

I. Introduction

In March 2011, there was a rare diplomatic crisis between Taiwan and European Union (EU) over the issue of death penalty. The crisis was ignited by Taiwan's sudden executions of five death row inmates on March 4, 2011. Not only local and international human rights activists protested; but some EU countries also reacted blisteringly. German Federal Foreign Office unprecedentally summoned the Taiwanese Representative in Berlin to the German Federal Foreign Office.[1] After the meeting, Markus Löning, German Federal Government Commissioner for Human Rights Policy and Humanitarian Aid, issued a statement, strongly condemning executions in Taiwan.[2] On the same day, EU High Representative for Foreign Affairs and Security Policy Catherine Ashton openly expressed a deep regret at the executions and urged Taiwan "not to undertake further executions."[3] Few days later, the president of European Parliament Jerzy Buzek openly criticized Taiwan's executions. He called on Taiwan's authorities to reinstate a moratorium on the death penalty.[4] Some EU

---

1   Due to the pressure from the Chinese government, the German government officials generally do not meet Taiwanese delegates publicly. Therefore, the open official statement from the German government on Mar. 04, 2011 was an ironic diplomatic "achievement" for the Taiwanese government. See NEW TALK, *The Executions in Taiwan has given Taiwan an unexpected diplomatic breakthrough* (Mar. 05, 2011) 〈http://newtalk.tw/news_read.php?oid=12499〉 (visit: July 03, 2011).

2   *Human Rights Commissioner Löning on the latest wave of executions in Taiwan* (Mar. 04, 2011), 〈http://www.auswaertiges-amt.de/EN/Infoservice/Presse/Meldungen/2011/110304-MRHH_Taiwan.html〉 (visit: July 03, 2011). Also see German Institute Taipei, 〈http://www.taipei.diplo.de/Vertretung/taipei/en/Execution3.html〉 (visit: July 03, 2011); CHINA TIMES, Mar. 06, 2011.

3   *Statement by the High Representative, Catherine Ashton, on the executions in Taiwan*, 〈http://www.consilium.europa.eu/uedocs/cms_data/docs/pressdata/EN/foraff/119612.pdf〉 (visit: July 03, 2011); CHINA TIMES, Mar. 06, 2011.

4   *Buzek opens March plenary session in Strasbourg: executions in Taiwan, victims,*

parliamentarians allegedly considered to scrap Taiwan's EU visa-waiver, because Taiwan's sudden executions on March 4, 2011 made them wonder whether Taiwan has taken human rights seriously.[5]

Facing harsh criticisms from EU and the possible revocation of Taiwan's newly-granted visa-waiver, the Taiwanese authorities, including President Ma Ying-jeou and the leader of the parliament, were mobilized to solve the crisis. Even though this diplomatic crisis seemed to be eased within a week - EU later issued no further statement or took no further action against Taiwan, the fact that Taiwan did not execute while EU was reviewing Taiwan's visa-waiver application, and the efforts that the Taiwan government has made to get an understanding from EU in March 2011 suggest EU's policy on the death penalty matters to Taiwan. Despite of Taiwanese government's preference of defining the death penalty as a purely domestic criminal policy issue, the diplomatic crisis in March 2011 shows that this preference is unrealistic in the global era.

The diplomatic crisis ignited by executions in March 2011 has thus raised an important issue about the role of the international anti-death penalty movement on the death penalty policies and practices in Taiwan. Since the Amnesty International (AI) launched a campaign against the death penalty in 1977,[6] and EU became an active actor in this campaign in 1990s,[7] the worldwide death penalty policies have changed considerably.[8] Thanks to the efforts of abolition-

---

⟨http://www.europarl.europa.eu/president/view/en/press/press_release/2011/2011-March/press_release-2011-March-6.html⟩ (visit: July 03, 2011); Radio Taiwan International, European Parliament condemned the executions in Taiwan. (Mar. 08, 2011).

5   See CHINA TIMES, Mar. 06, 2011.
6   Herbert Haines, AGAINST CAPITAL PUNISHMENT: THE ANTI-DEATH PENALTY MOVEMENT IN AMERICA, 1972-1994 63 (1996).
7   Evi Girling, *European Identity and the Mission Against the Death Penalty in the United States*, in THE CULTURAL LIVES OF CAPITAL PUNISHMENT: COMPARATIVE PERSPECTIVES 115 (Christian Boulanger & Austin Sarat (eds.), 2005).
8   In 1977 when AI began its campaign against the death penalty, only 17 countries abolished this penal institution. More than thirty years later, 139 countries have abolished the death penalty in law or in practice. 58 countries are now classified as retentionist and far fewer use it. Amnesty International, DEATH SENTENCES AND EXECUTIONS 2010 (2011).

ists, the world has been moving toward abolition in a striking pace.[9] In the same period of time, death penalty policies and practices in Taiwan have also changed dramatically. The numbers of capital crimes, death sentences and executions have all dropped.[10] Since 2000, the abolition of the death penalty has become a state policy for Taiwan. The concurring developments toward abolition locally and globally make people wonder the correlation between the international and the local abolitionist movement. It also begs a question as to the extent the international anti-death penalty movement has affected the contour and content of the institution of the death penalty in Taiwan. An equally intriguing issue is: since Taiwan has been isolated from the international society since the 1970s, how could such an international influence be possible. This paper is intended to explore these issues by tracing the development of the anti-death movement in Taiwan.

II. The Anti-Death Penalty Movement in Taiwan

Even though the history of the death penalty in Taiwan strongly suggests that democratization since 1980s in Taiwan was a crucial force underlying the changes of the death penalty in the past two decades,[11] the proposal to abolish the death penalty came earlier than that. Evidence shows that when Taiwanese people lived in the shadow of state killing, some law journals curiously published articles advocating the abolition of the death penalty.[12]

---

9 *See* David Johnson & Franklin E. Zimring, THE NEXT FRONTIER: NATIONAL DEVELOPMENT, POLITICAL CHANGE, AND THE DEATH PENALTY IN ASIA 6-7 (2009). By 2001, Amnesty International was able to claim the majority of nations no longer executed. The growing number of abolitionist nations and the decline of capital sentences and executions have given AI the confident to claim that there is a clear global trend toward abolition. *See* Amnesty International, *id*.

10 *See* Fort Fu-Te Liao, *From seventy-eight to zero: Why executions declined after Taiwan's democratization*, PUNISHMENT & SOCIETY, 10: 153-170 (2008).

11 Professors Fu-Te Liao, Johnson and Zimring have made the similar attribution. *See* Liao, *supra* note 10; Johnson & Zimring, *supra* note 9.

12 Excluding those that did not directly discuss the issue of the death penalty, in the Index to Taiwan Periodical Literature System, we could find three papers discussing the death penalty published in the 1950s, twenty-four in the 1960s, and thirty in the 1970s. There are twenty-eight death penalty papers published in the 1980s. Thirteen of them were published before the lift of Martial law in 1987.

1. Academic Transplant in the Shadow of State Killing

The first three articles on the issue of the death penalty published in late 1950 s were translated work. One described the controversies over the abolition of the death penalty in UK.[13] The other two, written by Japanese scholars, explicitly advocated abolitionism.[14] They not only opened a window to the outside world for local researchers, knowing that the legitimacy of the death penalty was not unchallengeable, and whether to retain this very old punishment had become a controversial issue. They also unusually aroused similar discussion in Taiwan.[15] Since the 1960s, Taiwanese scholars began to explore and debate the issue of the death penalty. What happened in the countries were important references through out this period of time.[16] The discussion between the 1960s and the 1970s touched various issues that are commonly debated today.[17] But whether the death penalty could deter crimes effectively and whether the death penalty

---

13 See "*The Issue of the Abolition of the Death Penalty in UK*," translated from the New York Times Magazine by Jin-min Liu, THE LAW MONTHLY, Vol. 7, Issue 8, p. 15-16 (Aug. 1956) ;

14 See Yamaguchi, *The Death Penalty- An Unnecessary Punishment*, CHAS YANG LAW REVIEW, Vol. 24, Issue 11/12, P. 20-23 (Dec. 1958) ; Sugiura, *The Death Penalty must be abolished*. CRIMINAL LAW JOURNAL, Vol. 2, Issue 12, P. 67-72 (Dec. 1958).

15 See e.g. Zhan-shun Wu, *On the Deterrent Effect of the Death Penalty*, CRIMINAL LAW JOURNAL, Vol. 4, Issue 3, P. 30-39 (Aug. 1960) ; Dow-yuan Ding, *On the Issue of the Abolition of the Death Penalty, and the Method of Execution*. THE MILITARY LAW JOURNAL, Vol. 8, Issue 11, P. 13-17 (Nov. 1962).

16 See e.g. Zhan-shun Wu, *The Abolitionist Movement in Japan and its Trend*. CRIMINAL LAW JOURNAL, Vol. 5, Issue 2, P. 16-28 (Apr. 1961) ; Mon-jay Sun, *A Preliminary Proposal to Abolish the Death Penalty*, CRIMINAL LAW JOURNAL, Vol. 8 Issue 6, p. 39-52 (Dec. 1964) ; Zhan-shun Wu, *UK Has Abolished the Death Penalty*, CRIMINAL LAW JOURNAL, Vol. 9, Issue 6, pp. 13-22 (Dec. 1965). *Controversies over the Abolition of the Death Penalty*, INTERNATIONAL AFFAIRS WEEKLY, Issue 831, p. 16-17 (Feb. 1972) ; *Which Countries Have Abolished the Death Penalty*, NTERNATIONAL AFFAIRS WEEKLY, Issue 855, p. 23 (July, 1972) ; De-Kuan Liu, *The Capital Cases that Were Held Unconstitutional by the US Supreme Court*, CHINA LAW JOURNAL, Vol. 18 Issue 3, p. 15-20 (July, 1973).

17 The arguments included the development of civilization, the changed penal philosophy (from retribution to rehabilitation), the possibility of miscarriage of justice, dubious deterrent effect of the death penalty, respect for life, and the death penalty as a cruel form of punishment.

represented an outmoded penal philosophy (retribution) that should be discarded, were in the center of the debates. Even though these debates were no less serious than those counterparts today, they were confined within the academia. No evidence shows that these academic debates had affected public opinions, policies or practices.

2. The Anti-Death Penalty Movement and the Democracy Movement

In the early 1980s, the form of "involvement" of the international society with the death penalty in Taiwan had changed. It started with the international intervention in how the KMT government handled the political dissents arrested in the Kaohsiung Incident in 1979.[18] The political dissents were indicted with provocation and faced secret military trials and the death penalty. Thanks to the efforts of local opposition human rights activists and oversea Taiwanese, the case drew attention from Amnesty International (AI), the US Congress, and international media. Under increased local and international pressures, the KMT government was forced to let the political dissents tried and convicted at a public trial. None of them were sentenced to death.[19]

In fact, before the Kaohsiung Incident, AI had already suspected that the KMT government abused the death penalty to suppress the political dissents. After this Incident, it began to observe Taiwan's death penalty and to include it in its annual report. In 1981, AI issued a memorandum on Taiwan's death penalty, and asked the KMT government to stop executions and to abolish this cruel punishment. AI also mobilized its members to send letters Taiwan's

---

18 The Kaohsiung Incident was a political event, in which almost all leading political dissents in Taiwan were arrested in a rally to celebrate International Human Rights Day, and charged with provocation, aiming to undermining social order and national security, and subverting the government. See Shu-Fen Lin, "*Democratization*" *in Taiwan and Its Discontents: Transnational Activism and Human Right Movement as a Critique*', in Anders Uhlin and Nicola Piper eds, CONTEXTUALIZING TRANSNATIONAL ACTIVISM – PROBLEMS OF POWER AND DEMOCRACY 174-175 (2003).

19 Even though the KMT protested against unfavorable media coverage of the Incident, and insisted that ROC was a sovereign state whose internal affairs shall not be interfered in, it had no choice but to make tactical concession. After all, Taiwan had already suffered from a series of devastating diplomatic setbacks in the 1970s, including US's withdrawal of diplomatic recognition. *See* id, at 174-175.

government to revise capital statutes, to commute death sentences or to abolish the death penalty.[20] More evidence is needed to evaluate the impacts of AI's actions on Taiwan's death penalty practices, particularly on the executions of political dissents, in Taiwan in the 1980s. But AI's actions have essentially included Taiwan into its global campaign against the death penalty, despite of the fact that Taiwan was isolated from the international society since the 1970s.

Behind AI's actions, there was a changed notion about the issue of the death penalty. Before the 1980s, whether to abolish the death penalty was regarded as a question of criminal justice policy. Abolitionists questioned its effectiveness to deter crimes, and asked to abolish this ineffective form of punishment for humanitarian and policy reasons. In the 1980s, AI and some European countries collectively transformed the issue into a question of human rights and limits on government. The implication of this transformation was that the death penalty was no longer a criminal policy that each country could make its own decision. It was rather a human rights violation that no state shall use it as a legitimate criminal sanction.[21] Based on this transformed notion of the death penalty, AI launched an international campaign against this penal institution and tried to change death penalty policies and practices in Taiwan.

The inclusion of Taiwan into AI's global campaign against the death penalty was unilateral in the beginning. But soon, the campaign was joined by local human rights activists, particularly by the Taiwan Association for Human Rights (TAHR). TAHR was established in 1984 under the support of political dissents and human rights activists. Due to Taiwan's special political background, TAHR focused on freeing political prisoners and advocating political rights.[22] Its first involvement with the death penalty was its participation in the

---

20 AI-Taiwan, *Let the Death Penalty Disappear from the Earth — AI aggressively defends the Right to Life and Terminate the Humiliation of the Human Dignity*, JUDICIAL REFORM, Issue 77, p. 26-28 (May, 2010).

21 Johnson & Zimring, *supra* note 9, at 4-5.

22 Because the authoritative rule by the KMT government had comprehensively suppressed the development of democracy in Taiwan and the civil rights of Taiwanese people, the fights for human rights and the fights for democracy since the 1970s naturally blended. TAHR was established under the support of political dissents and human rights activists. It was not until the task of freeing political prisoners was accomplished that the human rights movement differentiated it

rescuing action of an aboriginal death row inmate Tang In-shen in 1987.[23] Out of the fear that the KMT government would still abuse the death penalty to kill political dissents,[24] and based on the transformed notion of the death penalty in the international abolitionist movement that the death penalty was a question of human rights and limits on government, TAHR decided to add this issue into its mission to fight for human rights and democracy in Taiwan.[25] While it was not clear whether and to what extent TAHR had collaborated with international human rights activists in the 1980s,[26] the position TAHR had taken and the question frames it had adopted conceptually connected the local action to the

   pursuit of human rights from the democracy movement, and turned to work on other human rights issues. *See* Feng-zhen Lin & Jun-yan Lin, *Retrospect and Prospect of Taiwan's Human Rights Organizations — The Experiences of Taiwan Association for Human Rights*. NATIONAL POLICY QUARTERLY, Vol 1, Issue 2, P. 145 (2002).
23 The case of Tang In-shen involved with a triple-murder. Tang killed his employer and the employer's wife and one child. Tang was thus described as a cold-blooded killer. But later, one investigative report revealed that crimes were actually triggered by the discrimination and the exploitation Tang had suffered. Tang's tragedy had aroused widespread sympathy and triggered a collective action to rescue him. Even though the rescue action failed, it gave the Taiwanese society the first opportunity to think about the death penalty collectively.
24 Yao-shuan Chang, THE ANTI-DEATH PENALTY MOVEMENT IN TAIWAN, Master Thesis, Department of Public Administration, Cheng-chi University 42 (2008).
25 In a forum on the issues aroused by Tang's case, the representative from TAHR explicitly appealed to the right to life and opposed the death penalty. *See* Taiwan Association for Human Rights (eds.), "*The Death Penalty and Human Rights*" *Forum*, in THE HUMAN RIGHTS ISSUES IN TAIWAN, p. 113-126 (1987). Besides, TAHR began advocating abolitionism in its newsletter. *See e.g.* Bu-ping Lee, *On the Abolition of the Death Penalty*, HUMAN RIGHTS IN TAIWAN, Issue 2, p. 3-4, (Jan. 1988).
26 TAHR did have contact with the international society in the 1980s. For example, in March 1985, Ms. Whitehead from Canada visited TAHR and shared her experience as a human rights activist. In April 1985, the secretary of TAHR Lin and another member participated in the World Conference on Human Rights in Dhaka. Lin delivered a speech in the conference. In 1989, TAHR worked with the international society to welcome exiles back to Taiwan (Cited from Lin & Lin, *supra* note 22, at 158-159) It was still not clear whether TAHR actually collaborated with the international human rights organizations on the issue of the death penalty in 1980s.

global campaign.

It was not long that the local action and the global campaign formally connected. Between 1989 and 1990, the capital case of Ma Shiao-bing aroused the attention of the Taiwanese society to the issue of the death penalty.[27] The case triggered discussion about the cause of crime[28] and the problem of the mandatory sentences. In the eyes of TAHR, Ma's case perfectly showed that the KMT government still abused the death penalty to control the society. Therefore, TAHR not only initiated a rescue action with other local groups, but it also launched a campaign to abolish the death penalty completely. The rescue actions were multidimensional. Some had a hunger strike in front of the Presidential Office. A few lawyers helped to file a petition to the Council of Grand Justices (CGJ, the Constitutional Court in Taiwan) to review the constitutionality of the mandatory sentences prescribed in the Bandit Law. AI issued an emergent call for an immediate action to its worldwide members to rescue Ma and his accomplices from executions.[29] Nevertheless, despite of the intensive local and international pressure, Ma and his accomplices were executed after CGI ruled against them.[30]

---

27 Ma's case involved with kidnapping for ransom. Even though Ma and his accomplice released the victim after they collected the ransom, the court still sentenced them to death under the Bandit Law. According to the Bandit Law, the offense of kidnapping carried the mandatory death sentence, regardless the kidnapper did not harm the victim. Their convictions were swiftly confirmed by the Supreme Court in June 1990. The fact that Ma and his accomplice did not harm the victim but still received the death penalty triggered collective actions to spare their lives. But the rescue action failed quickly. See Rong-Long Tsai, *The Disillusion of Freedom*, in MR. GRAND JUSTICES : PLEASE EXPLAIN THIS CASE TO ME 41 –57 (2003).

28 Ma, who fled from China in 1986, used to be an "anti-communist hero" lauded by the KMT government. But he was quickly "abandoned" by the government, and forced to survive on his own. He ended up with kidnapping rich people for ransom. Some thus believed that Ma was unfortunately corrupted by the capitalist society in Taiwan, and criticized the KMT government for failing to look after these "anti-communist heroes." *See id.*

29 *See id.*

30 The CGJ is consistently conservative on the issue of the death penalty. In Ma's case, despite of the fact that many legal scholars seriously challenged the constitu-

After Ma was executed, TAHR turned to deal with other human rights violations. AI was comparatively more active on this issue. It mobilized its member to write letters to the KMT government to advocate abolitionism, which forced the KMT government for the first time to commission scholars to study the issue of the death penalty and to conduct a national opinion poll to see whether the abolition of the death penalty was acceptable in Taiwan.[31] In November 1990, the AI Group in Taipei organized a forum to discuss about the abolition of the death penalty. TAHR was invited.[32] In 1992, AI Group in Taipei voluntarily went to France to attend the International Conference against the Death Penalty.[33] The connection between the local anti-death penalty movement and the global campaign was stronger.

In 1993, the case of Liu Huan-rong once again aroused debates on the death penalty in Taiwan, particularly on issues of remorse, forgiveness, reformation and rehabilitation.[34] Liu used to be a cold-blooded killer. But his reformation in prison awaiting trial had impressed quite a few people. A collective rescue action emerged. Based on Liu's remorse and reformation, rescuers not only appealed to compassion and forgiveness, but also worked on a new penal philosophy about reformation and rehabilitation. Even though rescuers did not

---

tionality of the mandatory death penalty, and three death row inmates' lives were at stake, the CGJ quickly made the decision in J. Y. Interpretation No. 263 on July 18, 1990, and upheld the constitutionality of the mandatory death penalty in Bandit Law on the ground that the law did not constrain the judge from considering mitigating factors when sentencing.

31 See Chun-Jin Hsu, et al. , THE STUDY ON THE ABOLITION OF THE DEATH PENALTY I (1994). The result of the research was announced in 1994. This report suggested that the death penalty shall still be retained. But the scope of capital crimes shall be narrowed, and the criminal procedure shall be reformed.

32 See Shian-hwa Chang (eds.) LIVE OR DIE — THE MINUTES OF THE DEATH PENALTY FORUM HELD BY AMNESTY INTERNATIONAL IN TAIWAN. (May, 1991).

33 See CHINA TIMES, June 10, 1992.

34 Liu Huan-rong was a professional killer, who committed quite a few murders in the 1980s. He was convicted of several accounts of murder and sentenced to death. But before all his convictions were final, he showed sincere remorse and signs of reformation. He asked the authority to spare his life, so that he could pay his debts to the victims and to the society. Some legislators, writers, and NGO groups initiated a rescue action for him in March 1993, but failed in two weeks.

ask to abolish the death penalty, their action inevitably aroused relevant debates. For the first time and the only time so far in the history of Taiwan, twenty-seven legislators formally proposed the government to abolish the death penalty.[35] Curiously, AI and TAHR did not participate in this rescue action.[36] However, after Liu was executed, AI, TAHR and other reform groups immediately held a public forum on the abolition of the death penalty.[37] The decisions by AI and TAHR suggest that abolitionism they favored was not founded on prisoner's remorse and reformation.

By the end of the 1990s, there was no large-scale public discussion on the issue of the death penalty like those in Ma and Liu's cases. During this period of time, AI continued to be the most active organization to advocate abolitionism in Taiwan, while TAHR was distracted to other human rights issues. In July and August 1993, AI issued two public announcements, condemning Taiwan for mistreating death row inmates and allowing them to donate organs. It also asked Taiwan to stop executions, to give clemency to all death row inmates, and to abolish the death penalty unconditionally.[38] When AI Taiwan was established in May 1994, it took chance to force Minister of Justice to publicly answer questions about the death penalty policies.[39] In August 1994, AI and TAHR visited Judicial Yuan to advocate abolitionism in the judicial system.[40]

In 1994, another high-profile capital case – Hsih-Chi Trio case drew the society's attention. Three young men, the so-called Hsih-Chi Trio, were accused of committing double murders in 1990. The court convicted them and sentenced them to death, despite of the facts that their confessions were suspiciously obtained by coercion, and the evidence against them was slim. Their case soon

---

35　See CHINA TIMES, Apr. 03, 1993.
36　One big difference between Ma and Liu's cases was the composition of the rescue team. THAR, which used to play a leading role in Ma's case, and the DPP, which was an important political ally for the activists, were relatively quiet in Liu's case. The Women's Rescue Foundation, along with one religious foundation and one ex-offender support group, played a prominent role in Liu's case.
37　See CHINA TIMES, Apr. 03, 1993.
38　See UNITED DAILY NEWS, July 22, 1993 ; CHINA TIMES, Aug. 21, 1993.
39　See UNITED EVENING NEWS, May 15, 1994.
40　See UNITED EVENING NEWS, Aug. 20, 1994.

aroused the human right groups' attention. Local activists organized a campaign to stop their executions. In March 1995, AI issued an emergent call for an immediate action to rescue Hsih-Chi Trio from executions.[41] In March 1996, the Deputy Secretary of AI Germany visited Minister of Justice to discuss the death penalty and Hsih-Chi Trio case.[42] On the next day, AI headquarter in London issued an announcement to ask the KMT government to stop executing Hsih-Chi Trio and to reinvestigate the case.[43] Under the increased local and international pressures, the executions of Hsih-Chi Trio were indefinitely postponed.

In retrospect, many activists believed that Hsih-Chi Trio case was the most important case in the history of the anti-death penalty movement in Taiwan. Participants in the rescue actions not only witnessed the problems of the criminal justice system in Taiwan. But they also felt the pressure of imminent executions. Such an experience had made many of them see the need to abolish of the death penalty (or strengthen their determination).[44] But except for AI, rescuers had never openly connected the abolition of the death penalty to this case. They feared that such a connection would be distracting. Nevertheless, the judicial reform directly inspired by Hsih-Chi Trio case still helped to lower the numbers of the death sentences. Mostly of all, this case had contributed to an aura that the judicial system was so corrupt that a comprehensive reform was needed. It was also in this aura that Minister of Justice (MOJ) responded to

---

[41] The Hsih-Chi Trio Rescue Team, LET THEM GO HOME ALIVE, Humanistic Education Foundation (1997). According to AI's organizational rules, AI members are prohibited from working directly on behalf of individual victims of human rights abuses within there own countries. Even though lobbying their own governments to abolish the death penalty was not banned, but participating in a rescue action for specific individuals still was. Herbert Haines, AGAINST CAPITAL PUNISHMENT : THE ANTI-DEATH PENALTY MOVEMENT IN AMERICA, 1972-1994 68 (1996). In order to be exempted from this "own country" rule, AI Taiwan communicated with AI headquarter in London, emphasizing that the Hsih-Chi Trio case was not a political case, and participating in the rescue action would not jeopardize AI's reputation. AI headquarter in London accepted this explanation. Thus, AI Taiwan joined in the collective action with TAHR and other groups. Chang, *supra* note 24, at 47.

[42] *See* UNITED EVENING NEWS, Mar. 08, 1996.

[43] The Hsih-Chi Trio Rescue Team, *supra* note 71, at 98-99.

[44] *See* Chang, *supra* note 24, at 43-51.

criticisms aroused by the case of Cho Shun-Shan in 1998 so quickly – Cho was executed before his lawyer received his judgment.[45] Since the problem in Cho's case was procedural, MOJ had no choice but to enact a rule to regulate the execution process.

One thing in the late 1990s that has also substantially influenced Taiwan's anti-death penalty movement in the next decade was the efforts by social movement organizations to "internationalize" themselves.[46] As noted earlier, TAHR had already collaborated with AI in various cases. Since the late 1990s, it had aggressively "internationalized" its activities and tasks. Under Peter Huang's leadership,[47] TAHR actively attended international human rights conferences,

---

45 Cho Shun-Shan was convicted of violating the Bandit Act. His conviction was final on Oct. 13, 1998. His lawyer received the Supreme Court judgment one day after Cho was executed. Cho was thus deprived of the right to file a special appeal to stop his execution. This unfortunate event has aroused vehement criticisms from lawyers and human rights activists. See *The Joint Statement by Taipei Bar Association, Taiwan Human Rights Association and Judicial Reform Foundation* (*Dec. 08, 1998*) ⟨http://www.jrf.org.tw/reform/file_4_1a.htm⟩ (Visit, July 11, 2011).

46 With the development of globalization, more and more local social movement organizations seek to participate in the transnational advocacy network to increase their leverage on the domestic policies. For example, feminist groups in Taiwan successfully use the transnational advocacy network to promote their agendas, such as gender mainstreaming. See Wan-Ying Yang, *From Committee for Promotion of Women's Rights to Committee for Gender Equality--A State Feminism Study from Comparative Perspective*, POLITICAL SCIENCE REVIEW, No. 21, p. 117-147 (Sept. 2004).

47 TAHR's former chairman (1998-1999) Peter Huang was an important pusher of this trend within TAHR. He believed that the local human rights advocacy must follow the development of the international human rights. It also must collaborate with international human rights organizations, and participate in transnational advocacy network to increase its leverage on the domestic policies. Huang pointed out that because Taiwan had been ruled by the authoritative regime and isolated from the international society for a long time, most Taiwanese people knew and cared very little about the development of the international human rights. This lack of knowledge and concern had caused that a lot of human rights abuses had been over-tolerated. He believed that this twisted situation must be changed by

and sought to join in transnational advocacy networks, such as FIDH, Human Rights Watch and Forum Asia. It also proposed to bring international standards for human rights into domestic law.[48] In 1999, it followed the Paris Principles and worked with 21 local human rights groups to promote the establishment of a national human rights institution.[49]

TAHR's pursuit of "internationalization" has two impacts on the subsequent abolitionist movement. First, it has brought in more international allies to Taiwan, which has increased local activists' leverage on the domestic policies and practices. The second impact was more direct on the state policies and practices. TAHR's proposals, including the abolition of the death penalty, were accepted by the DPP government in 2000 as parts of its "human rights state" policies. The anti-death penalty movement in Taiwan thus moved to a new stage since then.

3. Weak State and State Abolitionism

"State abolitionism" is a term borrowed from state feminism, meaning that abolitionism was created or approved by the government of a nation. The government either sets up an official commission or to put activists in important positions to implement top down strategies to achieve abolition.[50] The discussion of state abolitionism is particularly meaningful in a country like Taiwan where most people and politicians oppose to abolish the death penalty. The government could not abolish the death penalty as it wished, but has to implement strategies to achieve the goal.

In Taiwan, state abolitionism was pre-announced by president-elect Chen Shui-bian when he responded to the pope's call for abolition.[51] It was strength-

---

domesticalizing the international bill of human rights. TAHR should help to push the change. Peter Huang, *Selling Everything in this Grocery Store*, in Eternal Resistance & Forever Dissents 34-35, TAHR (Fall, 2009).
48 Lin & Lin, *supra* note 22, at 152-153.
49 *Id*, at 153-154.
50 *See* Yang, *supra* note 46.
51 *See* China Times, Apr. 29, 2000. In fact, Chen did not promise to abolish the death penalty right away. When asked and urged by Catholic Cardinal Shan Kuo-his, he said he hoped to that the death penalty could be abolished in the future. But it was

ened in Chen's inaugural speech on May 20, 2000. In this speech, Chen set up human rights policies that would support abolitionism – Taiwan would seek to include the international bills of rights in its legal codes, and to establish an independent national human rights commission, and to invite International Commission of Jurists and AI for advice with regard to the implementation of human rights instruments.[52] Chen also emphasized his goal was to bring Taiwan back into the international human rights system. State abolitionism under the DPP government was formally confirmed in May 2001 that Minister of Justice Chen Ding-nan announced that MOJ planned to phase out the death penalty within three years.[53] In the years that followed, MOJ sought to narrow the ambit of capital crimes and quietly lowered the numbers of executions. On different occasions, President Chen openly endorsed the gradual abolition of the death penalty.[54] The Basic Human Rights Law drafted by the advisory committee on human rights affairs asked the government to abolish the death penalty completely.[55] Taiwan seemed to move gradually to the final abolition.

For the anti-death penalty activists, however, the pace of reform was not fast enough. The relationship between activists and the DPP government became

---

the congress power to abolish this penal institution. As a president, he could not promise to stop executions or to give administrative clemency to death row inmates. Before the law is changed, he would still follow the law. He also pointed out that because most people worried about their safety, supplementary measures had to be taken before abolishing the death penalty. Even though his statement was conservative compared to most anti-death penalty activists, it was the first time the political leader in Taiwan openly supported abolitionism. It signified the rise of state abolitionism in Taiwan.

52 Lin, *supra* note 18, at 178. In the first two years, the DPP government did work hard to achieve its goal to build a human rights state. It asked the congress to ratify the International Convention for Civil and Political Rights (ICCPR) and the International Covenant on Economic Social and Cultural Rights (ICESCR). It set up an advisory committee on human rights affairs under the Presidential Office, an inter-ministerial Human Rights Protection and Promotion Committee presided by the premier and Human Rights Education Committee in the Ministry of Education. Id.

53 *See* CHINA TIMES, May 18, 2001.

54 *See* UNITED EVENING NEWS, Oct. 16, 2002.

55 *See* CHINA TIMES, July 25, 2003 ; LIBERTY TIMES, Nov. 19, 2003.

ambivalent. On the one hand, activists welcomed state abolitionism, and were willing to provide expertise to help the DPP government. After all, to achieve the goal of the abolition needed the support of the government. They wanted to keep the DPP government on the same side, and to maintain the access to the policymakers.[56] Besides, they knew the majority of the public supported the death penalty, and the parliament was unfortunately dominated by the conservative KMT. The DPP government just lost uglily on the issue of the nuclear plant.[57] The government that advocated state abolitionism was politically weak from the beginning.

But on the other hand, activists' unsatisfaction with the DPP government began to grow. As old-time comrades, Activists expected a lot from the DPP government.[58] As time went by, however, many activists began to wonder whether DPP's human rights state policy was rather a cheap slogan than a serious policy.[59] Even if they could understand the difficulties the DPP government had faced, its reluctance to announce an official moratorium on the death penalty before the final abolition still upset activists.[60] In 2003, the moratorium was urgently needed, because the conviction of Hsu Tzu-Chiang,[61] a criminal defendant in a problematic criminal case, was final, and Hsu faced an imminent threat of the execution. Activists felt anxious that Hsu might be rashly executed just like Lu Cheng in September 2000.[62] They felt the pressing need to abolish the

---

56 *See* Chang, *supra* note 26, at 55-88.
57 *See* Ming-sho Ho, *Taiwan's State and Social Movements under the DPP Government (2000-2004)*, JOURNAL OF EAST ASIAN STUDIES, 5 : 401-425 (2005).
58 *See id*, at *405*-408.
59 *See* CHINA TIMES, May 17, 2001. Interestingly, MOJ responded by announcing the policy to phase out the death penalty within three years.
60 *See* Peter Huang, *Why Taiwan Should Stop the Executions Completely?* JUDICIAL REFORM, No. 38, P. 6-7 (Apr. 1, 2002) ; Peter Huang, *Why Should We Stop the Executions? See* CHINA TIMES, Apr. 27, 2002 ; CHINA TIMES, Nov. 27, 2002.
61 The case of Hsu Tzu-Chiang (1995) involved with kidnapping for ransom and murder. Hsu was convicted and sentenced to death based on codefendants' confessions without any substantial collaborative evidence. Judicial Reform Foundation (JRF) and TAHR believe Hsu was wrongfully convicted, and helped him to file special appeal to the Supreme Court and to file petition to the CGJ.
62 The case of Lu Cheng involved with kidnapping for ransom and murder. Lu was convicted and sentenced to death based on problematic confessions and weak

death penalty just like how they felt in the case of Hsih-Chi Trio. In September 2003, activists from various human rights groups decided to take action this time. They jointly launched a coalition to call for the moratorium - the Taiwan Alliance to End the Death Penalty (TAEDP).[63] Since then, the efforts to abolish the death penalty were turning into an organized campaign.

In hindsight, TAEDP was established in time. The DPP government was weaker after the presidential election in 2004. Even though the DPP government could still ask the congress to revise certain outmoded capital statutes, and evidence showed that state abolitionism still had impact on the death penalty practices, particular on the numbers of death sentences and the execution rate, the controversy-ridden and the scandal-ridden government could hardly seek any radical reform or lead the country to openly debate the moral issue of the death penalty.[64] The abolitionist movement needed a different locomotive.

As the first coalition in Taiwan to advocate for the abolition of the death penalty, TAEDP tried to launch a comprehensive campaign from the start. It continued to urge the DPP government to stop state killings, and to offer legal assistance to defendants in capital cases. It began to lobby legislators and to

---

collaborative evidence. JRF and TAHR believe Lu was wrongfully convicted. One Control Yuan member agreed to investigate Lu's case. But before the investigation started, Lu was unexpectedly executed in September 2000.

63 TAHR, *A Public Petition Letter for establishing the Taiwan Alliance to End the Executions* 〈http://www.tahr.org.tw/site/death/030910_2.htm〉 (visit : July 28, 2011). This coalition was called the Taiwan Alliance to End the Executions first. One month later, it was changed to the Taiwan Alliance to Substitute the Death Penalty. In December 2005, it took the current name the Taiwan Alliance to End the Death Penalty.

64 Even though abolition did not happen by 2004 as promised, MOJ reaffirmed its position by releasing a five-page statement entitled "The Policy of the Ministry of Justice of Taiwan with Regard to Abolition of the Death Penalty." In this statement, the ministry called human rights "the foundation of the nation" and encouraged "extensive discussion and research" in order to "form a popular consensus for abolition," after which legislation would be enacted to eliminate the death penalty all together." Johnson & Zimring, *supra* note 9, at 214. This policy was unsurprisingly criticized by human rights activists for being too slow. But in hindsight, it was a position that the DPP government had to take.

communicate with the public. In order to raise public awareness about the problems of the death penalty, it periodically held seminars, lectures forums, film festivals, and photo exhibitions.[65] Besides the advocacy work at home, it endeavored to connect with the global abolitionist movement. Such a connection was substantively assisted by DPP's policy for human rights diplomacy.[66] By 2006, TAEDP successfully connected the International Federation for Human Rights (FIDH), and jointly initiated the Anti-Death Penalty Asia Network (ADPAN). It assisted FIDH in 2005 to produce a report on Taiwan's death penalty system.[67] The report was released in 2006. Even though the DPP government could not publicly adopt a clear timetable for the abolition of the death penalty as the report recommended, it was willing to change certain practices and policies.[68] The collaboration between local and international human rights activists have successfully increased their leverage on the domestic policies and practices.

What was more successful was the collaborative efforts by local and interna-

---

[65] TAEDP held its first death penalty film festival in December 2004, and the first photo exhibition featuring the work of a New York-based photographer Toshi Kazama on juvenile death row inmates in May 2005. TAEDP & Legal Aid Foundation (LAF), *The Taiwan Alliance to End the Death Penalty*, in STAYING OFF THE EXECUTIONER: TAIWAN UNOFFICIAL MORATORIUM 64-65 (2009).

[66] Human rights diplomacy was DPP's foreign policy between 2000 and 2008. It aimed to change Taiwan's international isolation by taking an indirect route. Instead of seeking formal diplomatic relationships with other countries, it promoted unofficial dialogues. The Minister of Foreign Affairs (MOFA) set up a special NGO committee and appointed 'ambassadors-at-large' with an emphasis on gaining entry for Taiwan to international non-governmental organizations and Taiwan's participation in intergovernmental organizations. *See* Lin, *supra* note 18, at 179.

[67] FIDH & TAEDP, THE DEATH PENALTY IN TAIWAN : TOWARDS ABOLITION? (2006).

[68] Among the criticisms this report has raised, the media targeted two issues : the abuse of shackles on the death row inmates, and the removal and the use the organs of executed prisoners. MOJ promised to reconsider these practices. Even though the practice of organ donation continues till now, the abuse of shackles on the death row inmates has greatly improved. In 2007, the DPP government pushed the congress to abolish the mandatory death penalty for all crime as the report recommended.

tional human rights to stop the execution of the death row inmate Chong De-shu in December 2006.[69] In order to stay Chong's execution, TAEDP filed an extraordinary appeal for Chong, and later a petition to the CGJ. It also worked with international human rights organizations. AI launched a global urgent action for Chong.[70] Meanwhile, the German Institute of Taipei contacted Taiwan's Minister of Foreign Affairs (MOFA) to convey the EU's opposition to the death penalty and urged Taiwan not to carry out any execution.[71] FIDH released a joint statement with TAEDP, calling on President Chen Shui-bian to commute Chong's sentence to life in prison. The statement argued, "*by abolishing the death penalty, Taiwan would stand to gain an increased recognition from the international community as a modern democratic state, and would set an example for the entire region.*"[72] Facing the vehement pressures from the international human rights community, President Chen made a secret promise to local activists that there would no execution before the end of his term,[73] despite of the fact that there were equally strong pressures from the Taiwanese society to ask for the execution according to the law at that time.[74] The rescue action in 2006 not

---

69 Chong De-shu was convicted of arson and murders. His conviction and death sentence were confirmed in 2003. On Nov. 29, 2006, the Minister of Justice signed an execution order to execute him. Even though his execution was stayed in 2006, he was executed in March 2011. See TAEDP & LAF, *supra* note 98.

70 TAEDP contacted AI to look for international pressures on the DPP government. AI joined in the action right away, because in October 2006, Minister of Justice just made a promise to AI that he would give serious thoughts to AI's suggestions to abolish the death penalty, and would not to carry out any execution in the next few months. Therefore, when AI learned about the execution order, it was frustrated and irritated. It started a rescue action, seeking to flood Taiwan's minister of justice, prosecutor-general and president with letters about Chong. See TAEDP & LAF, *supra* note 98.

71 Detlef Boldt, the then-director-general of the German Institute of Taipei (Berlin's de-facto embassy in Taiwan), learned about Chong's case in the news, Germany was about to assume EU's rotating presidency. Boldt contacted MOFA to convey the EU's opposition to the death penalty and urge Taiwan not to carry out any execution. See TAEDP & LAF, *supra* note 98, at 28-29; Chang, *supra* note 26, at 85-86.

72 See TAEDP & LAF, *supra* note 98, at 29. CHINA TIMES, Dec. 22, 2006.

73 See Chang, *supra* note 26, at 86-87.

74 Several retentionists openly spoke out to oppose to the staying of the execution.

only successfully stopped Chong's execution, but also brought about the de-facto moratorium until March 2010.

The promise by President Chen has given TAEDP space to adjust its structure[75] and to refine its strategies to campaign against the death penalty. It started to reach out to students, lawyers and judges. It turned to discuss specific issues, and endeavored to provide concrete strategies. In order to help the Taiwanese society to think outside the box, it invited experts from other countries to share the experiences and perspectives.[76] Some EU countries became zealous in the post-Chong campaign. They subsidized TAEDP's activities.[77] In addition to the collaboration with EU countries at home, TAEDP continuously sought connection with the global abolitionist movement. It joined in the World Coalition Against the Death Penalty (WCADP) in 2007, and met with a renowned abolitionist Robert Badinter. TAEDP's participation of ADPAN has increased its interaction with abolitionists in other Asian countries. By contributing to the regional and international abolitionist movements, TAEDP aimed to build international solidarity with abolitionists over the world, hoping such solidarity could increase its leverage on the Taiwanese government.

4. The Transformation of State Abolitionism

State abolitionism under the DPP government did not satisfy local abolitionists, but it surely reduced and even stopped the execution, and helped activists

---

See UNITED DAILY NEWS, Dec. 07, 2006 (from a DPP legislator) ; APPLE DAILY NEWS, Dec. 22, 2006 (from a journalist) ; CHINA TIMES, Dec. 22, 2006 (from a well-know actress) ; UNITED DAILY NEWS, Dec. 31, 2006 (from a senior journalist) ; UNITED DAILY NEWS, Dec. 31, 2006 (from a prosecutor).

75 In 2007, the TAEDP was restructured into four for departments: advocacy, education, research and death watch. See TAEDP, *About the TEADP*, in MY COUNTRY KILLS — CONSTITUTIONAL CHALLENGES TO THE DEATH PENALTY IN TAIWAN 75 (2011).

76 For example, in 2007, TAEDP invited a US-based victim abolitionist organization — Murder Victims' Families for Human Rights (MVFHR) to share the experiences and thoughts. See TAEDP & LAF, *supra* note 98, at 65.

77 In 2007, TAEDP held the second death penalty film festival with the help of La France à Taiwan and the Italian Economic, Trade and Cultural Promotion Office in Taipei. In that year, it also got financial help from the British Trade and Cultural Office in Taipei to hold a series of forums. *See id*, at 65.

to expand the scope and scale of their campaign against the death penalty. Whether the presidential election in March 2008 would change government's support for abolition and to lift the de-facto moratorium has become a matter of concern for activists.[78] Activists tried to raise this issue before the presidential election. The goal was to get promises from both candidates to abolish the death penalty.[79]

KMT's candidate, later president-elect, Ma Ying-jeou was not willing to make such a promise.[80] But after he was elected, he appointed Wang Ching-feng, a well-known human rights lawyer and a committed abolitionist, as his minister of justice. He also insisted on keeping Wang despite of criticisms from his supporters about Wang's position on the death penalty.[81] Ma's decision has kept activists hopeful. Very soon, Wang's plan to substitute the death penalty with thirty-year imprisonment[82] and her friendliness to abolitionists[83] convinced abolitionists that the regime change in 2008 would not affect the death penalty policy. Abolitionists believed that the new KMT government would not resume the executions under the international pressures, even if it was not enthusiastic

---

78 See id, at 88-89. Activists tried to raise this issue in the presidential election. The goal was to get promises from both candidates to abolish the death penalty.

79 See UNITED DAILY NEWS, Feb. 26, 2008.

80 In responded to the questions raised by abolitionists, DPP's candidate Frank C. T. Hsieh gave a positive answer. But KMT's candidate Ma Ying-jeou was only willing to promise that he would narrow the use of the death penalty. See *Presidential Candidate Frank C. T. Hsieh's view on the death penalty*. ⟨http://www.peopo.org/taedp/post/12939⟩ (visit Aug. 2, 2011) ; *Presidential Candidate Ma Ying-jeou's view on the death penalty*. (Feb. 27, 2008) ⟨http://www.peopo.org/taedp/post/12938⟩ (visit Aug. 2, 2011).

81 Wang's position on the death penalty quickly aroused serious objections. Many of the objectors claimed that if Ma abolished the death penalty, they would withdraw their support for him. See e.g. APPLE DAILY News, Apr. 23, 2008 (from celebrity Pai Ping-ping, whose daughter died at the hands of a brutal murderer). UNITED DAILY NEWS, Apr. 25, 2008 (from the association of mayors). After Ma openly promised that the death penalty would not be abolished until the society has a consensus on this issue, the controversy gradually ceased. CHINA TIMES, June 19, 2008.

82 See CHINA TIMES, June 04, 2008.

83 See Chang, *supra* note 26, at 72-73.

to abolish this penal institution.[84] The ratification and the implementation of two international covenants ‑ ICCPR and ICESCR under the leadership of President Ma into domestic laws in April 2009 have further strengthened activists' optimism about the future. Since the goal of implementing international covenants was "to connect Taiwan to the international human rights standard," abolitionists were optimistic that the moratorium would persist, and the final abolition could be expected.[85]

Under the support of Wang, state abolitionism persisted. Activists continued to expand their campaign against the death penalty, including reaching out to students, lawyers, death row inmates, and abolitionists in other Asian countries. The interaction with the global abolitionist movement intensified. To name some: in June 2008, delegates from WCADP, ADPAN and AI visited President Ma, and urged him to let Taiwan lead the abolitionist movement in Asia.[86] In 2008, TAHR, one of TAEDP's member organizations, was invited to conduct fact-finding mission on Japan's death penalty system.[87] Later in that year, TAEDP collaborated with the German Institute of Taipei to hold a conference on the death penalty. German experts were invited to Taiwan to share their experiences and perspectives. In 2009, TAEDP became a member of the steering committee of the WCADP. In February 2010, TAEDP was invited to the annual World Conference Against the Death Penalty in Geneva to share Taiwan experiences in the moratorium on the death penalty. By February 2010, Taiwan seemed to be a successful example to show how the local and the global abolitionist movements collaborated to press the government to achieve the moratorium on death penalty.

However, things started to fall apart since March 2010.[88] One KMT legislator

---

84 See Chang, *supra* note 26, at 88‑89.
85 For abolitionists, the ratification and the implementation of two international covenants into domestic laws was a milestone both for Taiwan and for abolitionists. Abolitionists were optimistic about the final abolition of the death penalty. See TAEDP & LAF, *supra* note 98, at 5.
86 See CHINA TIMES, June 19, 2008.
87 See Chia-chen Wu , *What you don't know about Japan — the Barbarian Punishment in a Civilized Nation.* TAHR PAS, p. 8-12 (Oct. 2008).
88 The controversy over the de-facto moratorium actually existed since 2007.

openly questioned Minister of Justice whether and when the forty-four death row inmates would be executed. Controversies over the death penalty quickly burst into an unprecedented political storm, when Wang openly and resolutely defended the moratorium and refused to order executions.[89] Unfortunately, she did not have the support from her superiors this time. Facing vehement public outrages and the pressures of the upcoming election, the Presidential Office issued a statement, claiming that "the death penalties handed down must be carried out and that any suspension of executions must follow the law."[90] Wang was forced to resign later that day.[91] Not only did the capacity and the determination to "follow the law" become the criterion for selecting the new minister of justice. "Following the law" also became the guideline for Ma administration on

> Some concerned journalists published articles on this issue once a while, criticizing the government. (*See. e.g.* CHINA TIMES, Oct. 10, 2007 ; UNITED DAILY NEWS, Jan. 02, 2008 ; UNITED DAILY NEWS, Mar. 29, 2009 ; UNITED DAILY NEWS, Jan. 30, 2010). This issue came back in February 2010 and went into the political realm. Legislator Wu Yu-sheng questioned Wang about the execution of 44 death row inmates in the congress meeting. This controversy could have quieted down in a few days just like before. But on March 8, 2010, Huang Shih-ming, President Ma Ying-jeou's pick for state public prosecutor-general, claimed that he supported the abolition of the death penalty, but 44 individuals on death row should still be executed. The disagreement between the minister of justice and the future prosecutor-general immediately became a big political issue.

89 Wang's reckless speech and action were important reasons why she ended up with an involuntary resignation. In the middle of the controversy over the death penalty, Wang published a statement titled *"Reason and Forgiveness — Suspension of Practicing the Death Penalty"* to defend abolitionism and the moratorium. In the next day, she openly claimed that she would rather 'go to hell' for the death row inmates than to order an execution. TAIPEI TIMES, Mar. 11, 2010. Her statement agitated the debates of the death penalty, and provoked anger at and even resentment to all abolitionists in Taiwan. UNITED DAILY NEWS, Feb. 24, 2010.

90 *See* Presidential Office, *The statement regarding whether Taiwan would abolish the death penalty*, Mar. 11, 2010.

91 Wang's resignation did not stop the controversies over the death penalty. People from both sides still debated relentlessly in the public and private domain. TAEDP, which defended for Wang and abolitionism, was cursed or even threatened by phone calls or emails, and criticized in the newspapers or in the talk show. Protestors gathered in front of the presidential office, opposing to the abolition of the death penalty. *See* LIBERTY TIMES, Mar. 28, 2010.

the issue of the death penalty. On April 30, 2010, Wang's successor Tseng Yung-fu signed the warrants to execute four death row inmates "in accordance with the law."[92]

The sudden resumption of executions shocked the Taiwanese society as well as the international society. Local human rights groups protested in front of MOJ's building, attacking the legality of the executions.[93] One law professor criticized the hypocrisy of Ma's government by following the law selectively.[94] The international human rights community also voiced their discontent with executions. The German government issued an open statement, condemning the executions in Taiwan.[95] So did the European Parliament's Subcommittee on Human Rights. It claimed that the executions could impact on Taiwan's relations with the EU, and obstruct Taiwan's aspirations to join the UN and other international organizations.[96] In fact, before the executions, MOFA of Taiwan had already been approached by EU representatives in Taiwan, and received a warning about the potential negative impact of executions on the approval of visa-free access to Schengen countries.[97] Besides, quite a few international human rights groups or advocacy networks, including AI, FIDH, ADPAN, WCADP and Together Against the Death Penalty, issued open statements to urged Taiwan to rethink resumption of death penalty.[98] Prof. Roger Hood and Prof. William Schabas, two renowned international scholars on the issue of the death penalty, sent e-mails to the editors of one Taiwan newspaper to express

---

92　See LIBERTY TIMES, May 01, 2010.

93　TAEDP staged a protest outside the MOJ's offices, accusing it of illegally executing four death row prisoners because the CGJ had agreed to hear their cases. See UNITED DAILY NEWS, May 01, 2010 ; MOJ denied such an accusation. See TAIPEI TIMES, May 04, 2010.

94　Chueh-An Yen, *Following the Law or Making up Cheap Excuses?* CHINA TIMES, May 02, 2010.

95　See CNA-NEWS, May 03, 2010.

96　See TAIPEI TIMES, May 06, 2010.

97　See TAIPEI TIMES, Mar. 26, 2010. Some members of the European Parliament even explicitly argued so to Taiwan's media. Executive Yuan Secretary-General Lin Join-sane said that he would pass the EU's concerns over Taiwan's policy on the death penalty to MOJ. See TAIPEI TIMES, Mar. 27, 2010 & Apr. 3, 2010.

98　See Hsiu-chuan Shih, *Analysis : Taiwan urged to rethink resumption of death penalty*, TAIPEI TIMES, Mar. 29, 2010.

their concerns. All of these indicated that the death penalty in Taiwan was closely scrutinized by the international human rights community.[99]

In 2010, the pressure from the international human rights community on the death penalty system in Taiwan was apparently much higher than that in 2006. But the outcomes were quite different. One notable difference is that the pressure from the Taiwanese society in 2010 was much more intense than that in 2006. So intense that grand justices of the constitutional court did not want to get involved. On May 28, 2010, CGJ denied the petitions filed by the TAEDP on behalf of remaining death row inmates.[100] Since CGJ once again upheld the constitutionality of the death penalty, Ma administration was "free" to formulate its own death penalty policy. In fact, earlier than the CGJ's decision, Ma's government has gradually developed a new form of state abolitionism —— "There were no timetables for carrying out executions[101] and no timetables for the abolition of the death penalty.[102] The final abolition of the death penalty is still the state policy. But because Taiwan is a democratic country, and the government must follow the law,[103] death row inmates still have to be executed, and the execution needs to wait until the completion of MOJ's case reviews. The government would not and should not abolish the death penalty until there is a consensus on the issue of the death penalty in Taiwan." It does not matter whether this new state abolitionism logical and ethical,[104] it helps Ma's government to answer the pressures from the Taiwanese society and from the international society. Most of all, it has given the government the discretion to decide when and who to kill. This is what abolitionists have to deal with after the political storm in the spring of 2010.

---

99   See id.
100 See Cases denied certiorari, No. 8409 & 9741 in CGJ Meeting No. 1358 (May 28, 2010).
101 See TAIPEI TIMES, May 29, 2010 ; TAIPEI TIMES, June 26, 2010.
102 See TAIPEI TIMES, Apr. 06, 2010.
103 See CAN-NEWS, May 03, 2010.
104 British scholar Roger Hood points out the problem of Ma's state abolitionism : "*once the death penalty is recognized as a breach of the right to life and a cruel and inhumane punishment, then it is unethical to execute persons who were given the death sentence in the past — to 'clear the desk,*' Quoted from Shih, *supra* note 133.

New state abolitionism supported by Ma's government has several implications. Under this new philosophy, TAEDP is no longer an important ally for the "abolitionist" state. It merely represents *one* opinion of the society. The government has to listen to *all* opinions. Government funding for TAEDP is thus decreasing, which overall has a negative impact on the local abolitionist movement. New state abolitionism also affects the prison administration. It is now more difficult for TAEDP to visit death row inmates in the prisons, and thus to file extraordinary appeals or retrials for death row inmates. In the time that the state starts to kill again, the rescue action for individual death row inmate becomes more important but more difficult. Besides, judging from the statistics, Ma's new state abolitionism seems to encourage more death sentences.[105] (see table1) By the end of August, 2011, there are fifty one people in the death row. The increasing number of death row inmates will increase the pressure on Minister of Justice. Executions might be resumed soon.

Table 1 : Death Sentences by Different Levels of Courts in Taiwan, 1999–May 2011

Year	District Courts	High Courts[106]	Supreme Court
1999	32	183	26
2000	36	110	22
2001	34	107	11
2002	28	74	7
2003	41	93	6
2004	27	94	7
2005	26	91	8
2006	5	71	11
2007	6	71	5
2008	8	43	3

---

105 In fact, since President Ma stepped up, the number of death sentences curiously increased. Supreme Court justices seem to know better as to which government will execute.

2009	7	35	13
2010	7	31	4
Jan-August, 2011	5	22	12^{107}

Sources: Judicial Yuan

The executions might be resumed in anytime. But TAEDP seem to lose its leverage to stop state killings. Judging from how the press covering the sudden executions in March 2011, the only criticism that the government concerned was those by EU and EU countries. Even though both TAEDP and AI made harsh criticisms,[108] and MOJ did respond to them,[109] it was clear that Ma's government

---

[106] The Supreme Court vacates judgments by high court quite often. More than 50 percent of lower court felony cases were vacated to high courts. The Supreme Court is even more particular about capital cases. As a result, high courts have to retry the vacated cases quite often. It explains why high courts have more death sentences than the other two levels of courts.

[107] By September 2011, there are fifty-one people on the death row.

[108] Local human rights activists staged a silent protest outside the ministry building, holding up two white banners, saying "*President Ma Ying-jeou's government signs international human rights covenants on one hand, while killing people on the other,*" and "*Ma visited Chiang Kuo-ching's family and then executed death row inmates who might have been wrongfully sentenced.*" TAIPEI TIMES, Mar 05, 2011. Amnesty International's Asia-Pacific Director Sam Zarifi also publicly denounced the Taiwanese government for it blatantly disregarded the fallibility and irreversibility of the death penalty. Zarifi criticized the hypocrisy of the Taiwanese authorities, for they "*have repeatedly stated their intention to abolish the death penalty, but they have - yet again - acted contrary to their own commitments and against the global trend towards abolition of the death penalty.*" Amnesty International, *Executions of Five Men In Taiwan Condemned* (March 4, 2011). ⟨http://www.amnesty.org/en/news-and-updates/executions-five-men-taiwan-condemned-2011-03-04⟩ (visit: July 03, 2011); UNITED DAILY NEWS, Mar. 06, 2011.

[109] MOJ immediately issued statements, denying accusations that Taiwan's executions violated the International Covenant on Civil Rights, and emphasizing that the covenant recognizes the idea whether to retain or to impose the death penalty is a matter within the state sovereignty. MOJ news release No. 00-024 (Mar. 05, 2011) ⟨http://www.moj.gov.tw/ct.asp?xItem=224108&ctNode=27518&mp=001⟩; MOJ news release No. 00-025, (Mar. 07, 2011) ⟨http://www.moj.gov.tw/ ct.

only cared about whether EU would revoke Taiwan's visa-waiver. After all, EU visa-waiver was celebrated by Ma's government as one major diplomatic achievement. However, EU's influence should not be overstated. In addition to the fact that EU has other political and economic interests, and thus does not want to push the Taiwanese government too hard, there are backlashes from the Taiwanese society against EU's interventions in Taiwan's sovereignty. Some people accused international human rights organizations and EU countries of inappropriately interfering in domestic affairs.[110] Some even argued that the global abolitionist movement was motivated by colonialism.[111] Ma's government has never explicitly used nationalism to fight against EU's criticisms like what the Chinese government has done. But the backlashes from the Taiwanese society had undoubtedly eased the pressure on the government, and undermined the influences EU could have on Taiwan.

In the past two years, the anti-death penalty movement in Taiwan has faced the biggest frustration. The government resumed the state killings. Nine people were executed within one year. TAEDP and other local and international human rights groups have not only lost their leverage on the government, but also their creditability on the issue of the death penalty in the Taiwanese society. TAEDP has become an easy target to blame for any failure of the criminal justice system.

While the prospect for the anti-death penalty movement in Taiwan looks depressing, some new developments have given the movement hope. First, after the political storm over the death penalty in the spring 2010, more people have joined in the campaign against the death penalty, even though the percentage of the population that supports the abolition of the death penalty becomes even

---

asp?xItem=224270&ctNode=27518&mp=001〉 (visit : July 04, 2011) ; CHINA TIMES, Mar. 06, 2011.

110 In fact, the majority of people in Taiwan still believe that whether to abolish the death penalty is a question of criminal justice policy, and each country could make its own decision. Even though most people are aware that this issue has been defined by the human rights groups as a human rights issue, many of them do not buy it. Or even if it is a human rights issue, victims' human rights are more important.

111 See CHINA TIMES, Mar. 09, 2011.

lower. Feeling that the debates in 2010 were too chaotic, some supporters have organized forums or conferences to encourage rational discussions over relevant issues.[112] More papers from different disciplines were published in the past year to deal with the issue of the death penalty.[113] Besides, one book specifically on the issue of the death penalty—*The Difficulties of Killing* — was published in October 2010. It won book prizes and became a hit in the book market. The author, Chang Chuan-fen, has delivered almost a hundred of speeches in her book tour, and engaged discussions with various groups of people. She has her own campaign against the death penalty.

Second, the confirmation of the wrongful execution case of Jian Kuo-chien in January 2011 has changed the debates of the death penalty at least to a certain extent. Jian Kuo-chien was accused of raping and killing a young girl in 1996. Despite of his insistence of his innocence, he was convicted and executed in 1997. In 2010, his case was reopened. The new investigation shows that Jian's confession was coerced, and the DNA evidence against him was problematic. Jian's case has aroused public outrage against those who conducted the criminal investigation. For a few people, however, Jian's case reminded them of the problem of miscarriage of justice. Some people began to feel sympathetic to the abolitionist movement. When MOJ unexpectedly executed five people in March 2011, these sympathizers voiced their discontent with the hypocrisy of the government on the issue of the death penalty.[114] It would be too soon to say what these new friends and sympathizers to the campaign against the death penalty

---

112 For instance, in March 2011, the department of Philosophy of Huafan University, one Buddhist University, has held a symposium on the issue of the death penalty, which encouraged interdisciplinary discussions. 〈http://ph.hfu.edu.tw/app/news.php?Sn=1141〉 (visit : Sept. 30, 2011).

113 *See e.g.* Yuan-Wei Liao, Analyzing the Death Penalty from the Theological Perspective, in SOLITUDO : A MEDITATIVE JOURNAL OF TAIWAN CHRISTIAN THOUGHT, Vol 242, pp. 35-42 (June, 2010) ; Gao-Yen Hsiao, *On the Abolition of the Death Penalty, A Political and Philosophical Reconsideration*, REFLEXION, Vol 17, pp. 123-141. (Jan, 2011) ; Wen-Shan Chen, *Discussing the Abolition of the Death Penalty based on the Philosophy of Restorative Justice*, TAIWAN BAR JOURNAL, Vol 15, Issue 8, pp. 16-26 (August 2011).

114 *See e.g.* CHINA TIMES, Mar. 05, 2011 ; UNITED DAILY NEWS, May 06, 2011 ; APPLE DAILY NEWS, Mar. 07, 2011 ; CHINA TIMES, Mar. 10, 2011.

would bring. But they are undoubtedly reviving the anti-death penalty movement in Taiwan.

III. Conclusion

The diplomatic crisis between Taiwan and EU in March 2011 has calmed down with a few days. But it has told us a lot about the anti-death penalty movement in Taiwan. Who was involved, who was ignored and what has been said in this crisis all exist for reasons. Abolitionists have lost their leverage they thought they had between 2000 and 2010. But they have new friends and sympathizers to revive the campaign. As history is never predestinedly written, the contingency found along the development of the abolitionist movement in Taiwan might help to pave the way for the emerging possibilities in the next turn.

[4] How is China changing its Death Penalty Policy?

Wang Yunhai

Introduction

China sentences the most criminal defendants to death and conducts the most executions in the world today. My presentation consists of three parts : "Why are so many death sentences and executions possible in China?", "What is China doing in improving its death penalty policy?" and "What is important for the future of the death penalty in China?".

I. Why are so many death sentences and executions possible?
1. There are so many capital offences in Chinese Criminal Code.
2. There is a very easy and rapid criminal procedure for death sentences and executions in Chinese criminal procedure code.
3. There is a political style of enforcing criminal law and dealing with crimes that is enhancing death sentences and executions.

II. What is China doing in improving its death penalty policy?

China has turned to a new death penalty policy expressed as "firstly retain, then limit, eventually abolish", and has been trying to improve its death penalty system especially since 2000s.
1. Reducing the capital offences
2. Making the standards of death sentence stricter and trying to reduce executions
3. Completing a "Chinese Super Due Process" for death cases

III. What is important for the future of the death penalty in China?

Firstly, Chinese government should reveal the information on its death penalty sentences and executions. Secondly, it is a key point to allow the Chinese legal professionals to be independent in dealing with death penalty, both from the political power and so-called "public opinion" or "people's will". Finally, how to draw Chinese society out of the "Superstition" to death penalty is the final way for China to reduce and finally abolish death penalty.

Reference

Wang Yunhai, "The death penalty and society in contemporary China", *Punishment & Society : the International Journal of Penology*, Volume 10 Number 2, April 2008, p.137.

[Theme Session]

The Concept of Japanese Drug Court: from punishment to harm-reduction

We have researched rehabilitation programs for drug addicts whose models are "Drug Courts" in the USA. There core components include a scheme that the court suspends sentencing if a defendant pleas guilty of drug related crimes and if he/she agrees to take part in a rehabilitation program, and then if he/she finishes it without withdrawal, and then that he/she becomes free from any punishment. This is kind of diversion systems. Now, more than 2300 drug courts serve over 120000 drug addicts some programs.

In Japan, it is widely believed that an illegal drug user is the criminal who should be punished. Most addicts have no chance to be treated by medical systems nor to be supported by welfare staff members. As a result, they repeat drug abuse and are imprisoned again. Our concepts, Japanese Drug Courts, have proposed to change this punitive policy with overriding priority into a new balanced drug policy between legal, medical and welfare approach, and then concretely to divert a number of addicts who will engage who will engage in own treatment program from criminal justice systems.

We are proud to have developed effective and efficient treatment models in parallel. We call this drastic diversion "Japanese Drug Court" project under the slogan of "From punishment to harm-reduction".

Key Words: Drug Court, harm-reduction, drug policy, drug addiction

Languages: Japanese, English.

Chair:
Shinichi Ishizuka, Ryukoku University
Yasuhiro Maruyama, Rissho University

1. Yasuhiro MARUYAMA, Rissho University
"Contemporary Japanese Drug Policy : Compulsory and coerced treatment for drug addicts in criminal justice system."

In Japan, there was no treatment programs for drug addicts in the criminal justice system until the past a few years. According to recent public opinion poll on drug problems, most people think that illegal drug users should not be treated, but punished. However, new types of systems that are more curative for drug addicts has increased and been put into practice recently, for example, compulsory and coerced drug tests are used in criminal practices, and prisoner have to join some group meetings which are operating in prisons.

The trend of drug treatments in the criminal justice system is on the way to become more compulsory if the treatments have effective results. However, I think that the prisoners with addictions should have a choice whether to be treated or not.

We have to pay attention to compulsory treatment problems at first. First of all, I will check the effectiveness of coercive treatments. Secondly, I will discuss the coerced treatment's issues and recommend improve the treatment methods if there is a big problem in this area.

2. Tamaki Morimura, Kokusikan University
"Drug Court Today in the USA"

Drug Court have proliferated throughout the United States in the past two decades. Taking advantage of the unprecedented high level of prison population and economic recession, Drug Courts have been enjoying success as the most promising alternative to incarceration. This article sketches out current trend of U. S. criminal justice and examines what Drug Court are. It also shows the results of evaluation studies of Drug Courts and analyses their recent developments and critiques.

3. Tsuneo Kondo, Japan DARC
"Advances in support and treatment at DARC : Looking back on the 25years"

Drug Addiction Rehabilitation Center (DARC) was established by Tsuneo Kondo in 1985. Those who would recover from drug dependence came together as co-residents at a small house. DARC supported recovery not only of clients but also staffs. They accepted the 12 steps and concept of self-help, which was characteristic of neither paternalism nor authoritarian. The concept prompted their self-esteem in its activities.

[Discussion]

4. Makoto Oda, APARI Yoji, Miura, NPO Okinawa DARC
"Activity condition of APARI and promotes various activities in Asia"

Since July 2000, Asia Pacific Addiction Research Institute (APARI) in Tokyo JAPAN has been providing a drug treatment program for defendants on bail/probation in partnership with DARC. This program is for drug offenders on bail/probation and incorporates participation in self-help groups. It aims to enable offenders to return to a drug free life. As for drug use charges, first time offenders receive suspended sentences. It is very important to utilize this opportunity and provide recovery program for offenders on bail/probation. Mr. Oda presents his intervention methods for drug offenders in Japanese legal systems.

Developing a recovery meeting in Metro Manila is quite important due to a shortage of social resources for drug addiction in this area. Family Wellness Center, one of the private organizations that provide residential rehabilitation program in Makati City, Metro Manila, will be our counterpart for this project. Managed by recovered drug addicts, the center adopts 12-step model and, although many residents are from high or middle class, the center has dealt with recovery for low-income addicts too.

Thus, it will be strictly valid to develop a 12-step based meeting to help addicts with low-income in Metro Manila, Philippines, as JICA's grass-roots technical assistance project. This project expects participation of various people, such as program users (addicts) and their family members, NGO workers, and public/religious organization workers.

5. Leonardo Estacio, University of the Philippines
"Current situations and agenda in Philippines"
outlines Philippines drug policy and activities with APARI.

6. Sung Nam Cho, Bugok National Hospital, Ministry of Health and Social Welfare

"Current situations and agenda in Korea"
outlines Korean drug policy.

[Round table session]

"Talk a lot about what is Contemporary situation of Drug policy in Asia-Pacific"

Summary :

In Japan, it is widely believed that an illegal drug user is the criminal who should be punished. Most addicts have no chance to be treated by medical systems nor to be supported by welfare staff members. As a result, they repeat drug abuse and are imprisoned again. Our concepts, Japanese Drug Courts, have proposed to change this punitive policy with overriding priority into a new balanced drug policy between legal, medical and welfare approach, and then concretely to divert a number of addicts who will engage who will engage in own treatment program from criminal justice systems.

We are proud to have developed effective and efficient treatment models in parallel. We call this drastic diversion "Japanese Drug Court" project under the slogan of "From punishment to harm-reduction".

This round table session is following up the theme session, "The Concept of Japanese Drug Court: from punishment to harm-reduction".

[1] "Contemporary Japanese Drug Policy : Compulsory and Coerced Treatment for Drug Addicts in Criminal Justice System"

Yasuhiro Maruyama (Rissho University)

Key Words : Japanese drug policy, new criminal justice treatments, compulsory treatment, coerced treatment.

Summary

In Japan, there was no treatment programs for drug addicts in the criminal justice system until the past a few years. According to recent public opinion poll on drug problems, most people think that illegal drug users should not be treated, but punished. However, new types of systems that are more curative for drug addicts has increased and been put into practice recently, for example, compulsory and coerced drug tests are used in criminal practices, and prisoner have to join some group meetings which are operating in prisons.

The trend of drug treatments in the criminal justice system is on the way to become more compulsory if the treatments have effective results. However, I think that the prisoners with addictions should have a choice whether to be treated or not.

We have to pay attention to compulsory treatment problems at first. First of all, I will check the effectiveness of coercive treatments. Secondly, I will discuss the coerced treatment's issues and recommend improve the treatment methods if there is a big problem in this area.

By compulsory treatment, I mean an object person has no choice in an assertive way. And By coerced treatment, I mean an object person has some choices but he/she has to adopt some treatments which are indirectly-controlled. For example, the object person has a hard time choosing between the treatment in his/her "community-based treatment" or "in prison". In reality, they have no options.

contents

I would like to explain that current Japanese drug policy, new treatments and related issues. I must concentrate heavily on the points in this presentation. Incrementally, I would like to show you a little bit about "Agreement" of treatments in criminal justice" and "Ethical issues of treatments in criminal justice".

Commercial message

The methamphetamine. In 1941, were put on sale by Dai-Nippon-Seiyaku. It was said that methamphetamine can relieve sluggishness from lack of sleep and that can remove the scales from our eyes. In World War 2, they were distributed to workers in military manufacturing plants and to young pilots.

After World War II, these came onto the market. Many commercial messages were in newspapers and on TV. It was easy to get them at a pharmacy. As a result, methamphetamine had become popular within several years. Then a lot of patients suffering from drug addiction were produced by the distribution of methamphetamine. So The Stimulants Control Act (Act No. 252 of 1951) was established in 1951.

Number of persons cleared for stimulants control Act Violations

The figure 1 shows the number of persons cleared for Stimulants Control Act violations since 1951. Stimulants abuse began to become widespread during the chaotic postwar period, however, persons cleared fell sharply after a peak of over 50,000 in 1954. As a background, it has been pointed out that penal regulations were tightened, and that clearance by police was implemented thoroughly.

However, the number of persons cleared took an upward turn again in 1970 and reached over 24,000 in 1984, recording the second peak. After that, the number fell below 20,000 in 1989 and had leveled off until 1994. It started to increase again in 1995 and reached almost 20,000 in 1996, 1997, and 2000. After that, it has generally been on a decreasing trend.

Cannabis Control Act, Opium Act and Narcotics and Psychotropic Control Act

The figure 2 shows the number of persons cleared for Narcotics and Psychotropic Control Act violations, Opium Act violations, and Cannabis Control Act violations. Both the number of persons cleared for Narcotics and Psychotropic Control Act violations and that for Cannabis Control Act violations have generally been increasing since 2001, and as for Cannabis Control Act violations, the number registered the record high in 2006.

Certainly, Cannabis control act violations have been increasing, but Stimu-

figure 1

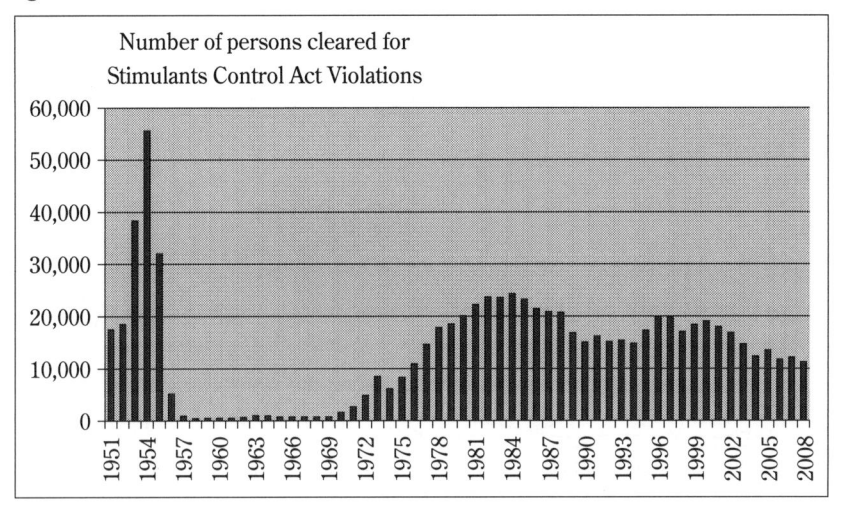

[Figure 1: Bar chart titled "Number of persons cleared for Stimulants Control Act Violations" showing values from 1951 to 2008, with y-axis from 0 to 60,000. A peak around 1954 reaches above 55,000, then drops to near zero in the 1960s, rising again from the 1970s with peaks around 1984 and 1997 near 20,000.]

lants control act violations have been over 5 to 6 times more than cannabis act violations. So, a major drug problem area of Japanese criminal justice is Stimulants.

Percent distribution of newly admitted inmates by type of offense 2007

The figure 3 shows the percent distribution of newly admitted inmates by type of offense in 2007. In examination of offenses committed by newly admitted sentenced inmates, the following five offenses had the highest percentages: (PP) 1 theft (32%), 2 Stimulants control act violations (20%), 3 fraud (8%), 4 injury (5%), 5 road traffic act violations (2%).

I think we have a focused agenda that results in effective programs for theft and stimulants control act violations in the Japanese criminal justice system. We can see a big difference between theft violations and stimulants control act violations in the next figures.

Persons sentenced to imprisonment for theft violations in the court of first instance by term of imprisonment

By the number of persons sentenced to imprisonment with work for theft violations in the court of first instance since 1980, by the term of imprisonment,

figure 2

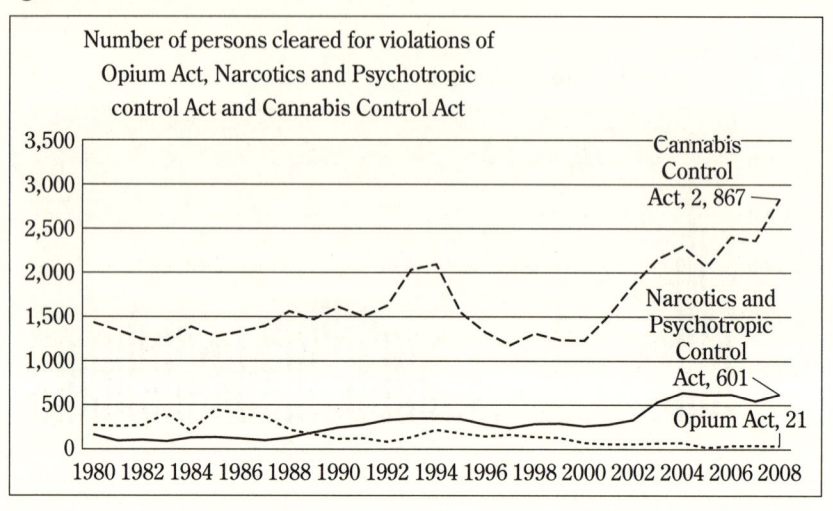

Number of persons cleared for violations of Opium Act, Narcotics and Psychotropic control Act and Cannabis Control Act

- Cannabis Control Act, 2, 867
- Narcotics and Psychotropic Control Act, 601
- Opium Act, 21

(1980–2008)

We can notice that this rate has been increasing as part of the total count. However, as like I mentioned before, the number of persons cleared for Stimulants control act violations has generally been on a decreasing trend. Please see the next figure.

Persons sentenced to imprisonment for stimulants control act violations in the court of first instance by term of imprisonment

By the number of persons sentenced to imprisonment with work for Stimulants Control Act violations in the court of first instance since 1980, by the term of imprisonment, Its total count has been on a decreasing trend. However, the term of imprisonment has been lengthening and toughening for persons convicted of stimulants control act violations. It's hard to see less than 1year.

Number of persons for probationary supervision by stimulant control act violations

By the number of persons on probationary supervision for stimulant control act violations, about half the total of persons are given a suspended prison term. And most of these are probation without probation officers. This mean effective treatment is not provided for drug addicts, too.

figure 3

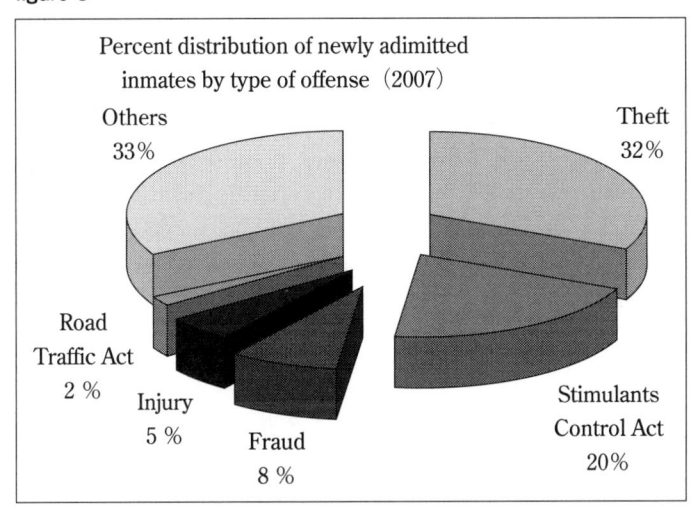

Percent distribution of newly adimitted inmates by type of offense (2007)
- Others 33%
- Theft 32%
- Road Traffic Act 2%
- Injury 5%
- Fraud 8%
- Stimulants Control Act 20%

The new treatments and these issues

In Japan, there were no treatment programs for drug addicts in the criminal justice system until the past a few years. According to recent public opinion poll on drug problems, most people think that illegal drug users should not be treated, but punished. However, new types of systems that are more curative for drug addicts have increased and been put into practice recently, for example, compulsory and coerced drug tests are used in criminal practices, and prisoners have to join some group meetings which are operating in prisons. So I summarize these points.

The curative methods of new treatment include actively promoting the use of probationary supervision with officers, use of special guidance reform in prison and use of analysis of urine in parole.

(1) Guidance for reform

Guidance for reform is guidance aiming to make sentenced inmates aware of their responsibility for offenses they committed, fostering their sound mind and body, and training them to acquire knowledge and attitudes necessary to adapt to social life. There is both general guidance for reform and special guidance for reform.

Special guidance for reform is provided for sentenced inmates who are considered to have difficulties in the course of reform and rehabilitation or smooth reintegration into society due to certain circumstances, such as drug dependency. The special guidance for reform carried out as special rehabilitation guidance : "guidance for overcoming drug addiction" (prompting inmates to think about specific methods of not using drugs again after making them understand their own problems concerning drug use, etc.),In 2007, among the penal institutions (including rehabilitation program centers) across the nation, the institutions that carry out special guidance are as follows : 1) "guidance for overcoming drug addiction" in 74 institutions. As a result, recovered staff are able to go into prison to set up group meeting programs. This trend brings a chance of recovery for drug addicts.

The others 2-1 and 2-3

In the categorized treatment system, drug offenders are classified into "stimulant drug offenders" and "abusers" and efforts to provide effective treatment for them are made through group treatment for probationers/parolees and lectures for their guardians and guarantors, etc. For prison parolees and offenders given suspension of execution of sentence with probationary supervision for stimulant drug offenses, treatment utilizing simplified urine tests based upon their voluntary willingness to participate in them started in April 2004.

In addition, and in accordance with the Rehabilitation Act, probationers and parolees who meet certain conditions such as those whose offenses include stimulant abuse, etc. are obliged to take part in the "stimulants offenders treatment program" as a special condition of their supervision. The program is a specialized treatment program consisting of simplified drug detection tests with the aim of strengthening and sustaining the willpower of offenders to stop using stimulants and education courses with the main aim of getting them to learn concrete methods of preventing relapses./During the program, they are obliged to take simplified drug detection tests in parallel with the education courses.

Conclusion; In the near future?

A new bill that provides for judges to give sentences with partial suspensions of executions of sentences. If the bills clear the Diet, it's to be anticipated that a lot of drug crime offenders will become involved in this system. We are careful not to use just monitoring by urine analysis. If the object persons breach some rules, he/she has to go back prison. These cases cause a problem that the persons receive longer-term intervention than with a traditional procedure.

The new treatments bring drug addicts more curative treatments and more welfare treatments than traditional criminal punishment. They could have many opportunities to get treatment.

However, there are some issues about these treatments. Ultimately, the new treatments are based on punishment. Therefore, the object persons have no choice of treatment. This is a big problem because The United Nations standard minimum rules for the treatment of prisoners and the actual condition of the penal institution Article 60 call for conforming to standards of liberated lifestyle out of prison. In addition, the UN standard minimum rules for non-custodial measures Article 3. 4 says that Non-custodial measures imposing an obligation on the offender, applied before or instead of formal proceedings or trial, shall require the offender's consent. However, almost all Japanese drug treatment in criminal justice are compulsory treatments.

〔2〕 Drug Courts in the USA

Tamaki Morimura (Kokushikan University)

What are Drug Courts?

The first drug court opened in Miami-Dade County in 1989, providing treatment instead of incarceration to drug offenders, stopping the 'revolving door' of punishment thereby reducing the overcrowded prison population in 'the cocaine capital of the world'. Two decades later, in 2009, there are 2459 drug courts in all over the U. S. and there are also 1189 Drug Court-inspired Problem Solving Courts such as Domestic Violence Courts and Mental Health Courts.

Every Drug Court varies in style. But their common idea is providing court-monitored treatment instead of incarceration to addicted drug offenders. Drug addiction is considered ill and drug addicts are seen more patients than criminals. Drug Courts try to force treatment to sick offenders by the fear of criminal charge, conviction and incarceration, along with care and support. In 1997, Drug Courts' Ten Key Components' were issued for operating an effective drug court.

Drug Courts don't take adversarial style. They are collaborative, meaning that judges, prosecutors, defense attorneys (also, polices, treatment providers, probation-officers etc.) all work as a 'team' for client's best interest.

Drug Court's team leader is a judge. Judges take very active role in Drug Courts. In so called 'status hearings', held often weekly in the early stages, judges talk directly with clients about their progress, check attendance to NA meetings and the result of drug tests. If the client is doing well, he will praise her verbally, might give her a coffee mug, or movie ticket, or reduce her supervision requirements. If her urine was 'dirty', or she missed NA meetings, the judge will rebuke her, require more frequent appearance at the court, order her community service, or even short stay in prison. Since relapse is considered inevitable part of recovery, just one slip does not mean neither terminating the treatment, nor going to prison. Most DC programs run 12 to 18 months. The duration time can be much longer. Clients must be clean for specified period and have to fulfill specific requirements for the graduation from DC. Graduation ceremony in DC is a big thing, with family, friends all gather to celebrate participants' achieve-

More than 12 times as many people are in prison for drug offenses as in 1980.

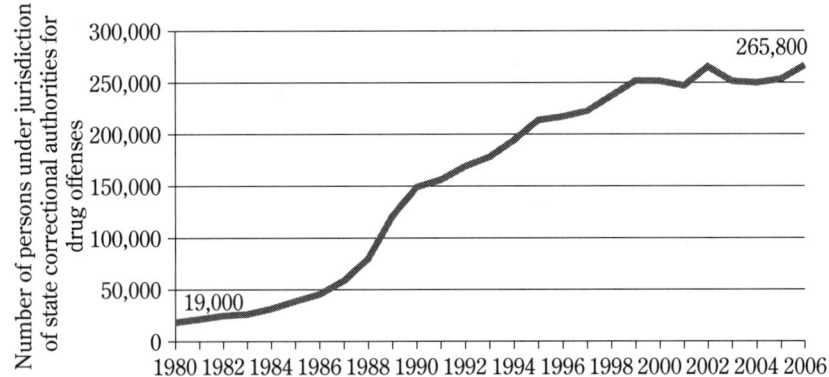

Source: Bureau of Justice Statistics, Key Facts at a Glance, *Number of persons under jurisdiction of state correctional authorities by most serious offense, 1980–2006* (Washington, D. C.: Department of Justice, Accessed January 2010)
http://bjs.ojp.usdoj.gov/content/glance/tables/corrtyptab.cfm

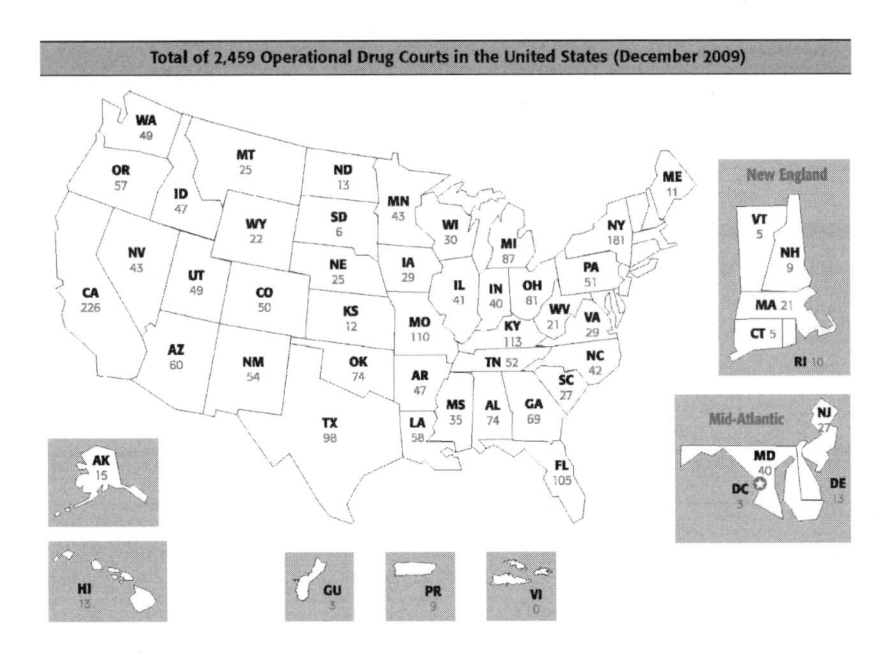

Total of 2,459 Operational Drug Courts in the United States (December 2009)

WA 49, OR 57, MT 25, ND 13, ME 11, ID 47, MN 43, WI 30, NY 181, VT 5, NH 9, WY 22, SD 6, MI 87, PA 51, NV 43, NE 25, IA 29, IL 41, IN 40, OH 81, MA 21, CT 5, UT 49, CO 50, KS 12, MO 110, KY 21, WV 29, VA 113, CA 226, AZ 60, NM 54, OK 74, AR 47, TN 52, NC 42, SC 27, RI 10, MS 35, AL 74, GA 69, NJ 27, TX 98, LA 58, FL 105, MD 40, DC 3, DE 13, AK 15, HI 13, GU 3, PR 9, VI 0

The 10 Key Components

1. Drug Courts integrate alcohol and other drug treatment services with justice system case processing.
2. Using a non-adversarial approach, prosecution and defense counsel promote public safety while protecting participants' due process rights.
3. Eligible participants are identified early and promptly placed in the Drug Court program.
4. Drug Courts provide access to a continuum of alcohol, drug, and other related treatment and rehabilitation services.
5. Abstinence is monitored by frequent alcohol and other drug testing.
6. A coordinated strategy governs Drug Court responses to participants' compliance.
7. Ongoing judicial interaction with each Drug Court participant is essential.
8. Monitoring and evaluation measure the achievement of program goals and gauge effectiveness.
9. Continuing interdisciplinary education promotes effective Drug Court planning, implementation, and operations.
10. Forging partnerships among Drug Courts, public agencies, and community-based organizations generates local support and enhances Drug Court program effectiveness.

(NADCP, 1997)

ment. Local politicians and celebrities are often invited to the ceremony.

Drug Court Models

Drug Courts can be divided into two types, which are (1) pre-plea and (2) post-plea. And post-plea models can be divided into ① pre-adjudication and ② post-adjudication. In pre-plea model, a defendant enters drug courts without guilty plea. When she completes drug court programs, her criminal charge will be dismissed. In ① post-plea/pre-adjudication model, she enters guilty-plea which is held in abeyance while she participates in DC. It will be vacated or withdrawn upon successful completion of programs. But when the defendant fail to complete the program, the deferred plea will be entered and sentence imposed.

② Post-adjudication model is more like a probation with judge's supervision. If a participant fails to complete treatment, suspended sentence will be imposed and she will be incarcerated.

Early Drug Courts were basically pre-plea/pre-trial diversion model. But gradually, they have changed into pre-plea model, and as of December 31, 2009,

58% of Adult Drug Courts are post-plea. Only 12% are pre-plea model and 20% are hybrid, which means serving both. As also experienced in NY's DTAP (Drug Treatment Alternative to Prison) program which started as a deferred prosecution model and sifted to deferred sentencing model because higher treatment retention follows an increased certainty of punishment.

Claimed Efficacy

There are vast amount of evaluative researches on Drug Courts efficacy. NADCP claims Drug Courts reduce crime more than any other programs. They also claim DCs save taxpayers considerable money. They also claim that Drug Courts are not reaching many of the citizens who need them and who could benefit greatly from them and need expansion.

Recent Criticisms against Drug Courts

Drug Courts have attracted lots of attention and criticism.

Recently, National Association of Criminal Defense lawyers (NACDL), Drug Policy Alliance (DPA) and Justice Policy Institute (JPI) have launched a large scale criticism against Drug Courts, claiming treatment through the justice system is no more effective than other treatment. Drug courts are not the best way to improve public safety. Drug courts are not as cost-effective as other options. Drug Courts widen the net of criminal justice control. Drug courts does not treat everyone equally, especially people of color. Drug Court research is often unreliable. Drug Courts limits access to proven treatment. Drug Courts may not reduce incarceration.

NADCP's Response

NADCP has made immediate response to these attacks claiming that Drug Courts save lives and Money and for that they are attacked by people who claim decriminalization of drug offence. They claim the DPA and JPI "studies" throw a disjointed slew of accusations at Drug Courts and their accusations lack in respect for science and are beyond unfair.

Conclusion

Japanese Drug policy has long punished the use of controlled drugs as a crime. The idea that addiction is disease and the addicts need treatment has been completely foreign to Japanese drug policy arguments. So the court-controlled coerced treatment by Drug Court with intensive supervision by DC judge was shocking and looked attractive.

Drug Courts have been increasing rapidly and have changed their early pre-plea/pre-trial diversion model to post-plea model, and becoming more like judge-supervised probation.

There are vast amount of evaluative and theoretical researches for and against DCs and recent criticisms by DPA and JPI of course are not the only one. However, there are still lot to learn from Drug Courts in the USA for Japanese Drug policy where the necessity of treatment for drug offenders is not yet part of the common sense.

[3] DARC (Drug Addiction Rehabilitation Center) for 25Years

Tsuneo Kondo (Japan DARC)

In the following statements, I will explain the reason behind the establishment of DARC and its history at first. Next, I will overview what DARC is planning to do against drug addiction and what DARC is doing now. And finally I will consider how and why DARC has remained for twenty six years.

1. The history of DARC

(1) As you know, I myself was once a drug addict. I began using a drug for a trivial reason - toothache. After that, however, I completely lost myself in drugs. Due to my addiction, I neglected my family and accumulated debts, resulting in my rapid downfall.

Meanwhile, I temporarily entered a mental hospital and met Father Roy Assenheimer, who was later to greatly change my life. At that time, however, I could not give up drugs and was eventually arrested. Only Father Roy visited me at the detention house. Although he was a father, he was alcoholic and eccentric. I gradually opened my mind to him.

Father Roy took me to Alcoholics Anonymous (AA), and I began to participate in its meetings. I was tormented by a feeling of inferiority and could not openly talk about myself at any other place than the meetings. I continued to participate in them every day. I was rather busy .because I had been told at court to undergo one and a half years' outpatient treatment and to participate in a self-help group.. Other ·AA members congratulated me for my abstinence from drugs for one month. However, my desire for drugs still remained strong. Around that time, I came to understand tile AA members' slogan : "Just for today," which means "Let's think only about today." I recognized that it would be all right to give up drugs just for today and think the same way the next day, two days later, three days later and so on.·

(2) Soon, I became a staff member of the Maryknoll Alcohol Center (MAC) and helped with Father Roy's work. At that time, Father Roy was trying to establish MAC in Sapporo. I helped him raise funds. To my surprise, when Sapporo MAC was established, I was offered the position as the first director. Sapporo MAC was a great success, and I did my best to promote MAC's

activities.

Through the activities, I was convinced that AA's recovery program was effective also for the recovery of drug addicts. As a result, I began to consider establishing facilities for drug addicts like AA's.

I began the search for a room, together with other NA members, and found a house in Higashi Nippori, Arakawa Ward. Because I did not have money to pay the rent on the shabby house, I borrowed 720, 000 yen from Father Roy, who, without my knowing, was suffering from heart failure.

On July 1st, 1985, DARC was established as the first private rehabilitation center for drug addicts. Since then, I have been responsible for DARC's activities. In 2010, DARC celebrated its 25th anniversary.

DARC is an abbreviation for Drug Addiction Rehabilitation Center. Jeanne d'Arc is the name of the French patriot and, as I discovered later, the biblical Noah's ark is also called "d'arche do noe." I think I was able to give the center a good name, as if guided by a great force.

2. Recent Activities of DARC :
Decriminalization, Diversion and Community-based Correction

(1) I am interested in the trend of dealing with drug cases by diversion or extrajudicial proceedings. I think it would be possible to impose a task on a drug addict as a condition for suspending the indictment at the investigation stage and hold a court trial only when the drug addict fails to complete the task.. If a driver is caught by the police for an overspeed or parking violation and a certain number of points are accumulated on the driver's license, the driver must have a lecture. The driver has to buy a stamp for the penalty, and see a video of miserable traffic accidents for many hours. Such program is far stricter than a court trial. I think it better to apply such a system to drug cases and give a drug lecture. If a court trial is held for a drug addict, it is very hard for us to intervene. At the police stage, however, we can take various measures, involving the social community. It is ideal and possible to create a system whereby drug addicts can be monitored in the social community so that they cannot be put in prison.

(2) If a drug addict has to take leave for about one week for the police investigation, he can stay in his job by falsely stating that a parent has died or

that there is a funeral or a wedding. However, for example, if a person is imprisoned for three years, this may lead to a family breakdown or divorce. All he possesses will be lost, including his job, livelihood and home. Although the cause of this situation is nothing other than his use of drugs, this situation is disadvantageous for the nation.. At the stage of the first offense, there are a lot of things that can be done to prevent drug addicts from repeating offenses. It is better to do something new as a model case instead of doing nothing because there is no established system.

In 2010, we set up a project in Tokyo for first offenders whose execution of sentence is suspended to take drug detection testing. The test used a kit called "i-Screen", which examines saliva, not urine, to detect a drug. After the test, we held a two-hour session where DARC's staff members talked about their experience.

(3) Regrettably, this program was discontinued one year later.· It would be good if such programs could be started in many prefectures. Such programs could prevent drug offenders from repeating offenses and ending up in prison. Drug addicts could participate in such programs without being absent from work. If the program was carried out every Saturday afternoon, offenders with suspended execution of sentence would be able to continue work and avoid a family breakdown. In other words, they would be able to rehabilitate themselves within the community. The number of offenders in Tokyo whose execution of sentence is suspended is about 1, 000 per year. These 1, 000 offenders are at large after release. Although most of them think it lucky to be released without having there sentence executed, they will be put in prison if they commit an offense again. Citizens must do something . to prevent this. At present, individuals and social communities completely depend on the police. Given this situation, we have to consider what we can do.

DARC's main activity is support from drug addicts for other drug addicts in each community. Because people who visit DARC are really in trouble and have no place to go, their risk of committing an offense again is very high. Although they have lost almost everything, they have a strong desire to use drugs. Our efforts to persuade them to give up drugs are useless, for they have heard the same advice thousands of times before. Because of this, I gave up persuading them to quit drugs.

A person who quitted drugs 20 years ago may use drugs again. If a person has not used any drug for several years, he may use a drug when he returns to society. Although drug addiction is similar to a chronic disease, Japan's social and administrative systems do not reflect this fact. What is important for treating a chronic disease is how to keep good company with it, which is the only way to treat drug addiction..

There is a system of parole and offenders released on parole for, say, three months have to be parole supervision for that period. But when the parole period expires, the offender will no longer have an access to the service. Such a system is not so useful for drug addiction. It seems as if drug addicts are running a marathon without a finish line. They are trying to give up drugs just for today and are continuing this effort every day. A system with a limited period – that is, a system where care is provided for a limited period but is discontinued at the expiration of the period – is useless for them in reality. Such a system is similar to the school system, where students have no relation with the school after graduating from it or being expelled from it.

Although I and other DARC members are often invited to give lectures at meetings of prefectural residents for the prevention of drug abuse, there are no drug addicts among the participants because the prefectural committees follow through the slogan "No drugs".

If a meeting is held on a theme such as "prevention of drug abuse" or "prevention of repeated drug abuse," some people with the problem of drug abuse themselves may feel like attending the meeting. Meetings of prefectural residents are places where drug addicts can never attend. It is necessary to reconsider this approach and create a system that encourages the actual people with the trouble to attend meetings.

First of all, it is important to prevent drug addicts from being isolated. If they are isolated, they will naturally become prone to committing an offense or become depressed and eventually go underground. Therefore, it is necessary. to take measures to bring the issue of drug addiction out into the Open. DARC members have carried out activities to this end.

The people with the drug abuse problem, high-risk juveniles, and people likely to use stimulants, marijuana, or MDMA if left without an appropriate care, need places like DARC, where they can communicate with each other without fear of being arrested.

Because drug addicts are highly conscious of doing wrong, many of them and their families are reluctant to confide in others. They have a firmly established mental scheme: if they consult with someone, they will be arrested. When I was using drugs and causing problems, my family phoned a mental health center. However, they could not easily visit it to discuss situation because they firmly believed that the mental health center was connected with the police. They also had an obsession that led them to believe that all administrative agencies are connected with each other.

For these reasons, now is the time to consider increasing the number of places where drug addicts can find consultant so that they can be diverted towards medical treatment. My greatest wish is to create new channels for drug addicts who cannot attend "the meeting of prefectural residents for the prevention of drug abuse".

3. Conclusion : Ambiguousness of DARC

DARC continues for twenty six years. Some reasons why DARC was retained so long are given.

One of them is that DARC has not been well organized. There are about sixty facilities of DARC in Japan. Although there is a facility named DARC Memorial Center in Tokyo it does not work as a headquarters of the entire. Each DARC that spread over Japan has it's own way to survive. One has been active as NPO, the other accumulate a fund from a private enterprise and so on. In other words each DARC takes a self-supporting accounting system.

The second reason is that DARC keeps a certain distance from the government offices concerned. Due to this we are not forced to do anything that the government requires. Instead of being given money from the government, we are free from any pressure groups.

As the third reason, we can mention that we do not force anybody to go out of DARC and we accept everybody that wants to join us. We also welcome even those who went out of DARC. This kind of security makes DRAC their second hometown and there is not a big trouble in it.

These kinds of situation require us to hold the ambiguousness. The attitude of distinguishing things one from another does not fit the addiction rehabilitation. The addicts need the circumstance which has a wide range of tolerance for their behaviors. The ability of holding such kind of ambiguousness leads DARC today.

[4] What is APARI (Asia- Pacific Addiction Research Center)?

Makoto Oda (Chief Secretary of APARI)

Today I would like to take this opportunity to explain to you about contemporary Japanese drug policy and my job in Japan. In Japan drug abusers are treated as criminals, not patients. Sentencing is becoming more sever year by year. But the programs for drug addicts have just started 5 years ago in the criminal justice system. Under the circumstances we have been doing assistance for drug addicts who are in the criminal justice system for 11 years.

By the way, what is the most difference between criminal justice system and assistant section such as drug rehabilitation centers, hospitals and so on? The answer is existence or nonexistence of the coercive power which obligate drug addicts what to do. Criminal justice system has the coercive power to put them into the prison, or on probation or parole. But assistant section has provide assistance to only whom want it.

Drug addicts have no sense of disease and they don't attend the programs for recovery from their addiction. That's why utilize some kind of actual coercive power in the criminal justice system to attend the recovery programs in the society.

Number of drug addicts who are under medical treatment in Japan. The number is presumed by Ministry of Health , Labour and Welfare. Please look at my handout which shows the Japanese statutory penalties of drug control acts. There are 6 drug control acts in Japan. For your information, in Japan, it is already against this law if you are using methamphetamine, without possessing it, meaning, if the drug is in your urine, you can be arrested and convicted.

By the way, I'd like to talk about the invention of methamphetamine. Did you know? Who first invented methamphetamine? Anyone? It's Japanese. Japanese call methamphetamine Kakuseizai or more commonly known as Shabu, formerly Hiropon. Methamphetamine was first synthesized from ephedrine by a Japanese pharmacologist, Dr. Nagayoshi Nagai in 1893, to be meant as a medicine against asthma. But then later, Shabu was sold at pharmacies as shaking up drug until 1951 when Stimulants Control Act was put in effect.

In 2009, according to the Japanese criminal statistics of drug offenses: Methamphetamine is most popular in Japan. In Japan, juvenile means under the age of 20. About 15 thousand people are imprisoned for methamphetamine abuse as of present.

This is a chart of the number of arrestees under violation of Stimulants Control Act. Recently every year about 12 thousand people are arrested under violation of Stimulants Control Act.

According to the Japanese criminal statistics of drug offenses: Methamphetamine is most popular in Japan. Second popular illegal drug is marijuana. Third popular illegal drug is thinner and toluene.

There is almost no Opium related crime in Japan. MDMA and cocain related crime is very low. Marijuana related crimes are relatively high.

Sentencing of drug abusers. They are treated by formulaic processing. Japanese judges have a wide range of discretion within the statutory penalty. Let me show you an example of a typical sentence in a case where a defendant used illegal drugs or possesed a small amount of illegal drugs.

For methamphetamine abusers: Statutory penalty is not less than one month but not more than 10 years with hard labor, but the sentence for a 1st time offender is 1 year 6 months imprisonment with labor but the execution of the sentence will be suspended for a period of 3 years. When a period of suspension progresses without rescission, the sentence shall cease to be effective.

And for a 2nd time offender it is 2 years imprisonment with labor and the execution will not be suspended. This is the standard.

For thinner & toluene abusers: Statutory penalty is not less than one month but not more than 1 year imprisonment or fine not more than 500 thousand Japanese Yen. It's about not more than 5 thousand US Dollars. And the sentence for a 1st time offender is usually a fine. And for the 2nd time offender it is also a fine. But for a 3rd time offender it is 6months imprisonment with labor but the execution of the sentence will be suspended for 3 years. And for a 4th time offender it is a 1 year imprisonment.

For marijuana abusers: Statutory penalty is imprisonment with work not more than 5 years. And the actual sentence for a 1st time offender is 6months imprisonment with labor but the execution will be suspended for 3 years. And for a 2nd time offender it is a 1 year imprisonment with labor.

In 24th May 2006 Japanese Prison Law has been updated to Inmates Treatment Law and then all prisons (78 facilities) must offer drug addiction treatment to drug addicts. Today all of the prisons without the prisons for traffic offenders invite the staff of DARCs as private collaborators at very low wage. But in the prisons only 10 times of 50 minutes course exists in several years incarceration.

Hereafter, I will explain the content of APARI's activity based on such a situation. Now in Japan, there are a little programs for drug addicts in the criminal justice system. And also there is no public drug addiction rehabilitation facility. But there are several private drug addiction rehabilitation centers. The most well-known one is DARC, where peer counselors use the 12 step recovery program to help recovering drug addicts. DARC was established in 1985 in Tokyo Japan by a person. His name is Tsuneo Kondo. His nick-name is Brut. He is an ex-user of shabu and now clean for 30 years. 30 years ago there was no NA in Japan but AA existed at that time already. Kondo attended AA meetings for 4 years and established the first drug addiction rehabilitation facility in Japan which he named DARC – that was 26 years ago. DARC is a private drug addicion facility in Japan. Presently, DARC has grown to 59 facilities all over Japan from Okinawa to Hokkaido, where peer counselors use the 12 step recovery program to help recovering addicts. All of the DARC staff consist of recovering addicts.

Now – what is the difference between this DARC and my APARI? Well, APARI is a separate organization that was established in 2000 for the support for DARC as its 'think tank' function. Therefore, APARI staff are consist of specialists such as psychiatrists, lawyers, researchers like me, so I'm a criminologist and so on.

Since July 2000, APARI has been proactively providing drug treatment programs for defendants on bail/probation/parole in partnership with DARC. APARI is now closely cooperating with DARC and especially focusing on drug addicts in the process of criminal justice system.

First : APARI provides support for trial in two ways.
(1) One is : drug addiction training program for criminal for defendants on bail
(2) Second is : guarantor for prisoner who is a drug addict

APARI manages the drug addiction rehabilitation facility in Fujioka, a small town in the deep nature of Gunma Prefecture (It is about 100km away from Tokyo). APARI offers an outreach program by sending peer counselors to drug addicts.

[5] DARC as a Cooperator of JICA in the Philippines

Yoji Miura (Director of NPO Okinawa DARC)

Today I'm going to talk you about "the supports for the drug addiction of the poor", which goes in cooperation of JICA.

This project started in 2004 when a probation officer who is a friend with DARC by chance, reported us the drug related situation of the Philippines.

Since then, we have proceeded with this project in cooperation with APARI, which is an aggregate of think tanks of DARC.

We have made an investigation into the situation of drug abuse in the Philippines a few times since December 2004.Our investigation was focused on Mindanao at first. However, JICA Japan told us they cannot make an program there because of the risk of terrorism. So we restarted an investigation focused on Manila in 2009.

We trained the core members of Philippine and have a meeting based upon 12 Steps at regular intervals at certain place called ARM (APARI Recovery Meeting) and make ARM continue even after our supports.

In Philippines the rehabilitation programs for drug abuse for the rich are substantial. Our task was taking attention of the rich class and bridging the gap between two classes. We met familiar people again through the activity in the Philippines.

Mr. Kondo, the executive director of DARC and I met Mr. Rich Costibal in 1999, who was the chairman of NA of Philippines. He established the drug addiction rehabilitation center in Philippines and he became a counter part of this project. His participation accelerated our project much.

We can have the core members that keep the ARM at least one day a month constantly by selecting from members that attend the NA meeting in Philippines. They have certain knowledge of drug addiction.

Children who have no food to have suck "rugby", that is thinner, to prevent hunger in the poor class in Philippines. There are also people who sell drugs to earn their daily bread.

DARC has tried to help addicts to recover from drug abuse for twenty six years. We then had trouble in Philippines because we had to also resolve a problem of poverty without the Livelihood Protection Law. It was different from Japan.

Now we are going to apply to JICA and try to make a similar type of activity. We would like to produce employments, for example to found a factory or something like that, and establish a system of NA program in the future.

[6] Current Situations and Agenda in Philippines

Leonardo Estacio, Jr. (University of the Philippine)

Introduction

Part one is discussion points where I will talk about the following : the drug addiction problem in the Philippines; the concept of recovery for drug addicts from the eyes of Filipinos ; and finally, as the main point of discussion, I will share with you, how the concept and practice of recovery of drug addicts is being played out in real life in the Philippines in treating and helping Filipino drug addicts in their road towards recovery from drug addiction.

Part two is take home messages where I will of course share with you some sour notes, good news that were drawn from our observations and experiences in helping Filipino drug addicts overcome their addiction and expound a bit on how these sad and promising stories can both be used as points of departure or "the way to go" messages that we can take note of in spreading the gospel of drug recovery from the Philippines to Japan and to East Asia.

1. The drug problem in the Philippines

To understand the drug problem in the Philippines, we need to look at the dynamics of drug use, drug trading and the drug law.

How serious is the drug problem in the country? What could account for this? What is being undertaken by the Philippine government to address this?

The magnitude of the drug problem in the Philippines is not well-established due to lack of continuous monitoring and prevalence studies. Currently, data that are relied upon are national data and official reports undertaken in previous years. For example, the baseline data that is still being used and well cited today that describes the current landscape of drug addiction is the 2004 National Household Survey commissioned by the Dangerous Drugs Board (DDB), the national agency responsible for drug policy matters in the Philippines.

According to the 2004 national survey, there are 11M lifetime users and approximately 7M current users in the Philippines. Majority of the users are characterized as 26 years old, predominantly male, single, high school educated, and residing mostly in urban areas like Metro-Manila. Most of the users are predominantly methamphetamine or shabu users, accounting for 65% of the drug-using population. Next are the cannabis users which account for 35% and inhalant users, 22%. The Dangerous Drugs Board report that most of the users are polydrugs users, which means that Filipino drug-users, either use a combination of drugs simultaneously or alternately or they can easily shift use based on availability, price, set and setting.

It can be argued that the drug addiction problem in the Philippines assumed a transnational character in the 1990s when shabu was introduced in the market (Porio & Crisol, 2004). With the increasing significance of the Philippines not only as a transshipment point of other high end drugs such as heroin and cocaine but also as exporter of locally produced shabu and marijuana, we can sense that we will never run out of supply of illicit drugs in the country. In fact, in the 2004 report of the United Nations Office on Drugs and Crime, the Philippines was ranked third in the world as a top producer of methamphetamine hydrochloride. Thus, we don't only drug our children and youth and productive adults, we also contribute in the drugging of the world.

Like most countries in East Asia, the use, possession, manufacture, and sale of shabu, marijuana, cocaine, heroin, opium, morphine and other drugs are considered illegal and are punishable as a criminal act. In the Philippines, Republic Act (RA) 6425, otherwise known as the Dangerous Drugs act of 1972, is an example of the first legal approach enacted to intensify the country's efforts against drug abuse and illicit trafficking. The law imposed death penalty for traffickers and instituted treatment and rehabilitation of drug-takers. It was heavy with law enforcement (supply reduction) and light with preventive-education and treatment (demand reduction). Proof of this is the death by musketry of Lim Seng, in 1973, a convicted heroin trafficker. It was a signal sent by the then Marcos regime that drugs are dangerous, illegal and deadly.

After thirty years of enforcement of the 1972 Dangerous Drugs Act, a new law, Republic Act 9165, otherwise known as the Comprehensive Drugs Act of 2002, was enacted. RA 9165 repealed its predecessor, Republic Act No. 6425, the Dangerous Drugs Act of 1972. The new law, being more stringent criminalizes all forms of drug abuse acts. For example, a life time sentence is meted out for possession, manufacture, sale of illicit drugs (shabu, marijuana, cocaine, heroin, opium, morphine and other illegal drugs) including equipment, instrument, apparatus and other paraphernalia, and cultivation. Mandatory testing is required for drivers, firearms owners, students, employees, military/police, candidates seeking elected office and for the drug users: 6 months mandatory rehabilitation for first-time offenders, 6 to 12 years imprisonment for recidivists with a fine of fifty thousand to two-hundred thousand pesos and for repeat-offenders, an imprisonment of 12 to 20 years with a corresponding fine of fifty to two-hundred thousand pesos.

The new law also led to the creation of two important agencies tasked to reduce the demand and supply of drugs. The Dangerous Drugs Board is held responsible for policy-making and strategy formulation while the Philippine Drug Enforcement Agency is tasked as the implementing arm of the law.

A cursory look of their performance in 2010 show that both the DDB and PDEA have shown remarkable and sterling performance in supply reduction such as arrests of drug personalities, foreign nationals, neutralization of drug syndicates, filing of cases with some successful resolution of cases filed against drug offenders, dismantling of shabu labs, and seizures of shabu, cocaine, essential chemical, marijuana plant and rewards to drug mules and informants, among others.

In terms of demand reduction efforts, DDB has been doing a lot of preventive education activities including providing alternative development projects such as crop substitution to reduce supply of marijuana and strengthening its regional and international cooperation by hosting and co-hosting international conferences.

Despite these accomplishments, however, we can sense that very little effort has been undertaken in terms of helping drug addicts recover from their addiction. In fact, there is lack of updated report on the status of treatment and rehabilitation services undertaken by accredited treatment centers nationwide. Information is absent on statistics of those who underwent for treatment for 2010.

However, we can rely on past reports and data from other sources for some information on the treatment statistics and information. For example, treatment admission in the years 2003 to 2005 in the Philippines totaled only to 24,000. With this data, we can infer that the Philippine government has failed miserably in helping millions of drug addicts from treatment.

One of the possible explanations are the gross lack of treatment facilities in the country [only 35 accredited treatment centers were reported in 2010], the prohibitive costs of private treatment, over-stuffed government treatment centers and the lack of funding priority given to treatment services in the country.

In sum, despite the relentless efforts of the Philippine government in running after drug traffickers and instituting amendments to the law such as making the law more stringent by imposing stiffer penalties and strengthening its supply reduction and demand reduction efforts, the drug problem in the Philippines remains a worsening social problem.

The New law had a sterling performance in supply reduction. However, it failed in 3 counts:

- It was not able to punish/penalize/neutralize BIG TIME DRUG SYNDICATES and DRUG LORDS;
- It was not able to stop proliferation of drugs;
- It failed to treat millions of addicted Filipinos
- [And/or probably it failed to empirically measure the number of drug addicted Filipinos]

2. The concept and practice of recovery

2. 1. Legal and psycho-social concept

Like most if not all countries in East Asia, drug addiction in the Philippines is a criminalized deviant behavior. Enshrined under the section 15 of the new law, the Comprehensive Drug Act of 2002, mandatory treatment of 6 months is required for first time offenders. If they fail to recover after 6 months and they turn 2nd offenders or recidivists, drug addicts will be imprisoned for 6 to 12 years with a corresponding fee of 50 to 20 thousand pesos. If again they failed treatment and become repeat-offenders for the 3rd time, they are subjected to a severe punishment of imprisonment of 12 to 20 years and a fine of 50K to 200K pesos.

As can be gleaned, the legal concept of recovery in the Philippines could be interpreted in two ways:

1. Recovery as treatment and rehabilitation (restorative justice)
2. Recovery as discipline and punishment (punitive justice)

Discipline and punishment as a form of recovery for addicts is a punitive type and may not be an ideal one by virtue of the argument that most addicts are victims of various circumstances that may have led to their falling into the trap of self-abuse through drug abuse. From the perspective of restorative and social justice, it violates the basic rights of the drug user as just a violator of a victimless and self-inflicted crime. In short, the provision of the law that pushes for incarceration of the drug addicts is to my mind a not so humane and right one. It should be amended using a more social justice driven view.

On the other hand, treatment and rehabilitation as a form of recovery is a type of restorative justice and an important feature of the demand reduction provisions of the Philippine drug law. Under the law, drug addicts are arrested and charged in court but, if they are found to be first time offenders, rehabilitation takes precedence over criminal action. Likewise, those who voluntarily surrender are given clemency and are immediately remanded to rehabilitation centers for medical examination and recovery treatment.

Since the enactment of the first drug law in the Philippines, the Dangerous Drugs Act of 1972, majority of treatment centers in the Philippines use only 2 dominant models of treatment. For example, in 2002, majority among the 60 treatment and rehabilitation centers in the Philippines were reportedly employing the therapeutic community (TC) and 12 steps facilitation (TSF) models in treating their clients (Colombo Plan, 2002).

One of the promoters of the TC model is the Self Enhancement for Life Foundation (SELF), a private treatment center accredited by the DDB in 1992. SELF adopted the Therapeutic Community (TC) approach and obtained its inspiration from the program of DAYTOP — an organization based in New York that originally formulated the TC approach in 1963. Like most other practitioners then, SELF inherited the methods from various people and operated its program through "best understanding". In following the model, most of the SELF staff were recovering persons who took charge of running the program. Only a minimal complement of professional staff were hired to support the program team. In their self-report, of the more than 700 clients they have so far served, 50% have completed the program. Of those that completed the program, 85% are successfully reintegrated into society (SELF, 2009)

TC's basic approach is treating the whole person through the use of peer community (De Leon, 2000: 3). According to SELF (2009), the Therapeutic Community (TC) model is a drug-free self-help program whose primary goal is the cessation of substance abuse behaviors and the promotion of personal growth. It is a scientific method of intervention founded on the "Enlightenment Model" of recovery where individuals living together empower each other to heal their dependencies through insights derived from group processes and "learning experiences" (SELF, 2009).

Twelve Step Facilitation (TSF therapy) refers to independent treatment interventions designed to familiarize patients with the 12-step philosophy and encourage participation in 12-step activities (Donovan, 2009), TSF consists of brief, structured, and manual-driven approaches based on the behavioral, spiritual, and cognitive principles that form the core of 12-step fellowships such as Alcoholics Anonymous (AA) and Narcotics Anonymous (NA). As in the 12 steps and traditions, this includes the need to accept that willpower alone is insufficient to achieve sustained sobriety. In TSF, the counselor is the facilitator of change (i. e., sustained sobriety) ; whereas the true agent of change lies in active participation in groups, including the guiding steps and traditions of the 12-step model (Donovan, 2009).

Some treatment facilities employed TC or TSF as a single treatment model and others combine them to produce what has been called as the eclectic model. The eclectic model is exemplified by the Dangerous Drugs Board- European Union Treatment, a government run center established in 1992 as a 3-year project funded by the European Union and proposed by key officials of the Dangerous Drugs Board. The Center was purposely set-up by DDB to provide the eclectic approach as a model for treatment and rehabilitation in the country. The eclectic model utilizes concepts mainly based on the spiritual "Twelve Steps" principles of Narcotics/Alcoholic Anonymous (AA/NA) Hazelden Model, Therapeutic Community and Multidisciplinary Team Approach. Put simply, the model is an embodiment of therapeutic center with an ambience of a home away from home. One feature of the eclectic model is the family recovery program which argues that drug dependency is a family disease and as such family members should also go through a recovery process through education (such as lectures, film viewing and discussions) and in this approach, the multi-group family patterned like AA/NA sessions. Another feature in this model is the Aftercare and Follow-up Program. This comes after the first 2 stages, the Intensive Residential Confinement Phase (3 months stay at the Centre) and the Trial-Re-entry Phase (6 months stay). After a rigid 6-month stay the patient graduates and is promoted to the Re-entry and Aftercare Phase for follow-up recovery services which could last up to 18 months. Aftercare services include group and individual counseling, family seminars, crisis intervention, medical counseling, among others.

Again, like most of the East Asian countries, the drug recovery interventions in the Philippines were generally western-derived and locally transformed to suit the needs of the client and the goals of the treatment institution.

However, despite the existence of approximately 60 treatment centers nationwide, these facilities are not enough to satisfy the wide gap between addicts needing professional treatment and the number of accredited treatment centers operating in the Philippines. As mentioned earlier, data shows that of the 7M current users in the NHS 2004 study, only 24,000 were reported to have been treated and rehabilitated (in 2003-2005). By extrapolation, less than 1 percent were treated nationally during that reporting year. Treatment demand is very high in the Philippines but treatment institutions are found wanting.

The gross lack of treatment facilities is further aggravated by the lack of funds allocated to address this need and the observably biased preference given by accredited privately-managed treatment centers to affluent clients. Privately run facilities charge as much as PhP PhP95, 000/mo. (Y ?) and as moderate as PhP40, 000-45, 000/mo. (Y?) ; with a socialized fee of PhP4, 000 to 8, 000/month (Y?). Even with the aforementioned fee of PhP 4,000, poor clients could still hardly afford to pay. Thus, the prohibitive costs, which apparently has not been subjected to regulations by the Dangerous Drugs Board promotes class bias and further alienation and/or exclusion of the economically poor drug addicts. On the other hand, despite the accreditation policy formed to assess the credibility of facilities to operate, the effectiveness and efficiency of these treatment centers are not well assessed and there seems to be a lack of instituting and implementing standards set in terms of providing quality treatment services to drug addicts. For example, quality of care assessments done both internally and externally should be institutionalized so as to ensure that proper and appropriate treatment protocols and services are delivered.

As an alternative response to the seeming lack of priority given by the government to treatments of addicts and by the biased nature of private institutions in catering to affluent addicts, small but well-meaning initiatives are being done by some people's organizations and non-government organizations in partnership with foreign institutions to provide recovery services to the urban poor or grassroots people.

One of these small initiatives is the JICA supported grassroots initiatives in the treatment of drug users piloted by APARI in partnership with KKPC and Addictus-Philippines in Tatalon, Quezon City that was implemented sometime in April 2010. The JICA-APARI-KKPC-Addictus-Philippines pilot project in Tatalon was conceptualized and piloted in response to the lack of available drug recovery program for poor drug users in the community. Although KKPC and Addictus-Philippines have been initiating community-based treatment interventions in the community prior to the project, the pilot project is an example of a transnational response to a village-level drug problem.

From the more than 1 year experience of implementation of the pilot project some ideas and concepts on recovery can be drawn that may provide important lessons or messages in designing models of drug recovery program for the grassroots.

2. 2 Recovery as a process of social/self -transformation : "*Mula sa Tamang Hinala, Tungo sa Tamang Tiwala*" (From "Distrusting Trip" to "Trusting Trip") :

The quotation above which was cited from an interview with a recovering addict in Quezon City encapsulates a concept of recovery that builds on the notion of mutual trust, mutual respect, mutual stake and mutual benefit. It suggests that recovery is an iterative process and is a social act, a form of human bonding based on a trusting relationship on three levels: among the addicts themselves; between the addicts and the treatment providers; among the treatment providers themselves. It invites a more engaged and humanistic approach to recovery rather than a distanced and mechanistic one. It promotes behavior change both at the social and personal levels. It is a product of the lessons drawn from the experience of implementing a pilot project in Tatalon, Quezon City. That pilot project is the JICA-APARI pilot project of drug recovery program in Quezon City, Philippines where the AA/NA model was used. It started in April 2010 and is about to end this month, March 2012.

In the project, we were able to recruit a mixed group of drug addicts whose age ranges from 18 to 46 years old. Although predominantly composed of males, one female member participated in the program. Half of the 10 members are married and most have no regular means of income and livelihood. For more than a year, the group met once a month and held an AA/NA meeting facilitated by an implementing partner of APARI, the Family Wellness Group. This is the first time for the members of the group to undergo an AA/NA recovery program that is piloted in the community and based on an assessment study (individual interviews and group discussions) undertaken sometime in October 2011 and just recently, in February 2012 (follow-through interviews and key informant interview),

the following are some of the significant findings from feedback of the participants regarding the pilot project:
- Positive effects:
- *"Nahinto ang paggamit"* (ceased using drugs);
- *"Nabawas ang pag-inom"* (lessened frequency of drinking alcohol);
- *"Bigayan ng opinion"* (sharing of opinions);
- *"Nagkapalagayan ng loob"* (became open/at ease with each other);
- *"Di nahihiya sa kapwa adik"* (don't feel inferior/shy with co-addicts);
- *"Unti-unting pagbabago"* (slowly changing for the better);
- *"Di na natutukso na gumamit"* (no longer tempted to drink/take drugs)
- Negative effects:
- *"Hindi sapat ang puro miting at sharing sessions lang"* (purely meetings and sharing sessions are not enough);
- *"Nahihiya sa mga attendees na may kaya"* (we feel intimidated by some attendees who are well-off);
- *"Kelangan ng iba pang pagkakaabalahan lalo na sa pangkabuhayan para maging kapakipakinabang naman kami at magkaroon naman ng sariling dignidad"* (We need to have other productive activities like livelihood activities to increase our self-worth and self-esteem);
- *"Yung iba di regular na dumadalo dahil walang nakikitang direktang material na pakinabang"* (Some don't attend regularly because of lack of direct material benefits);
- *"Sa tutulong dapat hindi pulitiko ang dating, dapat tapat "*(For those who wish to help, they should not appear like a politician, they should be honest);
- *"Feeling namin di-pantay ang pagtingin sa amin ng mga facilitators at nahihiya kami kasi di kami marunong mag-Ingles at di magarang magdamit"* (we feel that our facilitators are not treating us sincerely and we feel inferior because we don't speak English well and we are not well-dressed)
- Suggestions/recommendations:
- Family or conjoint approach, wherein the family is involved in the recovery sessions so that they will come to understand us better;
- Group sharing approach is very useful, listening to life stories of other individuals motivated us to change for the better
- Other group sharing activities are needed such as updates about the effects of drugs, lectures on self-recovery, livelihood training, etc.
- Health concerns, since long-term users like us are exposed to various

drugs and haven't undergone any medical check-up, we don't know anything about our health status
- Transitional outcome :
- As far as the transitional outcome of the pilot project is concerned, 20% are total abstainers and 40% have reduced their drug use.

3. Conclusion

In this presentation, I discussed the magnitude of the drug problem in the Philippines and showed how the dynamics of drug use, drug trading and drug law are played out to create the drug problem in the Philippines. I also discussed the concepts of recovery as informed by legal, psycho-social and social transformation perspectives.

Based on the discussions, I made, I wish to summarize and conclude my presentation by giving out to you 3 important take home messages.

3. 1. the sour note :
- Do we always have to borrow from the West? Do we always have to look up to the West for solutions to our local/domestic problems?
- Can we not develop our own drug recovery programs based on our own experiences and cultures? Do we always have to hybridize, indigenize, McDonaldize, re-program Western models to suit the needs of our clients and institutions?
- Do we always have to do recovery programs the formal, the legal, the universal and hierarchical ways? How open are we and intellectually honest are we to accept that most of the time, what works for Junichi may not work for Juan and vice-versa?
- Do we always work on the basis of distrust and not trust? Like, to what extent do we believe the addicts when they say that they are 100 percent sober? On the other hand, how honest are they in stating so? How open are we to entrusting the addicts or partner communities with monetary resources so they can directly manage their own drug recovery program?

3. 2. the good news or message of hope :
- There is always a road not taken. And if we take that road, it can always bring us to a new place.
- Sometimes, in our attempt to modernize and universalize things, we forget

the basics. And in our attempt at sophistication, we tend to ignore going back to the basics. One of our community leaders, an inspiration in drug prevention and treatment work, has shared to me this reflection a couple of weeks ago and I want to share it with you... She told me

- .."*Jun, simple lang naman magpatino ng adik. Tratuhin mo lang sila na tao at kaibigan at di parang mabangis na hayop, o nakakatakot na kriminal, o walang silbi. At madali na lang natin silang ma-engganyong magpabago. At kalimitan, di natin kailangan ng malaking pondo para gawin yan. Binilhan ko lang kamakailan si Nato, isa sa mga tinutulungan nating adik na magbago ng mumurahing sapatos at alam mo, naiyak siya sa tuwa. Sinabi niya sa akin na ngayon na lang muli siya nakaramdam na matratong espesyal na tao"*

- (Jun, treating the addict is very simple. Just treat them as a human being and as a friend and not as dangerous animals, or fearful criminals, or useless persons and it would be smooth sailing for us to enable them to change. Most of the time, we don't need to have huge funds to do that. I just bought Nato, one of the addicts we are helping to recover, a cheap pair of shoes as a gift and you know, he cried some tears of joy. He told me that this is the first time in so many years that he felt treated again as a special person.)

- Indeed, a gesture of kindness and caring even in the simplest and cheapest way can change lives. Which bring us back to the universal reality that mother's know best. Our group is now thinking of pursuing and implementing in a more studied way what we have started years ago, of tapping the mothers as community-based recovery facilitators. Mothers are naturally -born nurturers, protectors, caregivers, counselors and psychics. Tapping their expertise can transform lives.

3. 3. The way to go from Manila to Okinawa to East Asia]

From my almost 20 years of experience in the drug abuse field as researcher, trainer, community worker and project manager, I believe that the only way and the only best way to go in drug recovery work in the Philippines through the community-based model of recovery.

And I believe that that was what the UNODC has come to realize, likewise. For example, they now have demonstration projects in Cambodia and Vietnam that employs community-based models of recovery. I just hope that these are community-managed or community owned also. Because if the project is not owned or managed by the community, I firmly believe that that project will not last long. It will not be sustainable.

We, in the Philippines, in our small little way and with a little help from our friends in Japan, such as APARI and DAPC, are initiating what we believe would work as an antidote to the ineptness of our government in failing to provide treatment to poor addicts. Of course, we are also in the process of traveling the road of "*mula sa tamang hinala tungo sa tamang tiwala*" (from distrusting trip to trusting trip). We need to develop a trusting relationship in this transnational project in order for it to create an impact. It is our sincere hope that we can make a difference, by working together, in implementing a recovery program in the Philippines that challenges :

- Drug policies to go beyond punitive justice to restorative/transformative justice
- Treatment centers to go beyond facility-based treatment...
- Treatment interventions to go beyond psychotherapy ...toward a more socially-transformative and holistic approach that includes livelihood, health services, etc. as part of the recovery program..and
- Peoples organizations and NGOs to go beyond treatment and recovery towards building drug resistant communities

As an post-script, I wish to quote our Vice-President Jejomar Binay who emphasized in a meeting among law enforcement officials in the Philippines that

- "....*The most important police work is not sufficient. We have to go beyond police work. We have to do more. We need a comprehensive drug program*" (Philippine Daily Inquirer, 30July2011, A7)

- Maraming salamat po!!!

[7] Current Situations and Agenda in Korea

Sung Nam Cho, M.D. (Bugog National Hospital)

1. History of Substance Abuse in Korea

Drug problems meant abuse of opium and heroin as from 1950's to 1960's in South Korea. The government enacted the Act on the Control of Narcotics in 1957. Methadone, barbiturates and marijuana prevailed there in 1970's, when public entertainers, for example singers, actors etc., used them, and then the Act on the Control of Addictive Drugs in 1970 and the Act on the Control of Cannabis in 1976 became in force. Methamphetamine, tranquilizers and inhalants spread out in 1980's, when the government would control it through the Act on the control of Psychotropic drugs and the Act on the control of Toxic Chemicals in 1980. Someone abused glue, butan gas, gasoline, thinner, etc., too.

From 1990's to 2000's,dextrometorphan, cocaine, heroin, LSD, YABA, MDMA and Nalbupine brought about new drug problems, which should be controlled by the Act on the Control of Narcotics and abused drugs in 2000 to unify Acts about narcotics, psychotropics and marijuana and to delete doctor's duty to report the substance abuser who was treated in his hospital to the police. It resulted to activate voluntary treatment.

2. Perspectives of Substance Abuse

Drug Offenders have arrested over 10, 000 per a year since 1999. South Korea was changed from a safe to a dangerous country concerning to substance abuse. Substance abusers have been increasing now.

The Influx of new abused drugs from other countries created so-called "Club Drugs", for example MDMA, GHB, Ketamine, YABA, LSD, etc..

(2) Expansion of The Abusers expand over various classes, for example businessman, housewives, farmers, adolescents etc.. Some medical personnels abuse propofol. Increasing international travels brought with smuggling of illegal substance, and internet makes illegal trade easier than yet. Now most abused drug is methamphetamine.

3. Three Types of Treatment by Government

The government can use following three types of treatment : (1) orders of Medical treatment and protection ; (2) orders of Medical treatment and custody

[table 1] Drug Offenders

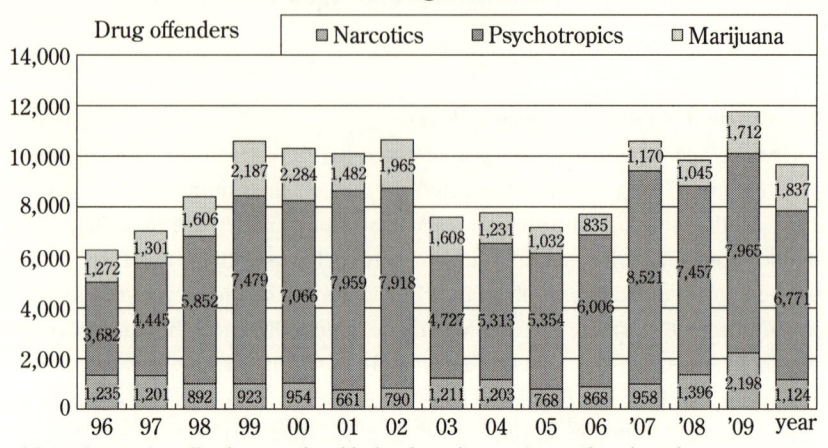

Drug offenders ■ Narcotics ■ Psychotropics ▫ Marijuana

year	96	97	98	99	00	01	02	03	04	05	06	'07	'08	'09
Marijuana	1,235	1,201	892	923	954	661	790	1,211	1,203	768	868	958	1,396	1,124
Psychotropics	3,682	4,445	5,852	7,479	7,066	7,959	7,918	4,727	5,313	5,354	6,006	8,521	7,457	6,771
Narcotics	1,272	1,301	1,606	2,187	2,284	1,482	1,965	1,608	1,231	1,032	835	1,170	1,045	1,837
Total														1,712 / 2,198 / 7,965

—Most of narcotics offenders are the elderly who culture opium rather than abuse
—Most of psychotropics are methamphetamine that is smuggled mainly from China
—There is a period of decreasing from '03 to '06 and that is due to clean-up of the Mafia in Korea and SARS (Severe Acute Respiratory Syndrome) in China

[table 2] Characteristics of drug offenders

Characteristics of drug offenders

	<19 years	20~29	30~39	40~49	50~59	>60 years	unknown	Total
Total	19	1013	3460 (32.4%)	3939 (36.9%)	1173	709	336	10649 (100%)
Opium	0	20	41	136	199	536 (60%)	26	958
Psychotropics	13	778	3080 (36%)	3431 (40%)	831	125	263	8521 (100%)
Marijuana	6	215	339 (29%)	372 (32%)	143	48	47	1170 (100%)

—Recidivism rate is over 40%
—37% of them have no employment
—87% of them are lower education level
—Male : Female =6 : 1

[table 3] Abusers who have treatment and protection

Abusers who have treatment and protection

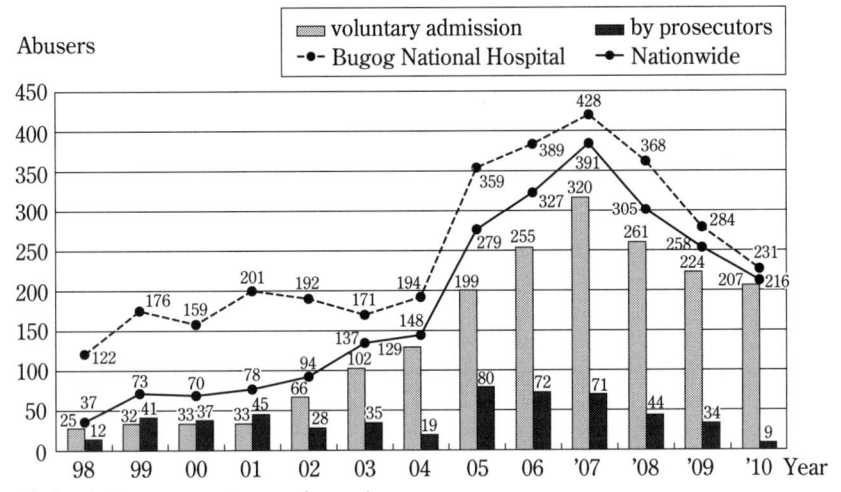

- voluntary admission
- by prosecutors
- Bugog National Hospital
- Nationwide

Year	98	99	00	01	02	03	04	05	06	'07	'08	'09	'10
voluntary admission	25	32	33	33	66	35	19	279	255	320	261	224	207
by prosecutors	12	41	37	45	28	102	129	80	72	71	44	34	9
Bugog National Hospital	37	73	70	78	94	137	148	199	327	391	305	258	216
Nationwide	122	176	159	201	192	171	194	359	389	428	368	284	231

- Referrals from prosecutors are decreasing, but voluntary admisions are increasing
- There are 11 hospital which can treat abusers but has no special ward
- Bugog National Hospital is only one hospital which has special substance abuse treatment wards (200 beds) in Korea
- Ninety percent of abusers having treatment are in Bugog National Hospital

[table 4] Methamphetamine abuse and Psychosis

Methamphetamine abuse and Psychosis

	Methamphetamine user		P value
	Without psychosis	With psychosis	
Age at first use (yr)	27.1	22.7	0.04
First faced social and occupational problems (yr)	33.4	29.1	0.044
Period of abstinence (mon)	21.9	16.9	0.736
Number of admission	0.6	1.8	0.01
Period of addiction (yr)	10.3	11.1	0.594
Total number of uses	1536.6	2527.0	0.023

Bugog National Hospital

[table 5] Most abusers have no treatment
Most abusers have no treatment
▶ Substance abusers : 300, 000~1, 000, 000 (?)
　▶ No epidemiological study about substance aduse
▶ Arrested drug offenders : 13, 000/yr
　▶ 70% of them are abusers
▶ Abusers in prison : about 3, 500 (7% of prisoners)
　▶ No facilities for treatment
▶ Abusers having treatment : 400~2, 000/yr
　▶ 0. 1% of total abusers
　▶ Order of Treatment and protection : 300~400/yr
　▶ Order of Treatment and custody : 50/yr
　▶ Order of Attending a lecture : 1000/yr
　　▶ For 40-50 hours
　▶ Private clinic : ? (1, 000 or less/yr)

and (3) orders to attend a lecture

(1) Order of Medical Treatment and Protection

Prosecutors can suspend his prosecution to order medical treatment and protection in the case of voluntary surrenders, or voluntary admission by oneself or family members. This period is one month or less for testing and two months or less for treatment. The government charges it for 12 hospitals in presence.

(2) Order of Medical treatment and custody

The Medical Treatment and Custody Act permits the discretion for courts to order medical treatment and custody to criminal offenders with substance abuse for over 3 months. National Custodial Hospitals, which run by the Ministry of Justice, should accept those who are criminal offenders with mental illness or substance abuse.

(3) Order to attend a lecture

Courts and Prosecutors could suspend execution of punishment or prosecution in order to attend a lecture about substance abuse between 40 and 50 hours with a monitoring of urine test. The order should mainly enhance their motivation to rehabilitation

4. Narcotics Anonymous (NA) in South Korea

In 1996 NA started once a month, every 2nd Tuesday. The Meeting with Abusers was held in the National Custodial Hospital. NA Korea was opened formally in 2004, Seoul. The meeting whose members consist of 50 addicts was held from 7. pm, every Tuesday. NA Korea registered as a member of NA World Service in 2005. The first Korea-Japan NA Convention was held in 2006, Busan. The theme is "It's OK". The 100 members from Korea and 50 ones from Japan took part in the convention.

The second convention whose theme is "Not Alone, All Together was held in 2007, Seoul. The 150 Korean NA and 40 Japanese NA member attended it. The third convention whose theme is "Just for Today"was held in 2010, Seoul. Five NAs activates in Seoul, Incheon, Yangju, Busan and Bugog National Hospital.

5. Conclusion

(1) Epidemiological study

We don't know how many abusers are there in Korea because of no epidemiological study about substance abuse in Korea, so Korean government have no idea about the severity of substance abuse and no actions about the treatment and rehabilitation of abusers.

(2) Drug Court

There is no conference or meeting about the treatment and rehabilitation of abusers between legal system and health system, so policies about treatment are limited. Prosecutors prefer arrest and imprisonment rather than treatment. Treatment order by court is necessary

(3) Treatment Programs in Prison

This year, treatment programs in prison were started by way of showing examples at 8 prisons with 2 hours lecture per a week for 3 months and this programs will be extended. Treatment facilities within prison are needed with systemic treatment programs like Therapeutic Community (TC).

(4) Narcotics Anonymous and half-way houses

In Korea there are only five NA and only one half-way house. Roles of NA must be extended and rehabilitation centers like DARC in Japan are needed.

(5) National Institute on Drug Addiction

We, staffs of National Center on Drug Abuse in Korea, have published following four articles in 2009:

(1) "Dose-dependent frontal hypometabolism on FDG-PET in metham-

phetamine abusers", *Journal of Psychiatric Research*, vol. 43 (2009) p. 1166-1170.

(2) "Reduced corpus callosum white matter microstructural integrity revealed by diffusion tensor eigenvalues in abstinent methamphetamine addicts", *NeuroToxicology*, vol. 30 (2009), p. 209-213.

(3) "Frequency of osteoporosis in 46 men with methamphetamine abuse hospitalized in a National Hospital", *Forensic Science International*, No. 188 (2009) p. 75-80.

(4) "Alterations in cortical activity of male methamphetamine abusers performing an empathy task : fMRI study", *Hum Psychopharmacol*, vol. 25 (1), p. 63-70.

[8] Mie DARC's Case : Discussing the Fundamental Value Behind Supporting and the Importance of Staff Education

Takehito Ichikawa (Director of NPO Mie DARC/Psychiatric Social Worker)

1. Mie DARC's Case
The Fundamental Value Behind Supporting and the Importance of Staff Education

DARC established a recovery-based community, where addicts who have had experience with addiction alike, could support each other. Mie DARC was the 17th DARC to be opened out of the current 70 facilities (June 2009) that are open today. It was established during the earlier era of DARC expansion.

(1) Mie DARC's Features

One of Mie DARC's leading features is the intimate relationship that it holds with the local community. Not only merely does it provide support to help addicts "quit using drugs", Mie DARC programs aim to help clients regain their dignity as members of the local community. With staff members who have attained various professional qualifications, such as becoming a psychiatric social worker (PSW), on stand-by, Mie DARC is capable of supporting clients with a professional approach and "personal recovery" approach, for most staff are recovering addicts themselves.

Also, through the interactions with people from the local area, clients get the chance to challenge their addiction, by working together towards recovery with these people. Building relationships with addicts and also non-addicts, we strive for recovery. In this way, Mie DARC can be considered as a new form of rehabilitation community, as it continues to grow today.

(2) Mie DARC's Basic Program Outline
A3 Step Recovery Program
[STEP ONE-Treatment]
This step can be divided into 2 phases:
Detox and Problem Analysis (Developing a Rehabilitation Plan).
[STEP TWO-Rehabilitation]

Step 2 can be divided into 2 major groups:
Social Skills Training and Addiction Care.
〔STEP THREE-Work/Returning to Society〕
 During this phase, clients are given the opportunity to either Go to School and Acquire Qualifications, Find a Job in the Local Area, Do Farm Work at Higashi-Kishu.

 Furthermore, Mie DARC pushes to support clients with multiple disorders (handicaps), and holds the support of clients that are developmentally-handicapped (intellectual disability, Asperger syndrome, ADHD) as a strong point. Based upon the nature of the disorders that are being dealt with, non-verbal communication tactics and visual based programs are provided to such clients.

(3) About Staff Education
 DARC itself is a non-professional rehabilitation organization. Although this trait is one of its valued characteristics, at Mie DARC, staff who have spent a certain amount of time at the facility as a client themselves, support the current clients while they devote themselves in strengthening their expertise through enrollment and studying at colleges (in which the majority are health and welfare related colleges or correspondence courses). By doing so, they become "socially-significant" people, and therefore their services do not only end up only as a "DARC based" inner-focused movement. Also, in support of these staff's efforts, Mie DARC acknowledges such college schoolings as a part of the facility's staff-training, setting an environment that encourages education.

2. Survey on Recoverd Counselors

 A survey taken in June 2011 shows that 14 Ibaragi DARC branch facilities and Ibaragi DARC itself hold 277 people.
 190 clients, 87 staff members of which 17 are directors

(1) DARC Staff and Their Clean Time
▶81.6% of the staff members became staff when they had 0-2 years of clean time
▶88.2% of the directors became directors when they had 2-7 years of clean time
 In response to the question "what was the main reason that you decided to become staff", (64.3%) staff/directors answered, "Because the director/staff at

that time advised me to do so". All 17 directors said that their previous job was as staff.

Furthermore:

Up until the year of~2000:

Directors had 0-2 years of clean time when they were assigned to open a new DARC.

From the years 2000~2009:

Directors had 3-6 years of clean time when they were assigned to open a new DARC.

After 2010~:

Directors have more than 7 years of clean time when they are assigned to opening a new DARC.

From this data, we can distinguish that the amount of clean time that the directors have when they are assigned to a new facility, has become longer in the recent years.

In concern to this (staff criteria), Mr. Iwai, the representative of Ibaragi DARC has stated as follows:

"After entering Ibaragi DARC as a client, one regains their health, character traits, and attains some clean time. As a result, if they have spent more then 5 years at Ibaragi DARC, we ask them once again what they would like to do, for their next step. If they reply that they want to become a director, our standard is that they must have over 3 years and under 5 years of clean time. However, before appointing them to a director position, we put them in charge of a new facility as a trial era. If they are capable of handling that for 2 years, we then come up with our decision."

(2) Being a Staff and One"s Own Recovery

"Has becoming an employee of DARC been beneficial for your recovery?"
To the question above:
▶94.2% of the staff and
▶100% of the directors replied that being a DARC employee supports their own recovery.

On the other hand, the
▶93% of the clients＜97% of the staff＜89% of directors
who said that their relationship with DARC has helped them in their personal recovery, did not mention any aspect on how it has helped them to feel like a

productive member of society. This indicates a connection that lacks between DARC facilities and society as a whole. I think it is fair to say that many of the DARC staffs don?t consider "DARC staff positions" as a "legitimate social status".

3. Couflict between Addict A and B

DARC was started by Tsuneo Kondo, with the intent to provide a communal area where addicts with the desire to stop using drugs could live together. One of DARC"s main features is that "addicts share their own experiences" with one another. This style of recovery was inspired from "self-help" groups. The objective is simple and solely focuses on "helping another addict who wants to stop using drugs". However, "addicts" can be categorized into 2 groups :

Addict A : a person who is trying to recover from drug use

Addict B : also a drug addict, but one who has a sufficient amount of clean time and is trying to support "Addict A"

Representatives from various locations said that "because the staff are addicts themselves we are capable of understanding our clients", "supporting the next generation of recovering addicts provides us a sense of self-value, thus we don"t relapse", and "feeling that our services are ?needed? allows us to forgive ourselves, and nurture self-esteem". From this we can say that "Addict B" has benefited from being a staff, for it has supported their personal recovery. So in actuality, although DARC"s ideal is in "helping Addict A", we can see that "Addict B" is the one who is actually being supported.

The fact that the country (Japan) and local governments were unwilling to support DARC when it first began its "one addict helping another" movement, (ironically) gave drug addicts, who are usually considered as "patients" in other facilities, a place where they could feel that they themselves were contributing service to another, thus had enabled DARC to become a "self-governed" entity. When addressing what DARC has achieved, the fact that one"s "recovery experience" is utilized as a potential service factor of DARC (for those that desired), should be recognized. In other words, as long as a person has "experience" in recovery they are able to be employed, regardless of their academic background or lack of qualifications. (Although social significance and evaluations by professionals are low) I believe that it is fair to say that, DARC itself was "a movement of independence for addicts" and that it exemplifies "empowerment".

The feeling of "being of assistance", the recognition of one's own contributions, is what supports the minds of DARC staff. But in reality, when one progresses in recovery, their identity as a "former drug user" becomes a distant past as well. For newcomers, senior staffs are not their closest peers. It would be ideal if there were an educational system that could train "peer staff" to evolve a step ahead (becoming "Addict B+"), but unfortunately in Japan there is no such system. Within the past 5 years or so, there have been multiple cases where "recovering addict counselors" with 10-15 years of clean time have relapsed or died.

In recovery from drug addiction, "Addict B" standing by the newcomer as a "peer supporter" is vital. However, with the main reason behind why most members chose to become a DARC staff being "because it was difficult to picture any other way of living", they have ended up with the dilemma of having their personal rehabilitation and "job" co-existing in the same boundaries. When engaging in this line of work, staffs understand that they have gained a "job", however they are usually unaware of the social significance that this "job" lacks.

Surely in a self-help group, "Addict B" stands out as the "role model of recovery". It would be wonderful if all "Addict A"s followed in the foot steps of an "Addict B", but to be a fully active supporter, relying only on "recovery experience" itself, has it's limits. If newcomers cannot relate to somebody's experience, it will be difficult for that person to guide them. Besides, not all clients will end up becoming "recovering addict counselors" of a facility. Hence, it is important for all "Addict B"s to secure their foundation of recovery, then pursue and present different career paths that hold social significance on top of that foundation. This message of "how to evolve" needs to be relayed to newcomers during their early stages of recovery.

It all boils down to balancing one's identity as a recovering drug addict and holding a new socially significant identity at the same time. This cannot be automatically gained just because one has made the transition for "Addict A" to "Addict B". It must be formulated newly from that point. This reality is no different for "recovering addict counselors". For DARC staffs as well, I believe that we need to create "a clear-cut identity for ourselves as supporters". Just being an "Addict B" is not enough anymore.

[9] DARC Faces Drug Addiction
Forgiveness and Tolerance Instead of Justice

Takeshi Kato (Director, NPO Kyoto DARC)

Introduction

DARC shares to support the peer who wants being off the drug every day. DARC is a drug addiction recovery institution and the origin of the name is abbreviation of initial of the Drug Addiction Rehabilitation Center. For recovery from drug addiction and live by sober needs the rehabilitation of the mind and body which suffered disease as well as the person who broke a foot undergoes the rehabilitation for curing a foot. So, there is case to need rehabilitation of the mind and body which suffered disease. Person using the drug loses to control feelings and the money and his or her life becomes difficult. DARC offers the place where they grow up and become useful member in the society and regain the way of sober life. DARC was founded by Mr. Tuneo Kondou together with his supporter 25 years ago.

Activity of DARC began as a person of the glue sniffer and person of the drug abuser of former Japanese yakuza were left at the door of DARC. Its activity has prevailed over 50 DARCs and related facilities until now.

Recovery support at Kyoto DARC is managed by 6 full time and 5 part time staff. In 2009, we recorded 3,400 accesses of addicts in number at our facility.

Kyoto DARC activities are as follows.
- Residence support.
- Care support.
- Practice of ordinary life.

Also, we are organizing in outside special lectures several times a year,
- Drug-free advice for prisoners: over 150 times per year
- Family mental program: 36 times per year.
- Various lectures: 44 times per year.

We have been carrying message that we do recovery. About problem of drug addiction, we wish another measure to medical service and welfare development not only measure biased to slogan of "Don't use drug".

It is important that we work on the program not at the isolated place but in the society. We guide to overcome various difficulties in daily life. But the rate of recovery has been noticed. More importantly, anyone can make use of DARC.

1. Recent drug problem in JAPAN

There seems to be various reasons for starting use of drug, not only curiosity.

Most of them use drug without being able to refuse the temptation from their friends or bad company. Once they start using drug, and they will find it hard to stop for seek its pleasure. Also, some people used stimulant for his job because lost distress and fatigue.

I suggest the following factors as the social phenomenon regarding drug contamination of young generation. They are getting public eyes by news and media.

The kind of various drugs has become diversified.

i.e. Thinner, Gas, Stimulant, Marijuana, Psychotropic, MDMA, Psychotropic, Other legal drugs etc…

The guilty conscience was lost by wrong knowledge. They can easily get a lot of information through internet and even purchase drugs totally unnoticed by anyone.

2. The policy for drug addiction in Japanese government

International diagnostic criteria exist as ICD-10 (WHO), DSM-IV (USA).

Japanese government authorized drug addiction as mental patient in 1999 by law revision. Drug addiction was possible to get medical care and welfare by this revision.

3. Tendency of users at DARC

Beginning, almost of users who had lost human relations asked for help to DARC. They had been divorced, and had been prisoner or patient of mental hospital.

However, recently users who had not lost all of them have increased. Also, users who have various troubles come to DARC-Autistic spectrum disorder included Asperger syndrome, Attention Deficit Hyperactivity Disorder (ADHD), Gamble addiction, Co-dependency -

We aim to create the environment where addicts participate our program while working like other people in a society. Policies of Japanese government are not enough. We expect further progress in future.

4. Effect of Meeting

We need meeting for a variety of reasons. Always we attend meetings to share our experience. Meeting offer us identification with where we've been and where we can go - identification we can't do without and can't get anywhere else. That keeps us coming back.

At the meeting, we sit in a circle, a newcomer in center.

A facilitator present a theme of the day along which an appointed person takes the lead and talk his/ her own story. No discussion or debate. All they have to do is to listen to other's talking and share the experience. In the end, hopefully, they are encouraged and regain hope to start their life again. Meeting is the meaningful in this sense.

5. Tackle for cravings

Our slogan is 'Just for today' which means 'let us be free from drugs just for today'. This is easier and accessible task compared with 'Never more'.

Also, in order to control cravings, we suggest them to find the way to enjoy life without help from drugs. It is important to understand their own external triggers (a person, place, time, situation etc.) as well as internal triggers (mood, emotion, way of thinking etc.), which greatly helps to control cravings. Longer the clean time, less disturbance from the absence of drugs. Our recovery needs time and new experience, and we find how to enjoy time. And gradually the goal is approaching.

6. Sponsorship and Spirituality

Sponsorship does not mean financial support in this context. Those who have been practicing the program for a long time will act as a mentor for newcomers. By doing this, they can develop self-fulfillment feelings providing positive influence for both who help and is helped. I will reflect on the spiritual awakenings I have experienced. The simple beauty of a flower may remind us that there is a Power greater than ourselves at work around us.

7. Relationship with family

It is important for the addicts to be released from all the negative feelings i. e. dissatisfied, bitterness, intolerance, loneliness etc. to build up a new relationship with their families assisted by sincerity, thankfulness, consideration and love.

Once, my mother told me "You are not my child. I am not your mother." When I achieved of 3 years soberer and married, I went to meet to say hello to mother.

But she refused me. She said to go back to home, closing the door of the entrance. When I kept clean time in DARC for 10 years, she let me come in her home.

Conclusion

DARC is not almighty.

External support from family, friends, paramedical, welfare, lawyer and all other local corporation and resources are indispensable.

We have to cope with drug addiction hand in hand with all the related parties sharing information and activities horizontally not vertically in order to provide better environment for those who are striving for getting rid of drugs and start a new life.

[10] Decriminalization and Depenalization of Drug Abuse and Possession in Germany

Sangyun Kim (Ryukoku University, Kyoto)

It is possible not to prosecute possessors of "a few" illegal drugs in German Law. This thought and method is extremely different from harsh-punishment in Japan, and also from drug courts in the U.S.A.. Prosecutor makes suit at once in drug courts system, so-called "post-trial diversion" on one hand, but he doesn't prosecute by courts on the other hand, so-called "pre-trial diversion".

It is the question at issue in German Supreme Court, whether is marijuana an illegal drug or not, and what means "a few" possession. Court decided that the control of marijuana by criminal law was constitutional. It is a new question what and how we can define the soft and hard drug since then in Europe.

The definition differs state by state because Germany is a federal state. Concerning to marijuana one state punishes more than 15 grams, another state don't punish up to 30 grams. The government in city Hanover defines 6 grams as "a few" amount, therefore if the suspected who has less than 6 grams marijuana can't be prosecuted and furthermore the prosecutor has discretion to make suit or not up to 15 grams. No possessor of less than 1 gram heroin, cocain and amphetamine shouldn't be punished according to a state's guideline.

If a client relapses during the treatment process, it is difficult whether supporters should report to the police or not. The clear definition of crimes makes them ease to decide this question. The definition of "a few" amount is convenient to the relapsed. All states have similar propositions for those who possess a few amount of drugs. Practically they couldn't be prosecuted by any courts.

When we visited to Frankfurt two years ago, one office supported some hard junkies to offer a appropriate amount of heroin and to support addicts under the health insurance. German policies base on the different thought and methods on drug problems. The city enforces another project by which clients are proposed a needle for injection of heroin which they bought from an illegal trader. The official can't inject them, because the injection is illegal. The project functions as an entrance to treatment and to prevent spread of HIV. The shelter is called "health room" where clients can inject themselves free. Recently officials could give heroin under health insurance. Someone evaluate this policy positive, but others do negative. This is a new way in any case.

A participant supported the decriminalization-policy. If those who will still take part in rehabilitation programs relapse in Japan, they have to return to jails because of crime and loose chances to be supported by medical or welfare authorities. Any programs can't function effectively enough. The families who find out the relapsed can't report any official, because these should be arrested and thrown in jails. Those refrain from forcing their families to go to prisons, and then unavoidably remain spectators.

【Q1】 From the point of "harm reduction" view which reduces pains and harms on health as many as possible, addicts should be proposed treatment programs and supported to rehabilitation as fast as possible.

【Q2】 There was a "health room", where addicts ware given not only needles but also heroin, in Bonn 10 years ago in order to prevent being suffered from HIV. In that time such experiments had been enforced in eight cities but were finished in 2007. The Act to give substances to hard addicts was enacted in 2008, because the outcomes ware evaluated positive. After the experimental phase, the government enforces the plans. Therefore giving heroin to addicts under due process becomes lawful.

[11] Drug Addiction for a Psychiatric Social Worker

Natsue Sainen (psychiatric social worker)

As a Psychiatric social worker I involved with recovery support from addiction at the mental hospital in provincial city of the Hokuriku region until the end of 2010. Currently, I am in charge of guidance for withdrawal from drug addiction as a treatment counselor (for drug addiction) at the two prisons in the Hokuriku region.

In the mental hospital, mainly I had charge of supporting recovery from alcoholism. During the approach to alcoholics, I had been facing "Denial against addiction" such as "I spend my own money to drink my favorite sake. What's wrong with that?", "I'm not annoying anyone.", "Drinking is not crime", "Therefore, I never stop drinking". By contrast, in the guidance for withdrawal from drug addiction in prisons, many participants declare with straight back "I give up using methamphetamine because it is crime", "I'm going to strengthen my willpower, to change my mind and do my best.". Maybe you think it is good that they are full of motivation, but it is not as it seems.

Alcoholics say "No problem since drinking is legal", drug dependents say "I will stop since drug is illegal". "To drink or not to drink", "To use drug or not to use", "legal or illegal", there is no significant difference in the sense that both of them are caught up in those conflicting axes.

Except for specialized facilities for addiction, professionals in many psychiatric care institutions still consider that not medical system but judiciary system must deal with dependence of illegal drugs and they display negative attitude to treat.

The goal of treatment and programs for alcoholism are often placed in "abstinence". Similarly, the goal of the program in prisons is placed on "Stop abusing".

In fact, those who involved with helping recovery are also caught in conflicting idea such as "legal or illegal", "judicial proceedings or medical treatment", "Drink or not", "Use or not". I doubt whether recovery could be possible in this conflict.

Recovery from addiction is compared to a never-ending marathon. To admit being powerless against dependency, to live with addiction as chronic disease, to seek a new way of life, to forgive yourself, to recognized your own worth like "You are great the way you are".

Recovery is such long journey to explore the true picture of Himself / Herself, I understand. Needless to say, Neither temporary approach in hospitals, prisons and supporting facilities nor to wander in the conflict could realize those process.

The biggest stage in recovery from addiction is this community where they and we live. "Do they live the way they are?", "We live the way we are?".

I am afraid if we lose this perspective in the midst of huge rapid stream of systems and policies. Through involvement with drug-dependent people, I once again stood at the origin of social worker.

〔12〕 **Dependency and Gender**

Kaeko Nomura (Kyoto Tachibana University)

I have studied the self-help group of eating disorders from a sociological viewpoint for the past 10 years. With this experience, I will make some comments on dependency problems and gender differences in this report.

Suppose that eating disorders (that is, repeated binge-eating, vomiting, refusal to eat) are a symptom of dependency or addiction. We could learn a lot from drug addiction. In the medical treatment of eating disorders, doctors often advise their patients to stop binge-eating immediately. However, this kind of approach may not work effectively, based on the experience of patients with eating disorders. This is because patients who stopped binge-eating as a result of this program may tend to look for alternate objects such as sexual partners, children, alcohols as long as they failed to remove the roots of addiction completely.

My question is what is the "true" recovery from eating disorders. Based on the results of my sociological research, the true recovery is the whole process in which persons with eating disorders interact with others and identify themselves as who they are. In this sense, the persons who are aware of their own problematic symptoms and are seriously trying to get rid of them could be regarded as practitioners of "the recovery process". Also, eating disorders could be regarded not as "illness concerning food" but as "a mean of pursuing a way of life." In this sense, we may consider a way of living together with eating disorders as one of options.

Most participants in self-help groups of eating disorders whom I have met are women (previous studies show that more than 90% are women). On the other hand, most participants in self-help groups of drug users (as long as I know) are men. Relevant studies classify drug addiction as "men's illness", just same as alcoholism. Treatment programs and self-help groups of eating disorders seem to be led and organized by women while those of drug users seem to be led and organized by men. While some of single sex-dominated groups have been successful, some of them have not. Female participants in male-dominated groups (self-help groups of drug users) or male participants in female-dominated groups (self-help groups of eating disorders) are examples of the latter. It is said that women with dependency problems tend to be sexually abused as children and often suffer from psychological conflict such as regret or guilt. Different complex situations may arise if the number of female (male) participants increases in male-dominated (female-dominated) groups. That is why I suggest that self-help groups of drug users need to make full use of experience and accumulated knowledge of self-help groups of eating disorders, or vice versa. In the case of women with dependency problems, it is said that "just paying attention to their life would be a great help for them" or that getting to express their own thoughts and feelings is regarded as an "element of recovering process."

It's important to note that drug addict women are "minorities" even among women with dependency problems. That is, they tend to be downgraded by women with other dependency problems. "We can understand eating disorders or alcoholism to a certain extent. But this is not the case of illegal drug." "Don't confuse people with eating disorders with drug addicts." We see a kind of competition among "minority" women there.

For the treatment of people with dependency problems, a universal program as well as individual treatment is required. I believe that sociological approach that employ both micro- and macro-level analysis would contribute to the development of treatment programs and group orientation.

［矯正施設参観記］

2011年度「矯正・保護課程」
共同研究・施設参観報告

加 藤 博 史（矯正・保護総合センター長）

＝もくじ＝
全体報告（加藤博史）
1　福井刑務所参観記（青木恒弘）
2　更生保護法人「福井福田会」参観記（宮内利正）
3　更生保護法人「福井福田会」参観記（井上見淳）
4　湖南学院訪問記（板垣嗣廣）
5　金沢刑務所参観記（畠山晃朗）
6　富山刑務所（池田静）

はじめに——希望と自尊心の芽生えへの支援——

　当総合センターの2011年度の矯正・保護施設参観研究は、福井刑務所、更生保護施設福井福田会、金沢刑務所、少年院湖南学院、富山刑務所において実施された。各施設の所長、施設長、院長はじめ職員の方々には懇切にご指導をいただいた。ここに改めて厚く御礼申し上げる。参観研究内容の詳細は各担当者に譲り、ここでは筆者の印象に深く残り、啓発を受けたことを記すことで、感謝の意に代えさせて戴きたい。

　第1点は各施設で就労支援に精力的に取り組まれていることに関して取り上げる。福井刑務所では、溶接・配管・電気通信設備の資格のほか、造園技能士、内装業務に携わるカラーコーディネーター・福祉住環境コーディネーターの資格が取れるよう支援を行っていた。また、需要が著しいホームヘルパーに関しても四つの福祉施設で実習させてもらっているとのことであった。

　金沢刑務所では、入所時に就労支援指導の希望の有無を聴き、専任の社会福祉士が中心になってハローワークに相談するなど、出所後の生活設計について支援を行

っている。協力事業主も多く登録され、直接社長と交渉して就職あっせんを進めるケースもあるとのことである。福井福田会は長い歴史を誇り、建設業界などに独自のパイプをもっていた。富山刑務所も種々の働きかけを行っていた。

　孟子（梁恵王下）に、「恒産なくして恒心あり。」「民に恒産なければ因りて恒心無からん。」とある。収入が不安定であっても心は常に安定したものでなければならない。しかし、民衆は収入が不安定であると心も不安定となるものである、との意味とされる。もとよりわたしたちは君子ではなく、生活基盤が安定しないと心は限りなく不安定となり、希望を失い、自暴自棄にさえ陥るかもしれない。まして、受刑者たちは‘前科’というハンディを負っている。のみならず多くの受刑者は、後に述べるように、メンタルなハンディと生育歴のハンディを複合された形で負っている。だからこそ、恒産、より安定した生活基盤が必要なのではなかろうか。

　安定した生活基盤は、「職業」だけの支援ではもたらされない。狭くとも清潔で採光と通風の良い、プライバシーが守られた「住宅」と、将来計画が立てられる安定した「収入」と、愚痴を聞いてもらえ心配してくれ話を聞いてあげられる「仲間」と、いざとなった時に信頼できる「相談相手」がトータルに保障されることが、ほんとうの生活基盤だといえよう。

　特に所属する「仲間」は重要である。受刑者は、暴力団や暴走族などのような「支配・威圧―服従・へつらい」関係の仲間や、「傷をなめあう共依存」関係の仲間、「外部を敵視する」関係の仲間など、問題のある「仲間」に所属していることが少なくない。このような仲間から脱し、自分の弱さや無力を認めあえる仲間、葛藤から逃避しない仲間、寛容な仲間、人格を高めあえる仲間に加わる支援が目的的に取り組まれるべきであろう。

　そして、このような仲間は、常に風通しがよく外部に開かれている。つまり、複属的で選択可能である。趣味のサークル、市民活動のNPO、勉強会、ゆきつけの喫茶店グループ、信仰の仲間など、複数の所属をもっていることが生活の基盤を安定させる。「エコマップ」をもちいると、社会での根の張り様が可視化されてアセスメントすることができる。矯正・保護施設で「エコマップ」の導入をぜひ検討してもらいたい。地域で暮らすとは、地域社会の人間関係のなかに根を張っていくことであり、多様で開かれた所属集団をどれだけもてるかが地域定着の進展度を測る指標となると考えられる。

　今後の就労支援活動は、退所後の生活像を本人とトータルに描きつつ見通しをもって進められていく必要がある。そうなると、いよいよ、出所後に地域で支える機関との連携が重要になる。矯正・保護施設の地域生活支援のコーディネーターが、

地域の個々の社会機関の支援員と連携するのではなく、地域における生活支援コーディネーターと連携していかねばならない。今後そのような連携のモデルケースを積み上げていくことが求められているのではなかろうか。

　ちなみに、セルフ・ヘルプ・グループ活動として、DARCの関わりは極めて有効である。上から目線の「指導」ではなく、対等な目線の「仲間」だからである。福井刑務所には京都DARCが、富山刑務所には富山DARCが関わっていた。ただし、DARCが矯正の指導業務の一環に取り込まれていくと、そのセルフ・ヘルプ・グループとしての意義を失ってしまう。DARCは独立性を十分主張し、矯正施設との緊張関係を維持しつつ連携をしていってもらいたいものである。

　第2点は、帰住先の確保に関して取り上げる。矯正施設を退所後、帰る場所がないものが増えている。かつて60％ちかくあった帰る場所のある人たちは、平成20年には半数以下に落ち込んだ。富山刑務所では60％が帰る場所がないとのことである。つまり、引き受け手がないのである。そのために、仮釈放ができず満期の刑期を務めるものが増えた。彼ら帰る場所がないものにとっては、刑務所のほうが温かい世界に感じられる。そのために軽微な無銭飲食などをして刑務所に戻ってくる事例が後を絶たない。

　福井福田会では、過去五年間の累計で50歳以上が65％を占めており高齢化が進んでいる。当然、親は老齢化しており、きょうだいは疎遠となっていく。就職の際にも身元保証してくれるものがいない。そのため保護観察所を通して「身元保証制度」を利用している。この制度は全国的なものであり、4万円の保険料で「NPO法人全国更生保護就労支援会」が雇用主などに身元を保証するというものであり、損害を与えてしまった場合に保険金が出るので、雇用主が安心できるというものである。こういった制度の実績も踏まえて、さらに総合的で実質的な身元引受のシステムを社会的に整えていくことが望まれる。少し突飛ではあるが、「里親制度」なども参考にできるのではなかろうか。

　第3点は、メンタルなハンディに関して取り上げる。金沢刑務所では、受刑者の知能指数の平均は70〜80だとのことである。生育環境との相乗作用もあって、中卒が約半数を占めており、高校中退（実質的中卒）を含めると77％に及ぶ。全国統計では知能指数90未満のものが75％となっている。知的障碍者として認定されるのは知能指数が70未満である。ただし、70以下90未満の人たちは、障碍の境界領域とされ、学業の遅れが目立つ人たちである。いきおい、学校で虐められたり職場で馬鹿にされ軽視されたりして自尊感情を低め傷つけられた人たちと考えられる。この人たちが自尊心を回復していく働きかけが体系的に整備されねばならない。

精神障碍についても同様である。近年認識が高まったパーソナリティ障碍やアスペルガー症候群については、正しい診断が行われ、それに応じた適切な働きかけが整備されていかねばならない。各矯正施設では、「怠業」の増加が報告された。金沢刑務所では「集団生活が嫌で」、富山刑務所では「他人と関わりたくなくて」との理由で「単独室希望」のため、「怠業」するとのことである。背景にメンタルな問題があると推測される。有効な対策は十分取られていないと見受けられた。

　この点参考になるのは湖南学院の取り組みである。ここに入院する少年たちの多くは、親に暴力をふるわれたり家庭が崩壊して放置されたりした生育歴をもつ。そのために内面的世界（リフレクティヴ・セルフ）が十分育っていない。湖南学院では少年たちにピカソのような絵で自由に自己内面を表現させることで、またその表現過程を評価してあげることによって、内面世界を育み自尊心の回復を促している。

　ここで肝要なのは「できるできない」という世界での自尊心の向上ではないということである。そのような業績能力に伴う自尊心は正しくは自慢心というにふさわしい。自分の存在丸ごとをなにか「できなくても」信頼してくれ大切に思ってくれる存在があって初めて、「自分が生きていることはそれだけで素晴らしいことなのだな」と自己を信頼することができる。そして初めて自己存在への自尊心が回復できる。その前提になるのは内面世界の育みである。

　湖南学院ではこのほか、「メダカを育てる」試みや、「意見発表会」が行われていた。人はケアすることを通して深くケアされる。また、自分の生きてもらってきた関係の恵み（痛み）を語ることによって、人生体験を受容することができる。前者は、フランク・リースマンによって「ヘルパーセラピー原則」として打ちたてられ、後者は「ナラティヴ・アプローチ」として定式化されている。このような少年院の実績から刑務所も学ぶべき点があるのではなかろうか。成人には精神的可塑性がないと断定するのは、非科学的との誹りを免れない。

　なお、福井福田会では、1913年、本願寺派真宗僧侶が中心となり、福井西別院を拠点として県内を14～15支部に分け、支部ごとに僧侶を支部委員として任命して更生保護活動を展開した。わが国の保護司制度の濫觴である。更生保護分野への市民参加が求められようとしている今日、保護司は、市民と矯正・保護機関をつなぐ媒介役として益々重要な役割を期待されている。先駆者の熱情と使命感に学び続けたいものである。

　矯正・保護施設は今、変革の渦中にある。主題は非行・犯罪を行ったもののリハビリテーショにあり、そのためには、社会保障と市民連帯が重要であることを、改めて自覚させられる参観研究であった。以上のべた生活の再生と非行犯罪予防の方

法論とシステムの開発は、矯正・保護の分野だけでなく、社会学、心理学、精神医学、社会福祉学との学際的なアプローチによって実現されていく。当センターは、現場に根ざした総合的な研究をさらに進め、教えをいただいた各矯正・保護施設にお返しをしていきたいと考えている。

1 福井刑務所参観記

青 木 恒 弘

　平成23年8月24日（水）の午前10時、本年度の「共同研究出張」一行12名は、北陸3県の矯正・保護施設を順に参観するために、ここ福井駅の改札口に集合した。昨年の夏も極めて暑い日々を送ったが、今年もそれを上回るかと思うほどの烈暑の最中であった。わたしたちは、事務局があらかじめ手配してくれていた3台のタクシーに分乗して、最初の訪問先である福井刑務所に向かった。
　車は、走り出してすぐに右折したあと、南方向に、つまり、JRの線路に平行した道を走り、やや広めの川に架かった橋を渡った。このあたりは平成16年夏の豪雨により大水害を受けたところであると、運転手氏が話してくれた。説明によると、当時福井駅周辺は高架工事を行なっていたために、この川（足羽川）には、工事用の橋脚が多く立っていたようで、そのために水流がせき止められて、より大きな水害をもたらしたらしい。車は、橋を渡ってすぐに左折して走るかと思う間もなく施設に到着した。所要時間は15分弱であった。昨夏訪れた松江刑務所は松江駅からほど近い場所にあると記したが、ここ福井刑務所も同様であり、あるいはもっと近いように思われた。昨今、多くの施設が市街地から遠く離れた地域への移転を余儀なくされているときに、市街地にあるのは貴重と言えるかもしれない。
　表門を入った正面に、2階建ての庁舎が立ち、庁舎の東側に外塀で囲まれた戒護区域が広がる。
　会議室に招き入れられ、すぐにパワーポイントを用いての説明が柴田房雄所長により開始された。施設の面積は約4万3千m²と結構広く、敷地の北側は足羽川の河川敷に連なるとのことである。
　説明の冒頭には、施設の沿革が語られることが多いが、ここ福井刑務所においての重要なポイントのひとつは、明治時代に福井監獄署として設置されたのが、大正時代に金沢刑務所所管の支所と位置づけられたこと、もうひとつは昭和23年6月に発生した福井地震によって建物が全壊に至ったことであろう。
　この地震はマグニチュード7.1という巨大なもので、関東大震災、阪神淡路大震災、それに、このたびの東日本大震災と並ぶ規模のものとされている。福井市の震度は6であったが、遠く、京都市や甲府市においても震度4の揺れを観測したほか、

関東から九州までの広範囲に影響を及ぼした地震であった。

　説明によると、地震当日の被収容者数は217名（未決57・既決160）に人的被害はなく、全員河川敷に誘導できたが、戒護の間隙を縫って59名（未決43・既決16）が逃走した。しかし、そのうち、21名が自主的に帰所しているのはさいわいなことであった。

　その後、昭和25年に、本所として独立して福井刑務所となりＡ級受刑者を収容する施設と指定された。また、昭和48年から全体改築を開始し、同62年に完成を見るに至っている。

　職員定員は8月1日現在121名で、平均年齢は44.5歳。うち、40歳以上は27名いるが、30歳台が15名もいて、処遇力の低下が危惧されるとのことである。このため、職員研修を昨年は4回実施したが、本年度は月に1回の割合で実施している。

　収容状況では、この日の開室人員は302名（未決31・既決271）で収容率は63.4％。本年4月には340名の在所であったが急減している。これまでの収容の最高は平成18年の580名である。

　罪名別では、覚せい剤が13％、窃盗が30％、強盗が10％であるが、全体の58％を占める財産犯を、窃盗事犯者のＡグループと、強盗事犯と詐欺事犯とを合わせたＢグループの2群に分けて指導を行なっている。

　刑期の平均は3年1月、最長は9年である。従来8年以上とされていたＬ級が10年以上と規定の変更がなされたために、9年の刑期の者も在所することになっている。2入や3入の者が少しいるが、これは準初犯の者たちである。また、累犯者が若干いるが、これは移送待の者である。

　被収容者の平均年齢は44.1歳で、最高は77歳（昨年は79歳）。60歳以上は49名（全被収容者の15％）いるが、そのうちで65歳以上の者は11名（全被収容者の4％）とのことで、これらは養護工場で対応している。

　反則事犯としては、本年4月以降けんかが2件あったのみで、作業拒否事犯は1件も発生していない。これは過剰収容の終息と関連していると考えるべきであろうし、6割強という収容率の低さのためでもあろう。不服申立を行なう者が若干いるとのことであるが、これはすべて累犯の未決者である。

　つぎに処遇面であるが、収容率60％の影響は大きく、過剰収容時に常態的に行なっていた2名個室は全くないし、また、共同室に入れていた二段ベッドも撤去している。テレビは自由チャンネルにしているし、給食面では、管理栄養士を配置して献立面に配慮するなど生活条件の改善は著しい。なお菜代指定額は402円とのことであった。

職業訓練は、溶接、電気通信、内装施工、農業園芸、ホームヘルパー、配管の6種を実施している。現在訓練生は80名定員のところに27名（33.8％）とのことであるが、昨年21年度は52名（69.3％）いたので、これに比べるとかなり少なくなっている。これは、PFI施設への移送促進が行なわれていることとの兼ね合いであると考えられる。やはり知的レベルが高く受講意欲の高い者ほど、PFI施設への移送適格者になりやすいからであろう。
　施設では、訓練生減少の対策として、本年度後期の溶接科訓練に、近隣の岐阜刑、富山刑などB級施設からの受け入れを検討しているとのことである。これは、現在B級施設に在所している者であっても、今後の生活について真摯に考えていて、かつ受講意欲の高い者に、訓練の機会を付与しようというものであって、ややもすれば硬直的になりやすい分類処遇に風穴を与えようとするもので、その成果を注目したい。
　また、内装施工科は、一昨年までは畳工を養成するだけの半年間コースとして運用されていたが、これを1年間に訓練期間を拡大し、社会的に需要の高いクロス加工をもあわせて指導する場とするようになった。
　この一連の職業訓練種目の説明の中で興味深い話題をうかがった。それは、これらの職業訓練種目のひとつである農業園芸科の実地訓練を、外部通勤作業、つまり塀の外での作業として行なったというものである。
　具体的に言うと、最寄りの福井少年鑑別所構内の樹木の剪定作業に取り組んだということである。この作業が訓練生の手によって、2日間に渡ってなされたと言う。刑務所と少年鑑別所とは直線距離で約4km、車で20分くらい離れている。
　参加した訓練生は5名。担当職員の戒護はもとより、少年鑑別所の職員や指導に当たる講師も参加しての訓練であったとのことであるが、発注者である少年鑑別所の要望にどのように対応するかとか、一般の車両や歩行者が通行している状況の中で安全対策をも考慮しながら、かつ限られた時間の中で効率よく作業を進めるための段取りなど、訓練生は、彼らなりに前向きに対処したらしい。
　この処遇はこれまでの刑務所事情からすれば、まさに瞠目ものと言えようし、訓練生に対して一定の効果を与えたものと思われる。
　こういった構外作業は、受刑者の自立心と責任感の涵養を図り、円滑な社会復帰を促すための最良の方策であることを再認識して、今後は、より積極的な運用を行なっていくべきことと思われる。
　作業関係の話題としてもうひとつ。本年6月に、社会貢献作業の実施という通達が発せられたとのことである。これまでは、刑務作業と言えば、生産作業、職業訓

練、自営作業の3種類であったが、これに第4の作業形態が加わったことになる。従来、釈放前の受刑者によって、公園清掃などの活動を実施していたが、これを一般工場就業者に拡大し、ボランティア活動として、社会に貢献しているという意識を持たせようとするもので、改善更生の意欲を強めて行こうとするものと位置づけられる。

　施設では、この方向で検討を重ね、市役所の公園管理課に相談して、近在の公園の清掃作業に従事させることとした。市当局のアドバイスのもと、周辺の自治会や幼稚園などと協議を続け、その趣旨に了承をいただき、本年の7月に1回と8月に2回除草作業を実施することにまでこぎつけたと言う。今後この活動がどのように展開していくことになるか楽しみである。注目したい。

　当施設の矯正展は毎年9月に実施している。昨年度は335万円の計画案のところ、422万円（102.2％）を達成したとのことである。開催は1日のみであったが、4,336名の参加があり盛況であったらしい。本年は9月25日の実施の予定である。

　話題をもうひとつ。ホームヘルパー科の訓練には現在2名の者が在籍していて、所内での講習のほか、開放実習として市内の社会福祉施設で実地研修を受けているとのことであるが、この2名の訓練生に、先日名古屋刑務所の医療センターに移送した末期ガンの患者を病棟において介助させていたとのことである。その患者は、人工肛門を装着していたそうであるから、訓練生は、身体の清拭や病室の清掃に従事するなど、まさに実地の訓練を行なっていたらしい。

　教育関係に目を転じると、一般改善指導と位置づけて工場担当による訓話を行なっている。また、高齢受刑者教育としては、所内の空地に小さな畑をつくり、野菜類の栽培をさせている。この7月には、じゃがいもダンボール5箱分の収穫をしている。

　医務関係では、職員配置として、内科医師1名、正看護師1名、准看護師2名が常勤している。また、歯科医師が週1回来庁されるほか、精神科医師、これは福井病院の院長であるが、月1回来庁されて診察をいただいている。また、臨床心理士が週1回来庁してカウンセリングに当たっていただいている。このようにサポート体制がしっかりしているので、医療面での問題は生じていない。

　仮釈放率は、このところ7割前後で推移しているとのことであった。また、昨年22年度の釈放時の引受人は、親族が53％、更生保護施設が43％、知人・雇主が3％であった。

　その後、構内の見学に移った。庁舎区域の北側には拘置区がある。ここには、多くの施設に見られるのと同様の扇形をした未決被収容者のための運動場があった。

しかし、ほかの施設の場合、監視台は、一段高い位置にあることが多いが、ここでは同一平面に置かれているのが興味深かった。
　拘置区の東側は作業場や居室棟のある区域である。
　その中で、ひとつ興味をそそる設備を見せていただいた。それは、新様式とも言うべき保護室である。従来の様式に比べて特徴的であったのは、天井が高いことであろうか、それから、窓を大きく採っているために部屋全体が明るいことがあげられる。また、室内に入ってみて分かったことだが壁面に弾力がある。いわゆる名古屋事件の発端ともなった旧来の保護室とは、かなり印象の異なる居室であった。そして、もうひとつ、忘れてならないのは、窓から見える壁面に時計が掲げてあったことである。これは、ある意味で、極めて画期的なことであると思われる。
　刑務所を初めとする拘禁施設では、掛け時計はもとより、腕時計、目覚まし時計など、時刻を表示する設備はこれまで一切置かれていなかった。時刻は、時報やベルの音等によりもたらされるものであって、受刑者みずから見定めるものではなかったのである。それは、被収容者が、一定の時刻にことを起こすのを未然に防止するという、保安上の観点から定められたと聞き及んでいる。
　それが、ここでは、みごとに逆転している。この新式保護室に収容された受刑者は、この時計に対して、どのような視線を向けるであろうか。彼らに一度尋ねてみたいような思いがした。
　もう一か所見せていただいたのが、「静穏室」という名称の居室である。これは、保護室を一段と小さくしたようなところで、保護室にまで収容する必要のない者を入れる居室として機能しているとのことであった。
　つぎに居室棟を見せていただいた。ここには、いわゆる「ふたり独居」は見当たらなかったし、共同室でのベッドの利用もなかった。これは、まさしく収容率の格段の低下のたまものであろう。過剰収容のころは、個室に二段ベッドを置いていたし、6名定員の共同室に8名が生活した。就寝時には、定員を超える2名がベッドに寝た。そこへ、さらに1名。6名定員の部屋に9名が入った場合、最後の1名はどの位置で就寝したであろうか。この駄文を読んでいただいている方は、一度考えてみてほしい。しかし、その状況も今はない。
　収容率の低下は、受刑者の生活レベルを確実に安定させている。これは、極めて喜ばしいことであるが、しかしながら、被収容者の生活レベルが、収容率の変動によって左右されるものであってはならないと思う。あの暑熱の中の「ふたり独居」など定員過剰の居室の状況は再現させてはならないと強く願うものである。

2 更生保護法人「福井福田会」参観記

宮 内 利 正

1 はじめに

　平成23年度の矯正・保護課程の「共同研究出張」で更生保護法人福井福田会を参観させていただく機会を得た。更生保護の現役時代からかなりの更生保護施設を見てきたものの、まだ見ぬ施設で、創設が明治からの古い伝統のある施設と聞いていたので、行く道中から何となくわくわくしていた。
　我々一行が午後2時に到着すると、玄関先には職員の皆さまが待っておられ、心温まる歓迎を受けた。挨拶を交わしながら玄関を上がると記念母子像が待っていた。「愛〜ほころびの　ころもに　つつむ　母の愛」梅林玄十（哲朗）氏の彫刻である。創立百周年記念事業で建立された由。母子像を見ながら奥の会議室に集合し、早速、施設概要の説明を受けることとなった。
　藤井建夫理事長から歓迎の挨拶を受けた後、この施設の名称の由来を聞く。「福井福田会」は仏教の言葉から出ているもので、聖徳太子の福田思想に因んだもの。宗教的な香り高い慈悲心を以って人づくりをなし、明るく住みよい社会（安楽浄仏国土）を創るという意味で名付けられたとのことである。名称の重みを感じながら施設長の前田利昭氏から縷々説明を受ける。

2 「福井福田会」の沿革について

（1）明治・大正期

　更生保護法人「福井福田会」の淵源はかなり古い。明治43年5月、金沢監獄福井分監の職員の寄附と南越地区真宗本派寺院の僧侶の出資で「南越福田会」として発足している。当時は福井市西別院内を利用。その後は民家を借り「免囚保護」を行う。大正2年1月、時の検事正唐渡房次郎氏の支援で県下各宗寺院が合同で経営。名称も「福井県福田会」と改称し、初代会長に唐渡検事正が就任。当時は借家のため一時保護しかできなかった。そこで県下全域を14・15の支部に分け、支部委員

(僧侶)を任命し、各支部委員宅に分散して保護を行う保護区制を採用。我が国の司法制度に委員制と保護区制を採用した草分けとのことである。以来、歴代の会長は検事正が就任して進展が図られた。大正9年4月に財団法人として認可を受け、大正12年3月、家賃が暴騰して経営困難となり、土地の払い下げを受け、福井刑務所に建築を委託して受刑者の労役で25坪の保護施設を建設し、会所有の収容施設を持つに至る。大正14年9月、総裁制を採用し、県知事である豊田勝三氏が初代総裁に就任し委員の任免を行うこととなる。

(2) 昭和・平成期

昭和10年8月、被保護者が増加したことから施設を取り壊し、二階建て148坪の保護収容所とし、階下に木工部、洋服修繕、織物芯張り等の授産所を設ける。同12年2月、少年保護施設建設のため隣接地57坪を買い入れ、同13年7月に二階建て42坪の少年保護施設と主事官舎を増設。靴修繕、竹細工などの授産所を設け、少年の保護施設を開始した。貴族院議員飛鳥文吉氏から3万円の寄附を受け、2万円で鯖江市内の雑木林13,500坪を購入。福田会経営の飛鳥農園を作る。同15年6月、検事正の会長制が廃止され、弁護士藤井浜次郎氏が民間人で14代会長に就任。この頃より支部委員は司法保護委員に変更され、福田会は本部のみとなる。同年7月、農園に作業場を建設し、製筵機10台、制縄機3台を購入し、被保護者を通勤させて作業を開始した。同18年12月、農園に鍛錬道場（明道学園）を設置し、県下の不良青少年の錬成を始めたが、同20年7月の戦災で本部が焼失し自然消滅した。同22年、時の検事正は戦後の混乱社会で少年の不良化が増加していることから協議を重ね、少年保護施設の創設の必要を唱え、200万円の寄附を受けて福井市経田町に福井学園を設立する。4,500坪の敷地を50万で購入し、二階建ての施設を建て、延べ392坪に事務所、精紡工場、反毛工場、そ綿工場等を建設して事業再開する。同23年6、福井大震災で施設が倒壊焼失し、バラック建てで再開したが経営困難に陥る。同24年9月、成人対象者の授産場を増やすため製材作業を開始。同25年11月、更生緊急保護法制定で、更生保護事業が認可される。同28年10月、都市計画で2,595坪を貸与しなければならなくなり、農園敷地は大幅に減少した。同30年2月、福井福田会と福井学園が併合し、鯖江市内の福田会土地建物を800万円で売却し、福井学園の隣接地に2,842坪を購入し、事務所1棟、収容棟一棟、作業棟一棟、豚舎一棟を新築し、福井福田会と改名して成人・少年の男子の保護施設とした。同30年8月、売春防止法に基づき、篤志家の寄附により女子収用施設を新築併設し女子収容保護を開始する。同41年3月女子の入寮者がなく、一時閉鎖とし、4月から民間商社へ土地建物を一部貸与。同44年8月旧収容棟が老朽化し、鉄筋コンクリート二階建て一棟

の新築着工。同45年3月に竣工し、4月に旧収容棟を解体して落成式を挙行した。同53年3月福井市から土地185.51㎡を購入。同58年7月、管理棟の老朽化と収容棟の狭隘で、改築工事に着工。総工事費は9,348万円。同2月本館竣工。同60年9月旧館収容棟の補修工事を実施。平成4年10月に藤井健夫氏が18代会長に就任。同8年4月、更生保護事業法が施行され財団法人から更生保護法人へ組織変更され今日に至っている。まさに歴史の重みを感じさせられる。

2 施設等の概要

全面積は9,166.19㎡もあり驚く広さであるが、この内、貸付地が約7,000㎡を占めている。建物は鉄筋コンクリート造り2階建てで、新館が472.81㎡で、旧館が390.59㎡である。1階に事務室、調理室、食堂、集会室、相談室等があった。居室は2人用（和室）が8室。個室（和室）4室があり、全室テレビ、冷暖房が完備されていた。洗濯設備は2階で、3台の洗濯機に2台の乾燥機（無料）を備えていた。娯楽室にはテレビ・ビデオ・囲碁・将棋・図書等がある。収容定員は20名（男子成人18名・少年2名）である。

3 処遇の内容等

（1）**指導方針**
　ア　集団生活の中で規則正しい生活をしながら、人間関係の在り方を身に付けさせる。
　イ　一日も早く仕事に就かせて勤労意欲を引き出す。
　ウ　金銭感覚を養い、早期自立を目標に浪費を慎み貯蓄させる。
　エ　社会生活の中のルールを守らせる。

（2）**給食**（常勤の調理員が調理を提供している。）
　ア　朝・昼・夕の食事を用意。就労者の昼は弁当を用意。土曜の夕・日曜の朝・昼・夕は外注。
　イ　冷蔵庫・電子レンジ・トースター・電気ポットは備えてある。食堂には感謝・静粛・清潔などの言葉が書かれていた。また感謝の心・敬う心・許す心・詫びる心・思いやりの心の「五つの心」が明記されていた。
午前6時に起床し洗面・清掃。午前6時から7時30分が朝食。正午から午後1時昼食。夕食は午後5時30分から午後7時30分まで。

（3）就職指導

ハローワーク、求人誌等での自己開拓を優先しているが、希望者には協力雇用主に協力を依頼している。建築廃棄物処理業者、土建業・造園業などで現在3箇所とのことで積極的である。

4　最近の収容状況

定員は20名である。事業成績をみると平成20年頃から実績も上がり、ちなみに収容率は20年が71.1％、21年が71.6％、22年が78.0％、今年は80％程度とのことで、日本海側にあって高収容率をあげられている。

本施設は「特別調整」である高齢者・障害者を受け入れる施設である。

社会福祉士の職員を1名置き、4人を限定に地域生活定着センターと連携して処遇が行われている。また病院との関係も、本施設の理事が済生会病院や松原病院の理事でもあり診療をお願いするなど円滑な関係ができていた。矯正施設入所度数は年によるが最高が11人から8人を受入れている。ほとんどが窃盗犯で、詐欺や道交法違反が次ぐ。覚せい剤事犯は軽い場合のみでほとんど収容していないとのこと。

ところで、各団体との協力関係では、毎月1回更生保護女性会員による昼食会があり、季節のご馳走、おふくろの味が提供されている。ほかに季節や行事の特別食（正月三が日、クリスマス、屋外レクリエーション）も提供している。

5　処遇の実施状況

（1）特別処遇プログラム

ア　毎週日曜日の朝、一斉掃除と集団処遇が行われている。

イ　レクリエーションを兼ねて、福井県内の温泉施設で毎月1回社会福祉士を招いて、SSTを実施されていたが、現在は中止しているとのことであった。

（2）レクリエーション

更生保護女性会の方が来て、絵手紙作成を月1回実施している。仕事以外は全員参加で、楽しくやっている。

（3）全体集会

年間かなりの数になる。

6　おわりに

　更生保護法人「福井福田会」はまさに伝統を受け継ぎ、今日まで堂々とその存在を示し燦然と輝いている。帰り際に藤井理事長からいただいた創立100周年記念大会誌を拝見すると、平成22年10月15日（金）福井福田会創立百周年記念式典が、東方には冠雪した霊峰白山を遠くに望み、眼下には福井城跡の石垣と老松の映えるお濠が望まれる記念式典会場（ホテルフジタ福井市）において、関係機関団体120余名の来賓を迎えて盛大に開催されている。100年と一言で簡単にいうことはできるが、その間に福井空襲、福井大地震と大打撃を受けながらも、当時の会長を始め、多額の寄附をされた方、はたまた数多くの方々の愛と情熱に基づく献身的なご尽力により不死鳥のようによみがえり、偉大なる業績を積み上げて今日に至っていることをしみじみと実感した。

　2階からみた広大な貸付地にはスーパーマーケットなどのお店が集合し、多くの車が駐車していた。これまで、国の委託費に依存する多くの更生保護施設を見てきたが、これも先達のチカラによるものだと確信しながら、感慨深く役職員の皆様とお別れして同施設を後にした。

3　更生保護法人「福井福田会」参観記

井 上 見 淳

　福井市内の入り組んだ道路を抜けたところに「幾久公園」という大きな公園があるが、その公園の通り向かいに、ひっそりとした佇まいで「福井福田会」はある。隣接するスーパーマーケットが昼時の買い物客で賑わっているのとは、いかにも対照的である。
　8月の終り頃でまだまだ蒸し暑く、断続的に雨が降り続く北陸独特の気候のなか、タクシーで到着した我々を施設の職員さんたちが笑顔で出迎えてくださった。通された部屋には大きな仏壇があり、並んだテーブルの上には資料とお茶が準備されていた。弁護士でもある理事長の藤井健夫氏と施設長の前田氏とが改めてご挨拶され、施設の概要についてしばらくお話しくださった。そして、その後は施設見学を行い、我々の質問のひとつひとつに、実に丁寧にお答えくださった。
　福田会は1910（明治43）年に、南越地区に住む浄土真宗本願寺派の僧侶の出資によって発足しており、歴史は古い。昨年の10月には創立百周年を祝う記念式典が盛大に行われている。発足当初は「南越福田会」と名称されたが、その後、紆余曲折を経て現在に至っている。この施設は、刑務所を出所した人や、保護観察処分を受けた人たちが、社会復帰できるように、6ヶ月を1クールとして衣食住を提供し、支援を続けている。聞くところによると、ここは保護司制度発祥の地とも言われているらしい。この「福田会」という名称は、頂戴した資料によれば、
　　仏教の言葉から出ているもので、聖徳太子の福田思想に因んだもの。宗教的な
　　香り高い慈悲心を以って人づくりをなし、明るく住みよい社会（安楽成仏国土）
　　を創るという意味で名付けられたもの。
とある。つまり浄土真宗の僧侶の出資により、仏教の理念を骨格としてこの施設は誕生したのであった。
　ここで福井と浄土真宗の結びつきについて触れておく。この福井を含めて富山・石川の北陸三県と浄土真宗の結びつきは古く、いまも強い。現在も真宗教団連合に加盟している宗派のうち、真宗出雲路派・真宗誠照寺派・真宗三門徒派・真宗山元派の四つは、この福井に本山を構えている。全国的にみても広島県とこの北陸地方は浄土真宗の篤信地として、頂点に君臨しているといっても過言ではない。

福井と浄土真宗といえばまず思い浮かぶのは、本願寺第八代宗主蓮如（1415—1499）であろう。蓮如とは、比叡山の一末寺としてさびさびと存続していた本願寺を、事実上、一代で日本最大の教団に育て上げた立役者である。彼は比叡山の執拗な攻撃から京都を離れ、1471（文明3）、越前吉崎に進出している。このことが、わずか四年の滞在ではあったものの、蓮如自身にとっても非常に大きな転換点となった。彼がこの地で本格化させた数々の斬新な伝道方法は、急速に教線を拡大させた。これらの方法が後の真宗教団に与えた影響は計り知れないものがある。

　歴史はさらに遡る。北陸地方に浄土真宗が接触した初めは、本願寺の実質的な創建者である本願寺第三代宗主覚如（1270—1351）の時代まで行き着く。時は鎌倉時代である。覚如は、熱心に伝道活動をしていた如道という男に対し、1311（応長1）年5月、この地で『教行信証』の伝授を行っている。『教行信証』とは、言わずと知れた親鸞畢生の大著であり、正式には『顕浄土真実教行証文類』という。真宗教団においてはこの書を根本聖典と位置づけるので「本典」とも呼んでいるが、それを宗主が、わざわざ出向いて伝授した（伝授自体は、共に出向いていた長子存覚〈1290—1373〉が、一時的に門主権を与えられておこなっている）ことの意味あいは、相当に重いものがある。なお、伝授に際しては、あの有名な親鸞の寿像「鏡の御影」（1956年に国宝に指定）をかけて儀式は行われたという。のちに、北陸の地は「真宗王国」と称賛されるほどの大輪の花を開かせるが、その種子はこのとき決定的に植え付けられたといえよう。

　以後、第七代宗主存如（1396—1457）も北陸重視の姿勢をとり、続く蓮如にいたると、先に述べたように滞在期間はわずか四年であったものの、越前を中心にした北陸の地は、本願寺が教線を、急速にかつ濃密に拡大していく震源地となった。土着の者たちや、北国街道を往来する者たち、あるいは遠方からの参詣者、そしてそれを迎える出店や多屋……。かつて「虎狼のすみか」と評された吉崎の地は、蓮如のいる吉崎御坊を中心として、またたく間に「宗教都市」ともいうべき容貌を呈するようになる。突如出現したその町はいつも群参する者たちで人が溢れかえり、けが人が出ることもしばしばの大盛況で、蓮如は何度か参詣を制限したこともある。そんな中、吉崎御坊には、群参した者たちによっていつも地鳴りのような念仏の声が聞こえ、蓮如のひと言ひと言に耳を傾けた多くの人々が、そこで阿弥陀如来に出遇っていった。そんな濃密な時間が、北陸の地に流れたのである。

　爾来、五百年以上の月日が流れている。その間に浄土真宗の僧侶が、仏教をその理念に据え、こういった施設を誕生させている。この地で教えを肌に感じた人たちが、それを社会に具現化した形で示したのがこの施設であるとは言えないだろう

か。

　ところで、お二人の話に興味深い話があった。それは施設の禁止事項についてである。この施設ではあまり厳格に日々の行程というのは決められていないようであったが、飲酒は禁止されている。そこで、我々のメンバーのうちの誰かが「破った者はどうなるのか」という質問をしたところ、二人は少し笑まれ「もちろん退所を命じてもいいんですが、この寒い土地で外に放り出すわけにもいかんでしょう。まあ、よくよく注意するってところですかねえ」とのこと。この言葉に何ともいえない温かみを感じた。言い方を換えれば、他宗と違って戒を持たない仏教である浄土真宗らしさのようなものを感じたと言った方が当たっているだろうか。

　うかがえば、いま施設内で宗教的な取り組みは、特にはやっておられないとのことだった。いくぶん残念な気もしたが、その精神性はいまも脈々とこの施設全体に生きているのだろう。我々が迎えられた部屋の大きな仏壇は、浄土真宗の仏壇であり、中にはこれまでこの施設に関わってきたとおぼしき方々の位牌がずらりと並べられていた。この地に、このような施設の創設を発想した方、その理念に賛同し施設を存続させてきた方々、そしていま現に存続させ運営されている方々が、みなここにいるように感じた。

　この厳しい時代にあって、こうした施設を存続させていくことは並大抵ではない。称賛されるべき努力であり、そこに流れる精神性に心から敬意を表したい。

4　湖南学院訪問記

板 垣 嗣 廣

はじめに

「湖南」という名称は、創設当時の学院の所在地から名付けられたものであり、近くに大きな湖のあることが想像される。金沢駅から北に延びる北陸鉄道淺野川線の電車に乗り9つ目の駅が蚊爪（かがつめ）駅であるが、その東側に東蚊爪町が広がる。この町が海につながる河北潟の南に当たり、昭和24年開設の少年院はこの地にあって「湖南」という名を頂いたのであった。沿革によれば、昭和46年、現在地に移転とあり、以来40年にわたってこの地で、この建物で多くの少年たちが教育を受けてきたことになる。かなりの歴史があるのに建物は非常に清潔にきれいに管理されており、職員の方々がとても大事にこの建物を使ってきたことが伺える。それは処遇規則22条にある「自ら範を示すことにより、秩序を尊び自他を敬愛し、併せて物を大切にする習慣を養成する」、という教官の基本姿勢を身をもって真摯に指し示しているものであろう。

お尋ねしたのは8月25日、強い雨が降ったり晴れ間が覗いたりという天候不順の日であったが、施設の中を参観させていただく間は幸い青空も見えた。案内された中庭は木槿が満開で、そこから新築中の寮舎外観を望むことができた。古都金沢の色調で統一され落ち着いたおしゃれな印象を受けた。定員50名の新施設は、今年度中には完成予定のことで、新しい歴史がまた始まろうとしていた。

施設の概要等

1　収容少年

定員は55名。岐阜・福井からの送致が多数を占める。現在員は、短期生活訓練課程の少年13名と少ない。全国的に短期処遇への送致が少ないとのことであるが、少年法改正による厳罰化や被害感情（短期では許せないと考える）が影響しているのであろうか。

保護処分歴を見ると、保護観察歴と審判不開始・不処分歴が、それぞれ約54％と40％となっている。一般短期処遇という施設収容が初めてである対象者であるのでこの不開始・不処分の比率は他の少年院に比して高いようである。

2 教育活動

お伺いしたときはちょうど友禅科と木彫科が実施されていた。友禅科は、金沢らしい科目だと思った。色彩や構図など美的感覚が要求されるが、院外から専門家を招聘して指導に当たっていただいているとのことで見事な作品が多く見られた。夏休みに作った美術部の作品（花火をイメージしたもの）が並べられていたが、配色もよくとても美しい仕上がりとなっていた。情性の陶冶に力を注いでいるように見受けられた。

寮内をご案内頂いたときに、黒板に討論のテーマが板書されていた。「赤ちゃんポストの是非―身勝手な理由で預ける、妊娠や出産で悩む人たち―」。命についての討論と思われた。ある意味価値の対立するような問題を私たちはどう考えてよいのか、どう捉えどう対処すればよいのか、困難なテーマであろう。どのような話し合いになるのか大変興味をひかれ、時間が許せば参加（傍聴）してみたいプログラムであった。

その他、意見発表会には家庭裁判所の裁判官や調査官、保護観察官等関係機関の方々も参加され、終了後は少年に面接をしてくださるとのこと。院外活動は、春は写生会、夏は海水浴、秋は遠足、冬はスキーと四季を感じながらの行事となっている。青少年交流の家に協力を仰いでいるとのことであった。豊かな自然の中での学び直しと位置づけられている。

保護者ハンドブック

少年の9割以上は、ともかくも実の父か実の母がおり、短期処遇少年の家庭状況は長期処遇のそれに比べこの面では相当よいといえる。しかしながらその関係はかならずしも良好とはいえないのが実情である。今般の少年法、少年院法改正によって、少年院は保護者に対し指導・助言等の支援ができることとなった。湖南学院においても「家族の絆を深めるための働き掛け」は教育の大きな柱となっている。「親子交流会」や宿泊面会等は、保護者が少年院の活動に参加するプログラムであり、たとえば食事会などは親子のコミュニケーションの活発化を促しながら、関係の見直しや修復を進め、子ども理解、親理解を深められるよう配慮、支援している。少年の感想に、久しぶりに親と一緒に話をしながら食事をしたことを述べた

後、「社会にいるときは何も感じることがないあたりまえの食事だけど、今日はとても違う食事だと思いました。家族と食事をするのは、何でか分からないけどとても心が温かくなる感じがして、毎日こんな食事をしたいなと思いました。」とある。少年院のパンフレットのコラム「宿泊面会」の中に、少年が勇気をふるって「お父さんのむきになるところがきらいなんだ。」といったら、父は「お父さんはおまえのことが心配だからむきになるんだ」と応じたとのこと、そのことによって少年は父の本気で心配していたことに気づいたことが記されている。少年院に来てようやく父子の関係がつながった、新しい関係が結ばれたといえるのではなかろうか。

　湖南学院で特に注目したいのは、「REDO（やり直し、育て直し）」と名付けられた保護者ハンドブックについてである。全ての漢字に仮名が振られており、少年院の独特な言葉遣いが容易に保護者に理解されるように配慮されている。また、「8 保護観察について」の記事が非常に丁寧に編集されていることである。ほとんどの少年が保護観察に移行すると言うことが一つには考えられるが、先にも述べたように、4割の少年が保護観察未経験で、5割の少年が保護観察の失敗者といっていいからであろう。他施設のハンドブックにはない周到な配慮であろうと評価できる。

部外者の視点

　この訪問は龍谷大学の矯正・保護課程の教員の方々とであったが、実は、その10日ばかり前に、教育学や心理学の大学教員、児童福祉関係、看護学の専門家、病院の看護師等少し異種の方々と一緒に訪問していたのであった。そこでこれら外部の訪問者の違った視点からの、つまり多くの矯正施設を見慣れた方々の視点とはまた違った角度からの感想があり、紹介してみたい。

(1) 施設建物等生活環境について
・学校と旧来の精神科病棟と驚くほど似ていると思いました。ただし精神科病棟はこのように清潔に保たれていませんが。短期処遇で生活環境を整えることと、出院後の生活環境との隔たりをどのように埋めるかということを考えてみたくなった。
・社会と少し離れた場所で自分を見つめ直すということが行われているように思いました。部屋の窓が広く取られていてプライバシーを保つのが難しそうに思いました。他の人から見られていることで自分のあり方に目を向けることができそうな反面、そのような目が無くなった時にどのように自己を保っていけるのか興味を持ちました。

・個室に植物があるお部屋があったり、廊下に熱帯魚がいたり、心和む環境への配慮を感じました。
・全体に大変ゆとりのある落ち着いた環境という印象でした。床もぴかぴかで気持ちよく、至る所に職員の方々の教育的配慮が感じられ、たたずまいの清廉さが在院生の内観を促すことを環境が物語っていると感じました。
・Cozy そのもの。湖南学院にかぎらず、少年院は「恵まれて」いる。私立大学とは雲泥の差。
・少し難を言えば、部屋が殺風景な感じがしました。新しく作られるときはもう少し暖かい雰囲気にできないでしょうか。社会的に排除された存在ではなく、自分は大切にされているということを感じさせる生活空間を作ってあげて欲しいと思います。それから6ヶ月という短い期間で育て直しをすることは大変だろうなと思いました。
・古い建物だということでしたし、そのように思いましたが、とてもきれいに整備されていて、生活環境としてよい状況にあると思いました。
・古い建物ですのに、大変きれいに大切に使っておられました。とても大事なことと思います。教育的にも。
・経年使用のため、施設の古くささは感じられますが、清掃が行き届いているため清潔感がありました。今年度中に完成する新しい施設の模型も拝見しました。普通の学校でしたら、あの程度の年数で建て替えることはないと思いますが、一般人の視点からすると、どうして学校よりも優遇されるのかと疑問をもたれるかもしれません。

（2）処遇・教育内容について

・人格の変容というよりも社会の中に統合できるように行動変容と発達保障の教育目標になっていると思いました。個室が現在あるにもかかわらず、何故保護室が必要なのか分からない。精神科医療でも保護室は適正に利用されなかった歴史がある中で精神保健指定医や処遇改善請求の制度ができることになった。医療少年院や精神障害をベースとした対象者の処遇や教育で必要があるのであればまだ分かるが。
・6ヶ月で何ができるのかということについて、長いようで短い期間で、よい生活の体験をすること、相手の気持ちを共感する心の構えを持つこと、社会の中で生きる術を多少身につけること、苦難に耐えていく力をつけること、他の人と心を通わせることの喜びの体験をすること、などが行われているのだと思いました。子が再犯しないように見守っていく親の力を育てる取り組みは何があ

るのか、そこは保護観察の役割なのか、疑問がわいてきました。
- 短期間であるにもかかわらず、退院していく際に子どもたちが両親に対して「ありがとう」といえるようになったりする、そのように子どもたちが「生きやすく」なるような変化を可能にしている教育について、もう少し詳しくお話を聞かせて頂きたかったです。
- 他分野では立ち入ることがなかなか難しいと思うので、とても貴重な経験となりました。もっと閉鎖的なイメージがあったので、そういったイメージを変えることができました。前々から精神病棟と似ているところがあると思っていましたが、精神科病棟よりも生活を重視していると思いました。食事に力を入れていらっしゃるのも団欒の基本でいいなと思いました。
- 創造（物をつくりだす、開発する）という点に力を注がれているところが印象的でした。友禅染め、木彫等専門家の指導を受けながら、感性を豊かに発達させること、このことが認知的情緒的発達を相互に高めていく作用に通じるのであろうと感じました。
- 数種類のプログラムがあり、その期間に計画的に教育がなされているように感じました。短期処遇ということでスタッフに心理職が配置されていないのだろうかと思いました。
- 注目点：意見発表会
- 少年院の教官の方々が、少年の更生自立を目指して、真摯にお仕事をしておられることが伝わってきました。また、少年院での生活や学びを通して、少年たちの潜在能力や可能性が引き出され、自尊心の回復を図ることができるのだと感じました。社会性の発達のためには、共有体験、待つ力、役立ち感の三つが大切だと岡田隆介氏は述べていますが、少年院の生活は信頼できる職員との共有体験であり、待つ力を育て、人の役に立つという体験にもつながっているのだと思いました。
- 少年院における新しい試みがいくつか始まっていることは存じておりましたが、たとえば被害者の講演会など具体的な内容を教えていただき、さらにイメージが細かくなりました。友禅は湖南独自でいいですね。
- 討論（ニュースフォーラム）で「赤ちゃんポストの是非」が取り上げられていました。どんな意見が出され、どう考えられたか興味のあるところです。
- 少年院の教育内容、処遇内容は、内省、内観、進級など使用される言葉も独特で、一般人の感覚では、それが実際にはどのようなものであるのかイメージしにくいのではないかという印象を受けました。また、説明内容も一般の見学者

用だけではなく、学生や研究者用のものも作成し、司法、教育、心理、社会、福祉、医療など、それぞれの研究分野の視点からも説明ができ、理解が得られるような工夫も必要ではないかと感じました。特に学校教育や児童自立支援施設でも注目されている「発達障害」「虐待」などの少年に対して、どのような分析をしてどのような教育をしているかなど、理論の裏付けに基づいて説明ができると、矯正教育の価値を再認識していただけるのではないかと思いました。
・地域ならではの課業があり驚いた（物作り等）。

(3) その他
・精神科ととても似ているところがあり参考になりました。コストを考え短期でという考えは精神科にもあります。入院中に出来ること、出来ないこと、地域でやるべきこと、入院中にやらなければいけないことなど考えてみたいと思います。
・少年法の厳罰化の下で管理統制が強化されるような傾向がある中においても、教育・発達を核とした人間の可能性を開花させるべく生活丸ごと指導、支援に関わっていらっしゃる職員の方々のご尽力に触れることができ大変勉強になりました。
・大いに評価。もう少し時間がとれ、入院生の指導に当たる担任との懇談があるとなお良い。
・少年院を見学する機会はなかなか無いため、貴重な体験をさせていただきとてもためになった。感謝。
・学院において、共通認識、価値の共有が職員の方々にあるように感じられましたので、職員の方々への研修やエンパワーできるような職能開発の仕組みについて、院内そして、あるいは法務省管轄の仕組み、機会の在り方を知りたいと思いました。
・職員の制服について、「少年院はミニ刑務所」という印象を持たれないためにも、刑務官の制服とは全く違う別なデザインにすべきだと改めて感じました。
・新しい施設に移転することで寮のルールに変化が生じる部分が出てくると思われるが、その対応策について聞いてみたかった。また寒冷地の施設ならではの工夫があれば教えて貰いたかった。

最後に

　湖南学院における矯正教育の方針として3点が提示されている。
(1) 教育課程による体系的指導（在院者の特性及び教育上の必要性に応じた標準的な教育計画）
(2) 個別的処遇計画で一人ひとりに対応（少年一人ひとりの特性や必要性に応じた教育計画、教育目標や教育内容・方法、予定期間を策定）
(3) 個別担任制で信頼関係構築（入院から出院まで個別担任職員が一貫して指導）
　その上で、学院の矯正教育の特徴として、規律、ルール遵守、しつけ等の生活指導を中心とした「生活全般を通しての学び」をまず第一に挙げている。次に、集団寮の生活を基本に置いた「人と人との関わりの中での学び」を第二に、最後に、心身を動かす体験、施設外での活動等を通した「様々な体験を通じての学び」が挙げられているが、いずれも、生活全般を通しての学び直しを重視しながら、少年の発達を支援し、再非行防止と健全育成を図っていこうとしている。
　先にも述べたように、一人ひとりの少年の課題に対応したきめ細かな教育活動が準備されており、かつ構造化されているようにうかがえた。また、部外者の視点が示すように、少年院の活動が、非行からの回復と同時に発達支援であること、生活丸ごとの指導であること、さらにそれは少年たちが「生きやすく」なるような変化を可能としているということ、こういった面からも高く評価されていることは、元少年院職員としては大変嬉しいことである。一方で、処遇の説明を理論的な裏付けを軸にして行う必要性とか制服の問題など、一般の方々の理解を得るためには、外側から見て自然に写る姿、もまた大切なことであろうと思われた。

5　金沢刑務所参観記

畠 山 晃 朗

1　はじめに

　私ども龍谷大学矯正・保護課程の担当教授や講師等による恒例の夏期研修旅行は、例年通り酷暑の時期に実施された。今年は8月24日から26日までの二泊三日の日程で、北陸方面の矯正施設である福井刑務所及び金沢刑務所と湖南学園（初等少年院）並びに富山刑務所と福井の更正保護施設の福井福田会の5施設の研究参観を実施した。
　今回の各施設への参観の間は、天候不良で猛暑は一息ついていたが、途中で一時は物凄い雨が降るという悪天候で蒸し暑い中での参観となったが、参加者の心がけが良かったせいか各施設の所内見学中は不思議にぴたりと雨がやむという幸運に恵まれた。
　さて、最初にまずもってご多忙の中にもかかわらず懇切かつ丁寧な対応をしていただいた各施設の所長さん及び関係職員の皆様に心よりお礼を申し上げます。
　私は、今回の研究参観でお伺いする3箇所の刑事施設については、監獄法が平成18年に全面改正されて、「刑事収容施設及び被収容者等の処遇に関する法律」（以下新法という。）が施行され、5年が経過した今年が新法の見直しの時期にあたることでもあり、今回お伺いする各施設が、この新法の元で、どのような運営がなされて、どのような問題点が出てきて、どのような見直しが必要なのかという点に興味を持って参観させていただいた。最初にお伺いした福井刑務所はA指標の初犯者の多い総合職業訓練施設であり、さすがに改善が比較的容易とされる受刑者が入っている施設でもあり、その上、たまたま参観当日が、教育的指導日ということで、刑務作業が実施されていなかったので、工場は静かで施設も全体的に落ち着いた雰囲気であった。金沢刑務所と富山刑務所はB指標の累犯刑務所という違いがあったが、一時の過剰収容が解消されたこともあるせいか、両施設とも大きな問題もなく円滑に運営されており、非常に安定した運営がなされているように見受けられた。また、私が一番注視していた、受刑者に対する改善指導等の各種処遇の内容も、新

法施行後5年が経過したが、その間、各施設とも、新しい法律のもとでも、特段の問題もなく運営されている様子であったので、安心するとともに、新法により受刑者の処遇が大きく改善されたのではないかとの期待をしていたが、一部の処遇内容の変化が見られたものの、そんなに大きな変化は無いとの各施設の処遇担当者の説明に、若干の物足りなさを感じたのは、私の独りよがりの感想であろうか。勿論、短時間の施設参観なので、詳しくその状況を把握出来たわけではないので、その実態を正確に把握していたわけでないことをお断りしたい。

以下、私が担当することになった金沢刑務所についての参観記を述べたい。

2　金沢刑務所の概況

(1) 施設の沿革

金沢刑務所は、江戸時代の加賀藩の牢屋である公事場付設牢屋を、明治維新で廃止して刑法寮となり、明治14年に金沢監獄署となり、さらに明治19年に金沢監獄となったが、明治28年には元鶴間町に移転新築され、大正11年に金沢刑務所と改称された。さらに、昭和45年に金沢市の都市計画により、市内の中心部から少し離れた、現在地の田上町に新築移転したという伝統と格式のある施設であり、北陸地方の矯正施設の中核をなす施設である。

主として犯罪傾向の進んだ受刑者を収容し、彼らの更生復帰を目指して、多様な教育活動と処遇を展開している施設であり、収容定員756名、敷地面積920325㎡、建物面積2275㎡の施設である。建築後41年も経過している老朽施設とは見えず、所内は手入れが行き届いており、その管理が行き届いているようすが伺われた。

収容受刑者の平均年齢は46歳であり、最高齢は80歳であった。60歳以上の高齢受刑者は17%と他の刑務所と同様、高齢者が増加の傾向にあるとのことであった。また、平均刑期は2年8ヶ月で、平均入所回数は3．4回で、暴力団関係者は、186名で、全受刑者の36%を占めていた。

入所者の主な罪名は、窃盗35.8%、覚醒剤37%、その他27%であり、覚醒剤事犯者と窃盗犯の二つが圧倒的に多かった。

(2) 組織

所長を頂点として、総務部と処遇部という二つの部を有するいわゆる二部制施設であり、支所として七尾拘置支所を所管している。

職員定員は、181名であり、本所171名（内訳公安職167名、医療職4名）、七尾支所10名（内訳公安職10名）であった。

(3) 収容人員の状況

収容定員は756名で、内訳は既決661名、未決が95名である。

参観当日の収容現員は、本所が、既決677名（収容率102％）、未決44名（収容率46％）で、計721名で収容率95.3％であったが、受刑者の定員は依然として100％を越え、単独室への2名拘禁が継続されていたが、集団室の過剰収容状態は解消されているように見えた。

(4) 受刑者処遇の概要

同所における受刑者処遇の重点は、新法の趣旨を受けて、その者の資質及び環境に応じ、その自覚に訴え、改善更生の意欲の喚起及び社会生活に適応する能力の育成を旨とし、刑務作業、改善指導、教科教育を実施している。

そのため、各受刑者に対して処遇調査を実施して、個々の受刑者の処遇要領を作成して、各受刑者の問題性の改善、社会適応能力の向上による再犯の防止に力を入れた処遇を行っているとのことであった。

そのためにはまず、刑執行時の指導において、受刑の意義、矯正処遇に対する動機付け等について徹底した指導を行って、自発的な意欲の喚起を図っているとのことであった。

そして、その具体的処遇としては、刑務作業としては、生産作業若しくは自営作業に就業させているほか、職業訓練として、ビル設備管理科と溶接の二種目を実施している。また、改善指導としては、一般改善指導として、被害者感情理解指導、自己啓発指導、自己改善目標達成指導、対人関係円滑化指導を行い、そのために、酒害教育や、各種の通信教育、高齢者指導等をそれぞれのカリキュラムを組んで実施している。また、特別改善指導としては、薬物依存離脱教育と暴力団離脱指導及び被害者の視点を取り入れた教育を実施している。更に教科教育としては、補修教科指導を実施して、社会生活の基礎となる学力をつける教育指導を実施している。そして、これらの各指導等については、必要に応じて処遇要領の見直しを行い、さらに、定期的に目標達成度評価を行って、優遇措置や処遇の緩和を行っているとの事であった。

同所の制限区分別の受刑者の状況は、1種0名、2種A5名、2種B60名、3種517名、4種25名、区分なし70名（調査中）であるが、2種の処遇については、居室の不足もあり、3種との区分が難しいとのことであり、新法の目玉である制限の緩和が、明確に実施されていないように感じた。

また、優遇区分については、1類0、2類39名、3類283名、4類46名、5類125名、なし75名であった。無しというのは、調査中のものである。制限区分も優遇区

分も、B指標の受刑者の場合は、平均的なものが多く、1種や2種、あるいは1類や2類に該当するものは、どうしても少ないようであり、2種については、もっと増やすように当局からも指導がなされているようであったが、現場で直接受刑者を見ている立場の第1線の職員にとっては、その種別や類別に該当しない受刑者を、そう簡単に上位の種別や類別に区分することには抵抗があるようであった。私の体験から言っても、監督官庁からの指示の中には、現場の実態に合わないものが結構あり、中々その指示どおりには運営が出来ないことも多かったので、無理なからぬことだと思った。

(5) 刑務作業関係

同所の当日の就業人員は、636名であり、不就業人員は41名（内訳、釈放準備5名、懲罰中26名、免業5名、臨時休業5名）であり、就業率は93.9％であった。

最近の刑務作業は、各施設とも、新法の施行後の実質作業時間の減や、長引く不況の影響もあり、その内容の低落化が激しく、解約減産も多く、生産額や事業部作業の売り上げが大幅に減少しているが、同所の刑務作業は、活発に実施されており、達成率は99％であった。さすが、この難しい時代に、刑務作業関係の業務に長く携わっておられる所長がおられる施設は違うと感心した。しかしながら、金沢地方には、刑務作業に向く生産作業を実施している企業が少なく、また、同所の処遇の問題点である就業拒否のものが多いことや、60歳以上の高齢受刑者で養護処遇の必要な受刑者が増加しており、工場で生産作業に就業する適格者が減少していることもあり、施設の作業関係職員の活発な受注活動にもかかわらず、有用作業の維持に苦慮している状況がうかがわれた。

また、同所は、集合職業訓練として、溶接科とビル設備管理科を実施しているが、溶接科は、定員6名で年に二回実施して、修了者にはガス溶接技能工修了証及びJISアーク溶接免許を交付している。さらにビル設備管理科は、定員10名で、年に二回実施し、二級ボイラー技士免許及び乙種第四類危険物取扱者の免許取得をはかっているが、訓練受講者の能力の関係で資格取得にいたらないものも多く、外部講師による補習等による内容の充実を図る必要があるとのことであった。また、福井刑務所の総合職業訓練にも応募するが、B指標のものは、前科2犯までという縛りがあるので、同所のように平均前科4犯の受刑者では、受講できないので、B指標のものであっても幅広く職業訓練を受講できるようにしてもらいたいとのことであったが、同所の受刑者では資質的に職業訓練募集要領に合致できず、応募しても採用にならないことが多いとのことであった。

(6) 保安関係

次に、同所の保安関係であるが、同所は犯罪傾向の進んだ受刑者を収容している施設にもかかわらず、衆情はきわめて安定しているように見受けられ、最近5年間は、重大な保安事故（逃走、火災、自殺）は発生していない。

規律違反にしても、平成20年が807件であり、21年は892件、22年が883件であるが、特に重大な規律違反は、無いとのことであった。しかしながら、B指標の受刑者だけあって、職員暴行等は20年11件、21年6件、22年7件も発生しており、抗命事犯も20年40件、21年60件、22年92件も発生しており、B級受刑者の質の悪さを示している。さらに、受刑者同士の暴行等の事犯は20年85件、21年114件、22年114件も発生している。これは、ほとんどが受刑者同士の喧嘩事犯であるとのことであった。喧嘩に至らない争論という口げんかも20年52件、21年43件、22年92件も発生している。このことは、同所における職員の受刑者に対する行動観察が綿密に行われており、喧嘩にいたるまでの事前に、重大な事犯を防止しているという事が出来ると思われる。また、一番多い規律違反は、怠役であるが、20年273件、21年339件、22年373件と、圧倒的に多いが、これは単なる作業拒否を示しているのではなく、集団生活が嫌で単独室への逃げ込みをはかる事犯であり、わがままな同一の受刑者が怠役を繰り返す事が多く、そのような集団処遇が出来ない受刑者が多いため、単独室への二人拘禁をなかなか解消出来ないとのことであった。

また、受刑者の不服申し立ては、20年が182件、21年271件、22年151件である。その内容の多くは、職員に対する不満の申立であり、単なる不平の申立が多く、本省より改善を指導された事例はないということであった。

やはり、新法施行後の適正な処遇の実施や過剰収容の解消とともに、不服申し立ても規律違反も減少していると感じた。

それに同所の職員の規律正しい厳正な勤務態度が、随所に見受けられ、巡回する幹部に対する職員の報告態度も厳正であり、職員の士気の高さが伺われ、それが同所の厳正な規律の維持につながっていると感じた。

念のため、同所の職員の研修の内容を質問したが、職員の全体研修を年に10回開催されており、そのほかに各部門別に職務研究会も活発に実施しているとのことであった。特に最近は若年職員が増加していることから、採用後5年未満の職員に対する研修や55歳以上の職員に対するスキルアップ研修も実施しているとのことであった。それ以外にも柔道や剣道の訓練及び矯正護身術の訓練も活発に実施しているとのことであった。過激な勤務後に各種の訓練や研修を活発に実施するというのは、中々出来ないことであり、この研修や訓練の実施状況を見ても職員の士気の高

さを感じる事が出来た。

（7）教育活動

次に同所の教育活動であるが、新法により処遇の中心として刑務作業に加えて改善指導が受刑者の義務として実施することになるとともに教科教育も処遇の三本柱と規定されたことにより、教育部門の業務は驚くほど多くなったように思われた。

同所では、新法で規定された改善指導として、主に矯正指導日（毎月第2.4水曜日）を活用して、VTRで薬物、酒害等のビデオによる全体指導を行っていた。

また、最近実施されたものとしては、工場担当による担当訓話を一般改善指導として、毎月二回、各工場にて実施しており、これは、従来から各刑務所において伝統的に工場担当が毎日のように受け持ち受刑者に対して訓示を行っていたものを、内容を充実させて、実施しているとのことであり、職員の指導能力向上にもつながる効果的な方法であると感じた。

さらに、一般改善指導としては、全ての受刑者にたいして、「被害者感情理解指導」、「自己啓発指導」、「自己改善目標達成指導」、「社会復帰支援指導」及び「対人関係円滑化指導」を行い、その内容の細分化として、酒害教育、本人の社会復帰に役立つ各種の通信教育、高齢者指導等を実施しているとのことであった。

また、特別改善指導としては、改善更生及び円滑な社会復帰に特に支障があると認められる受刑者に対して次の通りの指導を実施していた。

「薬物依存離脱指導」（4ヶ月間、8回のサイクルで195名に実施、指導者は、刑務官以外にも民間の精神保健福祉士や富山ダルクの関係者に依頼している。）

「暴力団離脱指導」（4ヶ月間、8回のサイクルで35名に実施、指導者は、教育専門官及び石川県警の暴力団関係の担当者に依頼している。）

「被害者の視点を取り入れた教育」（生命犯をはじめ被害者に対して多大な悪影響を与えた受刑者に対して、4ヶ月間8サイクルで21名に対して実施、指導者は、教育専門官及び石川サポートセンター職員に依頼している。）

「就労支援指導」（受刑者に対して職場に適応する為の心構え及び行動様式を身につけさせると共に、職場において直面する具体的な場面を想定した対応の仕方を考えさせることを目的として、概ね3月間に6回のサイクルで、主に外部講師である石川雇用能力開発センターの職員による講義や指導を実施している。）

また、同所も他の刑務所と同様に余暇時間中における教育活動の一環として、通信教育を奨励しており、ペン習字や簿記等18名（公費8名。私費10名）が受講していたが、全受刑者のわずか2.6％に過ぎず、奨励しているという割りには少ないので、もっと受講生を増やす必要があると感じた。

また、外部ボランティアの活動としては、教誨師制度と篤志面接委員制度があるが、教誨師さんは、27名（内訳、仏教系20名、その他天理教やキリスト教等7名）であり、教誨の実施回数は、グループ教誨として、仏教系121回、キリスト教系11回、神道系52回、その他22回で206回実施されており、個人教誨は、仏教系53回、キリスト教系4回、神道系0回、その他0で57回実施されていたが、北陸仏教の活動が活発だったことや、金沢監獄以来の伝統を引き継いで、活発なグループ教誨活動が実施されていたが、個人教誨の回数が少ないのが少し気になった。

　また、篤志面接委員は、教育関係2名、法曹関係2名、文芸関係2名、宗教関係1名、商工関係2名、その他3名の12名であり、その活動状況は、グループ面接として、教養関係が12回、趣味関係が10回、その他70回ということであったが、その他というのは一般改善指導や特別改善指導の講師としての活動であるようで、篤志面接委員としての特有の活動ではないようであった。また、個人面接は、法律相談1件、職業相談3件だけであり、非常に少なく、外部資源の活用という意味からも、もっともっとボランティアの活動をしてもらう場面を増やすように、施設側で設定する必要があると感じた。

（8）医療関係

　同所には外科医師1名と内科医師1名の2名の医師が勤務していて、被収容者に対しては、入所時や臨時の健康診断を実施して、拘禁の影響により身体的及び精神的な健康を受刑者たちが損なわれないように注意しているとのことであった。今年に入ってからの休養患者は、感冒63名、インフルエンザ23名、腰痛10名、めまい10名、胃炎5名等であり、重病者はいないとのことであった。

（8）金沢刑務所視察委員会について

　同所の視察委員の構成は、弁護士1名、金沢市役所生活支援課長、福祉協議会会長、医師会代表1名、社会福祉協議会監事1名の5名で構成され、概ね2月に一回、施設において委員会を開催して、その都度、投書箱を開扉して、被収容者からの意見を回収して検討を行っており、必要に応じて投書受刑者に対しての面接を実施している。平成22年には、9回受刑者との面接を行って、その都度検討して、施設に対しての勧告等を行っている。最近の主な勧告内容は、歯科医師の治療に関するもの2件、医師の診察に関するもの1件、食事に関するもの1件、教育の充実に関するもの1件、就労支援に関するもの1件の7件であり、いずれについても、施設側において適正な措置がとられているとのことであった。

　同所は、所内に10個の投書箱を設置し、被収容者が視察委員に対して意見を提出しやすいように配慮がされていた。

3 新法施行後5年目で見直しが必要と思われる事項等

　同所では、新法施行御所内規定の見直しが積極的になされており、現時点では、大きな見直しが必要と思われる事項は無いとのことであった。
　しかしながら、新法の矯正処遇の目玉である改善指導については、私は新法施行後、色々な施設を参観させていただいているが、真に新法が求める改善の為の効果的な処遇が実施されているかということについては、指導者の増員もなされておらず、厳しい職員配置の中では、中々難しい現実にあるという感じを受けている。各施設ではそれぞれ特色ある取り組みがなされ、少年院や少年鑑別所の専門官の共助も実施されているが、累犯者が主体の施設では、配置職員と実施場所に限界があり、それほど効果的に実施されているとは見えなかったのは残念であった。しかしながら、まだこの制度が発足して5年しかたっておらず、各施設の体制や各種の基準の整備も整っていないが、各施設とも真摯に取り組んでおられるので、今後徐々にではあるが、効果が現れるのではないかと期待したい。ただし、現在の体制の如く、各施設がそれぞれ、同じような取り組みを実施するのではなく、特定の施設に集中して、効果的な方策を実施するように、収容区分の細則を改正して、同じようなA指標やB指標の施設を細分して、それぞれの施設で専門的かつ集中的な改善指導を実施することとすれば、より以上効果的に実施できるのではないかと感じました。

4 さいごに

　私ども矯正・保護課程の講師等が、短時間の施設参観で、正確な資料もなく、いつも勝手な感想を書いておりますが、この龍谷大学矯正・保護課程の夏期研究旅行における施設参観で、毎年お伺いする各施設では、真夏の暑い時期にもかかわらず、懇切丁寧に施設の案内をしていただき、私どもの見当はずれな質問にも丁寧に回答をいただいておりまして、毎回、心から感謝申し上げております。おかげ様で、今回も大変有意義かつ適切な説明をいただきまして、私どもに取りましては、非常に参考になりました。
　さて、この矯正・保護課程の修了生から、沢山の学生が矯正職員として採用されておりまして、その総数は現在180名に及んでいます。
　私どもは、出来るだけ優秀な学生を矯正の現場に採用していただくように努力い

たしておりますので、ここ数年、この課程修了生が各種の研修で優秀な成績を収めており、結構幹部になっているものも多くおります。また、今年も高等科研修に二名が合格して、現在研修を受けております。このように龍谷大学出身の矯正職員に対しましては、龍谷大学校友会の職域支部として、「ぎんなん会」というのがありまして、毎年二回、母校で矯正・保護課程との共同研修会を実施して、優秀な矯正職員の育成に努力いたしております。

　このような矯正との密接な関係にある矯正・保護課程でありますので、どうか、今後とも宜しくご協力ご援助をいただきますようお願い申し上げます。

おわり

6　富山刑務所

池 田　　　静

　我々一行12名は、2夜を過ごした金沢駅前のホテルを後にし、折からの雨の中を傘もささず、建物伝いに JR 金沢駅に到着し、午前9時13分発の「はくたか2号」に意気揚々と乗り込んだ。
　ところが、一昨日京都を出発するころから降り始めた雨が、昨日の金沢ではゲリラ豪雨と化し、いたるところで道路が冠水し、なおも降り続けているという状況であり、そのため列車は途中で減速運転を始め、富山駅には10分以上も遅れて到着した。確かに車窓からの眺めでは沿線の田畑の用水路は濁水が溢れ、所々で瀧のような勢いとなっており、そこそこ大きな川の水位は上昇して橋げたに届きそうな勢いであった。それにしても、35分で到着するところを50分近く費やしたことになり、その上、筆者の心ない振舞のお陰で、以後のスケジュールがひっ迫し、タクシー3台に分乗して富山刑務所に到着したのは、予定時刻の午前10時30分ぎりぎりであった。

概　況

　富山刑務所は、名古屋矯正管区管内に所在する B 指標の受刑者を収容する刑務所である。また、未決被収容者を収容する定員64名の拘置区を併設し、さらに、県下高岡市内に高岡拘置支所を有する。
　受刑者の収容定員は599名で、当日の収容現員は522名（収容率87パーセント）であった。また、受刑者の受け入れ先は、名古屋拘置所及び福井刑務所からそれぞれ30パーセント、岐阜拘置支所から10パーセント、残りは東京管内からとのことである。
　平成16年から同22年までの一日平均収容人員は、550名前後で推移してきたものの、同20年だけは改築工事のために444名にとどまったとのことである。本年度については約20名減となっている。
　富山刑務所は、明治5年に富山城西の丸の一隅に設けられた富山囚獄、徒刑場に端を発するが、その後同32年に市内西田（にしでん）地方に移転して富山監獄とな

り、昭和50年に現在地に新築移転している。移転当初の収容定員は、465名であったが、設備改造、増築工事により平成21年に現在の定員となっている。

職員の定員は148名で、うち13名が支所の定員とのことである。前述したように平成16年以降収容人員が横ばい状態であることから、職員も増員されることはなく、むしろ1名削減されている状況である。

刑事施設視察委員会は、弁護士、医師、市役所課長及び地元町内会長の4名で構成され、2か月に1回委員会が開催されている。これまでに委員長から施設に対する処遇改善等の意見が提示されたことはなく、所内の要所に設置されている提案箱の内容も、被収容者からの個人的希望がほとんどとのことである。

受刑者の状況

受刑者を罪名別に見ると、窃盗と覚せい剤が上位を占めるのは全国どこの施設とも同様であるが、大阪管内のB指標を収容する3施設（京都、大阪、神戸刑務所）に比べると、富山刑務所は窃盗の比率が高いのが目に付いた。すなわち、大阪の施設が窃盗、覚せい剤及びそれ以外の比率が大雑把にそれぞれ3分の1であるのに対して、同所は窃盗42パーセント、覚せい剤30パーセントとなっている。また、強姦等の性犯罪者が皆無であるのにも驚いた。

受刑者の平均刑期は、2年9月というのも、全国的に厳罰化の影響で刑期が伸長していることを考えれば、これまた驚きである。実刑期2年以下の者が130名、約25パーセントというのがその要因ではないかと思われる。

年齢別では、平均年齢が45.5歳で、60歳以上が16.3パーセントとなっており、全国的に見ても普通の数値であろう。また、50歳以上が全体の3分の1を占めているのもうなずける。そのため、養護的処遇を必要とする者が多く、その対応に腐心しているとのことである。

暴力団関係者の入所人員は121名で、全体の23.6パーセントを占めるが、これも大阪の3施設（28から30パーセント前後）に比べれば低い数値と言わざるをえない。所属組織別では、山口組が85名と最も多く、次いで稲川会20名、住吉連合10名の順とのことであり、ほとんどが、東京管区管内からの移入とのことである。

規律維持の状況

概況説明後、所内を案内していただいたが、各工場とも整理整頓が行きわたって

おり、担当職員の受持ち受刑者に対する目配り、気配りが厳正で、上司に対する報告態度もきびきびして声も大きく、施設職員全体の士気の高さをうかがい知ることができた。そのため、施設全体の規律は厳正に保たれ、ここ数年自殺その他の保安事故は1件も発生していないとのことである。

当日の規律違反取り調べ中の者は49名で、懲罰執行中の者が41名とのことであるが、ここ数年の特徴として、怠業で懲罰を受ける者が多く、昨年は年間で641件と前年の459件を大きく上回ったとのことである。本年もすでに340件を超えている。怠業が増えた原因としては、過剰収容によるストレスの蓄積、集団生活及び対人関係の煩わしさからの逃避、帰住先未定のため仮釈放が望めないこと等が考えられるだろうが、この問題は他の施設も抱えている頭の痛い問題であろう。

なお、先述した暴力団関係者についても施設内で特段の動きは見られず、特筆すべき問題も発生していないとのことであった。

作　業

富山刑務所の作業と言われて真っ先に浮かぶのは、全国的に知れ渡っている「神輿」制作であろう。日本の祭、特に農作物の収穫を神に感謝する行事としての秋祭には必ずといっていいほど「神輿」が担ぎ出される。その「神輿」を富山刑務所が刑務作業として導入し、受刑者が制作にあたっている。これには後継者不足の地場産業の継承という意味合いもあるようだが、各種の細かい作業工程に、受刑者が懸命になって取り組んでいるのである。戴いた資料によると、現在までに約5千基を全国の神社、町内会、自治会などに納品しているとのことであるが、筆者も某施設で勤務していたとき、官舎自治会の子供会のために子供みこしを購入した経緯があり、そのときの子供たちの喜ぶ顔を思い出し、一瞬ほのぼのとした気分にさせられた。

ところが、最近では販売台数が非常に少なく、最盛時には年間250基以上売り上げていたものが、昨年度はわずかに31基と低迷しているとのことである。「神輿」制作は、ユーザーからの注文を受けてから生産にとりかかるいわゆる受注生産で制作していることから、注文がなければ仕事がなくなり、受刑者に作業を課せなくなる事態も考えられるので、そういう事態を回避するため、関係職員は新規受注はもちろん、過去の納品先にダイレクトメールを送付して神輿修理作業の拡充に努めているとのことであり、そうした努力の結果として、現在21基の注文を得ているとのことであった。

なお、「神輿」については、伝統工芸・井波彫刻家の指導による木材工芸科の職業訓練も実施している。

中間期指導

新法は、「受刑者には、矯正処遇として、作業を行わせ、指導を行う。(第84条部分省略)」と規定し、作業と並行して、受刑者の改善更生及び社会適応能力養成のために「指導」を義務付けているが、富山刑務所では、刑執行開始時の指導及び釈放前指導のほかに"中間期指導"と位置づけして次のような指導を実施している。

① 勉強や教養のための指導

教科指導、自習教育、通信教育及びクラブ活動等を実施しているが、特に、教科指導については、円滑な社会生活を営むために必要な学力が不足している者を対象に、外部講師を招聘して国語、算数、英語及び社会科の基礎教育を行っている。

② 反社会性を除去するための指導

新法に規定する特別改善指導として、薬物依存離脱指導 (R1)、暴力団離脱指導 (R2) 及び被害者の視点を取り入れた指導 (R4) を行っているが、このうち被害者の視点を取り入れた指導については、富山被害者団体からの講話や富山少年鑑別所の心理技官による指導などを、6か月で12単元のカリキュラムで実施している。

そのほかにも、行動適正化指導、自己啓発指導、社会復帰支援指導等について外部協力者の支援を得て実施している。

また、一般改善指導として、専門医による講話やVTR教材視聴を通じて酒害教育を行っている。

なお、特別改善指導のうち性犯罪再犯防止指導 (R3) については、前述したように性犯罪者が在所していないため現在は実施していない。

③ 心を穏やかにするための行事

各宗教、宗派について、毎月一回の希望者による宗教教誨を実施するほか、彼岸法要、盂蘭盆会等の宗教行事を行っている。

また、民間協力者による生ディスク・ジョッキー「730ナイトアワー」も実行されている。

④ 生活をリフレッシュするための行事

毎日の運動や卓球、ソフトボール、囲碁等のレクリェーションのほか、演芸、舞踏、歌謡等の外部団体の慰問も極力取り入れている。

その他

　入所受刑者の入所度数は、平均４度で決して高い数値とは言えないが、引受人が確定している者が58パーセントで、その余は「不明」であり、更生保護会への帰住を希望している者が11.2パーセントを占めている。そのため、仮釈放についても芳しい数値は望めず、仮釈放率は40パーセントにとどまり、刑執行率も90パーセント前後である。さらに、いわゆる満期釈放者についても帰住先が決まらないまま釈放せざるを得ないケースが多く、釈放時保護の問題に腐心しているのが実情と言える。

　今回、富山刑務所を見せていただいての率直な感想は、総じて職員が若く、そのため処遇力に問題はあろうかと思われるが、これは団塊世代の退職に伴う世代交代の終期ということで避けられない現象であるため仕方のないことながら、職員の勤務態度に節度と覇気が感じられ、勤務意欲の旺盛さもうかがわれたことで、全体の士気の高さを実感したのと、各工場とも、脇見、雑談等の行為は見られず、受刑者の就業態度にも真剣さが見受けられ、施設全体の衆情が安定しているものと受け取ることができた。これもみな職員各位の日ごろの努力によるものであることは言わずもがなである。表面上は落ち着いているようには見えても、保安警備の場面や処遇の面で、更には作業、教育等々あらゆる面で、外部の者には分からない様々な問題が日々発生し、職員各位が真摯に対処しているからこそ、施設の規律秩序が保たれ、矯正処遇の実も上がるというものである。所長はじめ、職員各位の御努力に敬意を表したい。

　ところで、今年は新法が施行されて５年が過ぎ、その運用面での見直しの年に当たっている。先の全国刑務所・少年刑務所・拘置所長会同においても、この問題が議題となり、優遇措置の評価方法、懲罰手続きにおける保佐人の関与の在り方、単独室収容中の者の制限の見直し等々について協議が行われたとのことである。その結果は、やがて訓令、通達等の改正という形で現場施設に指示されるものと思われるが、すでにその準備に取りかかっている施設もあろうかと思われる。個々の施設にとっては、被収容者に対する告知や説明、処遇の公平性の確保、内規の見直し等々の作業に追われることとなろうが、より良い施設運営を実現するためだと考えて適切に対応していただきたいと念願している。

2011年 矯正・保護課程活動報告(2011年1月〜12月)

◆特別研修講座『矯正・保護課程』

　本学では、浄土真宗本願寺派の戦前から今日に至るまでの長い歴史と伝統を持つ宗教教誨を基盤としながら、日本で唯一の刑事政策に特化した教育プログラムとして、法学部を中心に矯正課程(現在の矯正・保護課程)を開設して以来、刑務所・少年院・少年鑑別所などで働く矯正職員を目指す学生や、犯罪や非行をおかしてしまった人たちの社会復帰を手助けする保護観察官等の専門職やボランティアとして活躍したいと希望する人たちを養成するための教育を行っています。

☆開講学舎と開講科目〔2011年度実績〕

開講学舎	開講科目
深草学舎	矯正概論、矯正教育学、矯正社会学、矯正心理学、矯正医学、成人矯正処遇、更生保護概論、保護観察処遇、更生保護制度、犯罪学、被害者学
大宮学舎	成人矯正処遇、更生保護概論、保護観察処遇
瀬田学舎	矯正概論A・B、矯正教育学A・B、矯正社会学A・B、矯正心理学A・B、成人矯正処遇、更生保護概論A・B、保護観察処遇、更生保護制度

☆経験豊富な講師陣

　講義講師は、矯正管区長、刑務所長、少年院長、少年鑑別所長など矯正関係の退職者や現職の法務教官、地方更生保護委員会委員長や保護観察所長など更生保護関係の退職者や現職の保護観察官です。豊富な実務経験に基づき実践的な講義や演習を提供します。

☆これまでの受講者数の推移〔1977～2011年度の実績〕

1977年度に当講座が開設され、これまでにのべ12,831名の受講生がこの講座を受講されました。下のグラフ①は、各年度における受講者数の推移を示しています。また、受講者数の主な変動要因についての説明をしています。法学部や短期大学部、社会学部（地域福祉学科・臨床福祉学科）において、正課科目（卒業要件単位科目）として取り扱った各年度に受講生が増加した傾向が見られます。

グラフ①　矯正・保護課程　受講者数の推移〔全体〕（1977～2011年度）

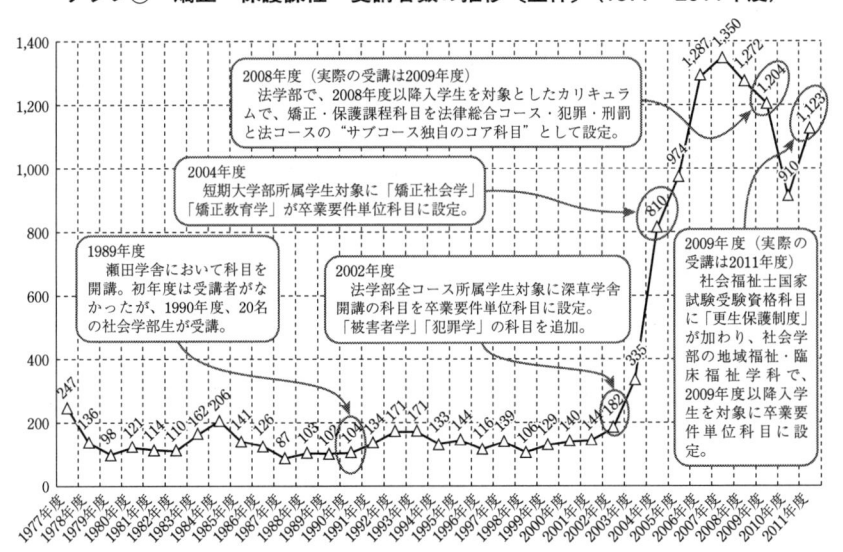

1989年度
瀬田学舎において科目を開講。初年度は受講者がなかったが、1990年度、20名の社会学部生が受講。

2002年度
法学部全コース所属学生対象に深草学舎開講の科目を卒業要件単位科目に設定。「被害者学」「犯罪学」の科目を追加。

2004年度
短期大学部所属学生対象に「矯正社会学」「矯正教育学」が卒業要件単位科目に設定。

2008年度（実際の受講は2009年度）
法学部で、2008年度以降入学生を対象としたカリキュラムで、矯正・保護課程科目を法律総合コース・犯罪・刑罰と法コースの"サブコース独自のコア科目"として設定。

2009年度（実際の受講は2011年度）
社会福祉士国家試験受験資格科目に「更生保護制度」が加わり、社会学部の地域福祉・臨床福祉学科で、2009年度以降入学生を対象に卒業要件単位科目に設定。

下のグラフは、各学部等における1977年度から2011年度までの受講者数（のべ人数）を示しています。法学部では、深草学舎で開講される矯正・保護課程科目を卒業要件単位に認めていることもあり、受講者数が他の学部に比較して圧倒的に多数の8,912名（69.46％）を占め、続いて文学部1,909名（14.88％）、社会学部975名（7.60％）、そして学外者（一般受講生）386名（3.01％）と続きます。学外者（一般受講生）は、2010年度に一旦のべ18名（2009年度はのべ37名）まで減少しましたが、2011年度は、過去最高となるのべ59名の受講者がありました。

グラフ②　学部別受講者数ののべ人数（1977〜2011年度）

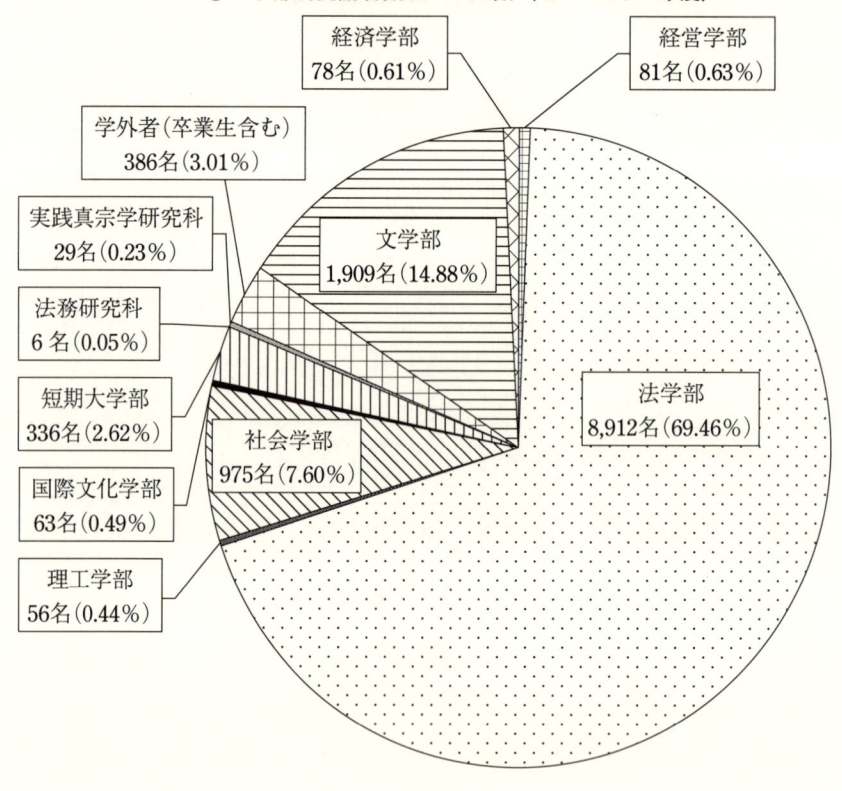

学部等	人数	割合
経済学部	78名	0.61％
経営学部	81名	0.63％
学外者（卒業生含む）	386名	3.01％
実践真宗学研究科	29名	0.23％
法務研究科	6名	0.05％
短期大学部	336名	2.62％
国際文化学部	63名	0.49％
理工学部	56名	0.44％
文学部	1,909名	14.88％
社会学部	975名	7.60％
法学部	8,912名	69.46％

◆施設参観

　矯正・保護課程の受講者を対象に授業で学修した内容を、実際の矯正施設や更生施設の現場を参観することを通じて、生きた知識として定着させるため、毎年8月下旬～9月上旬に、近隣の施設に協力していただき施設参観を実施しています。下表は、2011年度の実績を示します。

☆施設参観日程および参観先〔2011年度実績〕

参観日時		参観施設	施設の区分等
8月29日（月）	10：30～12：00	大阪医療刑務所	医療（男女）
	12：30～15：00	大阪刑務所	矯正（成人）
8月30日（火）	10：30～12：00	播磨社会復帰促進センター	矯正（成人）
	13：30～15：30	加古川刑務所	矯正（成人）
9月1日（木）	10：00～11：30	奈良少年刑務所	矯正（26歳未満の青少年男子）
	13：30～15：30	奈良少年院	矯正（少年）
9月5日（月）	14：00～16：00	大阪府立修徳学院	児童自立支援施設
9月6日（火）	13：00～15：00	和歌山刑務所	矯正（成人女子）
9月8日（木）	10：00～11：30	交野女子学院	矯正（少女）
	13：30～15：00	浪速少年院	矯正（少年）
9月9日（金）	10：00～12：00	京都少年鑑別所	矯正（少年）
	13：30～15：30	京都医療少年院	医療（少年）
9月12日（月）	10：30～12：00	更生保護法人　西本願寺白光荘	保護（成人女子）
	13：30～16：00	京都刑務所	矯正（成人）
9月13日（火）	10：00～11：30	更生保護法人　京都保護育成会	保護（成人）
	13：00～15：00	滋賀刑務所	矯正（成人）

　参観当日は、施設職員の方から施設の概要説明をいただいた後、実際に施設内の参観をさせていただきました。参観後は、質疑応答の時間を設けていただき、参観者からの質問に対して丁寧に回答していただきました。各施設職員の皆様には大変お世話になりました。ありがとうございました。

☆参観者の学部等内訳等〔2011年度実績〕

学部当	文学部	法学部	社会学部	短期大学部	法科大学院	実践真宗学	一般受講生	合計
人数	16名	109名	10名	9名	17名	13名	43名	217名

　法学部生がのべ109名と参観者数の半数を占め、学外者（一般受講生）の参観者が約2割を占めます。さらに、実人数が飛躍的に増加しており、2009年度が5名、2010年度が4名で、今年度は19名に増加しています。

☆一人における参観日数と平均参観日数〔2011年度実績〕

参観日数	1日	2日	3日	5日	7日	実人数	平均
人数	90名	38名	13名	1名	1名	143名	1.52日

◆国家公務員（法務教官・刑務官・保護観察官）採用試験合格者を囲む懇談会・懇親会
　毎年12月上旬に、その年度における法務教官と刑務官の国家公務員採用試験に合格した現役学生・卒業生から合格体験談を聞いたり、現職として活躍されている法務教官、刑務官、そして保護観察官の卒業生に現場のお話をしていただく機会を設けています。
　懇談会では、将来この分野へ進路を希望している多くの学生やこの分野に関心のある熱心な学生からの問いかけに対して、採用試験合格者と現職の卒業生、そして、矯正・保護課程講師や矯正・保護総合センター関係の教員がお応えいただけます。
　今年度、この分野を目指そうとする学生15名が、合格者や卒業生のアドバイスに熱心に耳を傾けていました。2011年度の開催内容は、次のとおりです。なお、現職の卒業生のお名前は、都合によりイニシャルにて掲載しています。

☆2011年度開催内容
　開催日程　　2011年12月9日（金）
　開催場所　　懇談会（18：00〜）深草学舎21号館602教室
　　　　　　　懇親会（19：20〜）深草学舎紫英館6階グリル
　主　　催　　矯正・保護課程委員会
　プログラム　懇　談　会
　　　　　　　1）委員長挨拶
　　　　　　　　加藤博史 先生〔矯正・保護課程委員会委員長／短期大学部・教授〕
　　　　　　　2）出席者紹介
　　　　　　　　本学出身の現職OB
　　　　　　　　　法務教官　S．Sさん（少年鑑別所教官／社会学部卒業）
　　　　　　　　　　　　　　T．Rさん（少年鑑別所教官／法学部卒業）
　　　　　　　　　刑　務　官　Y．Tさん（拘置所事務官／法学部卒業）
　　　　　　　　　保護観察官　K．Tさん（保護観察所保護観察官／文学部卒業）
　　　　　　　　2012年度採用試験合格者
　　　　　　　　　法務教官　岡崎健太 さん（法学部法律学科2010年度卒業）
　　　　　　　　　　　　　　中川裕介 さん（法学部法律学科在学）
　　　　　　　　　刑　務　官　村田康平 さん（法学部法律学科2010年度卒業）
　　　　　　　　　　　　　　仲平淑華 さん（法学部法律学科在学）
　　　　　　　3）合格者体験談
　　　　　　　4）現職OBからのアドバイス
　　　　　　　5）質疑応答
　　　　　　懇　親　会
　　　　　　　1）来賓挨拶
　　　　　　　　長上深雪 先生〔キャリア開発部長／社会学部・教授〕
　　　　　　　　畠山晃朗 先生〔本学客員教授／矯正・保護課程講師
　　　　　　　　　　　　　　　　／校友会矯正施設支部「ぎんなん会」会長〕

2011年 矯正・保護課程活動報告（2011年1月～12月）

■矯正・保護課程委員会
2010年度第5回矯正・保護課程委員会　2011年1月19日開催
2010年度第6回矯正・保護課程委員会　2011年3月12日開催
2011年度第1回矯正・保護課程委員会　2011年4月28日開催
2011年度第2回矯正・保護課程委員会　2011年6月23日開催
2011年度第3回矯正・保護課程委員会　2011年7月13日〈メール審議〉
2011年度第4回矯正・保護課程委員会　2011年7月30日開催
2011年度第5回矯正・保護課程委員会　2011年10月28日開催

■懇談会
2010年度第2回矯正・保護課程講師懇談会　2011年3月12日開催
2011年度第1回矯正・保護課程講師懇談会　2011年7月30日開催

■研究会
2010年度第2回矯正・保護課程講師研究会　2011年3月12日開催
講　師：大阪保護観察所次長　宇戸　午朗氏
テーマ：更生保護の現状について
2011年度第1回矯正・保護課程講師研究会　2011年7月30日開催
講　師：大阪少年鑑別所長　津崎　秀樹氏
テーマ：最近の少年矯正の動向～少年矯正を考える有識者会議の提言から

■2011年度施設参観

2011年度施設参観一覧

	参観日	参観施設	参加者数	受講者数	引率者
①	8月29日（月）	大阪医療刑務所 大阪刑務所	22	21	4
②	8月30日（火）	播磨社会復帰促進センター 加古川刑務所	28	27	3
③	9月1日（木）	奈良少年刑務所 奈良少年院	27	26	4
④	9月5日（月）	大阪府立修徳学院	14	10	3
⑤	9月6日（火）	和歌山刑務所	21	20	4
⑥	9月8日（木）	交野女子学院 浪速少年院	30	26	4
⑦	9月9日（金）	京都少年鑑別所 京都医療少年院	29	23	3
⑧	9月12日（月）	更生保護法人　西本願寺白光荘 京都刑務所	28	21	4
⑨	9月13日（火）	更生保護法人　京都保護育成会 滋賀刑務所	18	13	4

■2011年度共同研究出張
期　間：2011年8月24日（水）〜26日（金）
出張先：福井刑務所・更生保護法人福田会・湖南学院・金澤刑務所・富山刑務所
出張者：加藤博史・石塚伸一・井上善幸・井上見淳・斎藤司・金尚均・畠山晃朗・
　　　　宮内利正・青木恒弘・池田靜・板垣嗣廣・吉貞正流（順不同）
■国家公務員採用試験合格者を囲む懇談会
2011年12月9日（金）　18：00〜20：00
深草学舎：21号館602教室／紫英館6階グリル
講師：刑務官採用試験合格者2名、法務教官採用試験合格者2名
　　　法務教官・刑務官現職OB/OG 3名、保護観察官OB 1名

2011年度「矯正・保護課程」開講科目一覧

科目名（単位） 【講義テーマ】	担当者	学舎	開講	曜講時	受講者数	備考
矯正概論（4） 【刑事施設等の組織と業務及び被収容者の処遇等】	畠山晃朗	深草	通年	水3	76	
矯正概論（4） 【刑事施設等の組織と業務及び被収容者の処遇等】	池田　靜	深草	通年	水3	35	
矯正概論A（2） 【矯正関係法令及び国際準則と犯罪者の処遇】	中山　厚	瀬田	前期	火5	1	
矯正概論B（2） 【犯罪者及び非行少年の施設内処遇の現状】	中山　厚	瀬田	後期	木5	2	
矯正教育学A（2） 【少年院における矯正教育・総論】	藏田光秋	瀬田	前期	火4	2	
矯正教育学B（2） 【少年院における矯正教育・各論】	藏田光秋	瀬田	後期	火4	2	
矯正教育学（4） 【犯罪・非行少年に対する教育の場・機会・距離】	池田正興	深草	通年	木5	53	
矯正社会学（4） 【少年院の現状とその社会的役割】	逢坂俊夫	深草	通年	土1・2	51	隔週開講
矯正社会学A（2） 【非行・犯罪と社会の関係について】	浅田賢幸	瀬田		集中講義	5	
矯正社会学B（2） 【被収容者の矯正と、それを支える社会について】	浅田賢幸	瀬田	後期	火5	2	
矯正心理学（4） 【非行少年・犯罪者の心理と処遇】	青木恒弘	深草	通年	火2	58	
矯正心理学A（2） 【矯正心理学　基礎】	柿木良太	瀬田	前期	土1・2	3	隔週開講
矯正心理学B（2） 【矯正心理学　各論】	柿木良太	瀬田	後期	土1・2	3	隔週開講
矯正医学（2） 【矯正施設における精神医療を中心に】	西口芳伯 清水光明	深草	後期	月4・5	99	隔週開講
成人矯正処遇（2）	池田　靜	前期	深草	水4	127	

科目	担当者	校地	期	曜日・時限	人数	備考
【成人矯正施設においていかなる処遇が展開されているか】			後期 前期	大宮 瀬田	木5 木5	1 2	
保護観察処遇（2） 【保護観察処遇の理論と実際】	柴田由佳	深草	後期	土1・2	61	隔週開講
保護観察処遇（2） 【保護観察処遇の理論と実際】	冨田彰乃	大宮	前期	土3・4	5	隔週開講
保護観察処遇（2） 【保護観察処遇の理論と実際】	鈴木庄市	瀬田	後期	土3・4	2	隔週開講
更生保護概論（4） 【犯罪や非行に陥った者の社会内処遇を中心として】	松田慎一 宮内利正	深草 大宮	通年 通年	土3・4 土1・2	41 2	隔週開講
更生保護概論A（2） 【犯罪や非行に陥った者の社会内処遇を中心として】	玉柏ちづる	瀬田	前期	土1・2	2	隔週開講
更生保護概論B（2） 【犯罪や非行に陥った者の社会内処遇を中心として】	玉柏ちづる	瀬田	後期	土1・2	2	隔週開講
更生保護制度（1） 【犯罪者・非行少年の更生と福祉】	廣田玉枝	瀬田	後期	木3・4	144	前半開講
更生保護制度（2） 【犯罪者・非行少年の更生と福祉】	廣田玉枝	深草	後期	木1	69	
犯罪学（2） 【犯罪と非行の科学的認識〜犯罪は減っている？〜】	石塚伸一	深草	後期	木2	148	
被害者学（4） 【被害者支援の状況と被害者の権利】	板垣嗣廣	深草	通年	水2	74	

2011年度　矯正・保護総合センター活動報告（2011年4月～2012年3月）

■センター委員会
第1回センター委員会　2011年4月28日
第2回センター委員会　2011年7月28日
第3回センター委員会　2011年8月30日〈メール審議〉
第4回センター委員会　2011年10月6日
第5回センター委員会　2012年2月22日
第6回センター委員会　2012年3月14日

■運営協議会
第1回運営協議会　2011年4月14日
第2回運営協議会　2011年5月18日
第3回運営協議会　2011年6月19日
第4回運営協議会　2011年7月7日
第5回運営協議会　2011年9月29日
第6回運営協議会　2011年10月21日
第7回運営協議会　2011年12月21日
第8回運営協議会　2012年1月20日
第9回運営協議会　2012年2月3日

■研究委員会
第1回研究委員会　2011年5月18日
第2回研究委員会　2011年7月21日
第3回研究委員会　2011年11月24日
第4回研究委員会　2012年2月7日
第5回研究委員会　2012年3月12日

■月例研究会
第10回（通算89回）月例研究会　2011年4月18日
　報告者：フランス　ポワチエ大学教授　ベルナデット・オベール氏
　テーマ：フランス刑事司法における近年の動きと課題
第11回（通算90回）月例研究会　2011年5月19日
　報告者：フランス司法省青少年保護局研究部部長　リュック＝アンリ・ショッケ氏
　テーマ：要保護少年・非行少年の社会復帰と民事・刑事の対応―フランスの取組み
第12回（通算91回）月例研究会　2011年5月30日
　報告者：龍谷大学短期大学部社会福祉学科　講師　大場智美氏
　テーマ：ソーシャル・インクルージョン教育の取り組み
　　　　　―学校をエンパワーメントの場に―
第13回（通算92回）月例研究会　2011年6月17日
　報告者：広島大学大学院社会科学研究科　博士課程後期　荻野太司氏
　テーマ：更生保護関連法と事後法の禁止原則に関する一考察
第14回（通算93回）月例研究会　2011年7月12日
　報告者：矯正・保護総合センター嘱託研究員　本田宏治氏
　テーマ：日本のドラッグ問題の多角的検討
第15回（通算94回）月例研究会　2011年9月29日　都合により中止
　報告者：矯正・保護総合センター　リサーチ・アシスタント　田中久美氏
　テーマ：不快な行為の法的規制について
第16回（通算95回）月例研究会　2011年10月20日
　報告者：矯正・保護総合センター　リサーチ・アシスタント　田中久美氏
　テーマ：不快な行為の法的規制について

第17回（通算96回）月例研究会　2011年10月25日
報告者：矯正・保護総合センター　リサーチ・アシスタント　崎山右京氏
テーマ：少年犯罪に対する言説の変遷
　　　　―新聞報道における犯罪の「傾向」と「原因」―
第18回（通算97回）月例研究会　2011年12月12日
報告者：広島大学大学院社会科学研究科博士課程後期　荻野太司氏
テーマ：刑事施設医療と憲法36条の残虐な刑罰の禁止
第19回（通算97回）月例研究会　2012年3月6日
報告者：ポワチエ大学　ロランス・ルテュルミー（Laurence LETURMY）先生
テーマ：フランス少年司法の最近の動向と心理学の役割

■シンポジウム
矯正・保護総合センター開設記念シンポジウム　2011年10月8日開催
　統一テーマ「人間を大切にする刑事政策を求めて～ノルウェー犯罪学の実験～」
　基調講演「ノルウェー犯罪学の理論と実践」
　　ニルス・クリスティー氏（ノルウェー・オスロ大学教授）
　講演「ノルウェーから見た日本」
　　リル・シェルダン氏（ノルウェー・オスロ大学教授）
国際シンポジウム　沖縄からアジアへのメッセージ　2012年3月11日開催
　テーマ「日本版ドラッグ・コートを越えて～処罰から治療へ、そして真の社会参加をめ
　　　　ざして～」
　基調講演1「東アジアにおける薬物依存からの回復～フィリピンからのメッセージ～」
　　レオナルド・R・エスタシオ．Jr．氏（フィリピン大学）
　基調講演2「エビデンスに基づいた薬物依存への新しい取り組み～リラプス・プリベン
　　　　ションとハーム・リダクション」
　　原田隆之氏（目白大学）

■講演会
第1回矯正・保護ネットワーク講演会　2011年12月4日開催
　特別講演「私の学んだ人間教育」
　　山口良治氏（京都市立伏見工業高等学校・ラグビー部総監督）
　講演「保護司の現状について」
　　宮内利正氏（大阪府保護司会連合会理事・事務局長／本学客員教授）
第2回矯正・保護ネットワーク講演会　2012年3月4日開催
　特別講演「更生保護の課題と方向性について」
　　平岡秀夫氏（元法務大臣〈第88代〉／衆議院議員／弁護士）

■薬物依存症者処遇プログラム研修　薬物依存症者回復支援セミナー
第7回2011年6月11・12日開催
第8回2011年11月5・6日開催
第9回2012年1月21・22日開催
第10回2012年3月9・10日開催